SOUTH AFRICAN ESSAYS ON 'UNIVERSAL' SHAKESPEARE

South African Essays on 'Universal' Shakespeare

Edited by

CHRIS THURMAN

Routledge
Taylor & Francis Group

LONDON AND NEW YORK

First published 2014 by Ashgate Publishing

Published 2016 by Routledge
2 Park Square, Milton Park, Abingdon, Oxfordshire OX14 4RN
711 Third Avenue, New York, NY 10017, USA

First issued in paperback 2016

Routledge is an imprint of the Taylor & Francis Group, an informa business

British Library Cataloguing in Publication Data
A catalogue record for this book is available from the British Library

The Library of Congress has cataloged the printed edition as follows:
South African Essays on 'Universal' Shakespeare / edited by Chris Thurman.
    p. cm.
  Includes bibliographical references and index.
  ISBN 978-1-4724-1576-9 (hardcover: alk. paper)
  1. Shakespeare, William, 1564–1616—Study and teaching—South Africa. 2. Shakespeare,
William, 1564–1616—Criticism and interpretation. 3. Shakespeare, William, 1564–1616—
Appreciation—South Africa. I. Thurman, Chris, 1979– editor of compilation.
  PR2971.S6S68 2014
  822.3'3—dc23

                                                                                    2013035879

ISBN 13: 978-1-138-27200-2 (pbk)
ISBN 13: 978-1-4724-1576-9 (hbk)

Contents

List of Figures   *vii*

Notes on Contributors   *ix*

Acknowledgements   *xi*

Foreword   *xiii*
   David Schalkwyk

Introduction: Generation S: 'Southern' Shakespeares across Time and Space
   Chris Thurman   1

PART 1   **'Universal' Will**

1 On Being Human   19
   Natasha Distiller

2 Shakespeare without Borders   39
   Sandra Young

3 'Many in One': On Shakespeare, Language and Translation   53
   Pier Paolo Frassinelli

PART 2   **Shakespeare, Mediated**

4 Foxe and the Fat Man, Shakespeare and the Jesuit: Oldcastle Revisited   69
   Victor Houliston

5 'I, that am not shaped for sportive tricks': Playing with *Richard III*   81
   Chris Thurman

6 Traditions of English Criticism: Shakespeare's Late Plays in the
   Early Twentieth Century   99
   Brian Pearce

PART 3   **Butler's Shakespeare Reconsidered**

7 Shakespeare's Dramatic Vision   129
   Guy Butler

8 Shakespeare, Daniel and Augustus Caesar: Kingdoms in *Antony*
   and Cleopatra   139
   Guy Butler

9   Butler's *Lear*   167
    Laurence Wright

Bibliography   *183*
Index   *201*

List of Figures

8.1 Nebuchadnezzar's vision of worldly powers. Source:
Hugh Broughton, *Concent of Scripture* (London: Simson
and White, 1588). Location: William Cullen Library,
University of the Witwatersrand, Johannesburg.   148

8.2 *Daniel's Vision of the Four Beasts* (Hans Holbein, 1549).
Source: Wikimedia Commons / Arthur Mayger Hind, *Hans
Holbein, The Younger* (New York: Frederick A. Stokes, 1912).
Location: Available electronically courtesy of HathiTrust, at:
http://hdl.handle.net/2027/uc2.ark:/13960/t8qb9z703.   151

8.3 Illustration of the dream in the book of Daniel 8. Source:
Hugh Broughton, *Concent of Scripture* (London: Simson
and White, 1588). Location: William Cullen Library,
University of the Witwatersrand, Johannesburg.   152

Notes on Contributors

Guy Butler (1918–2001) was, for most of his career, Professor of English at Rhodes University in Grahamstown. He studied at Rhodes and, after serving in the 'Sapper' Engineering Corps during World War II, he read English at Brasenose College, Oxford. On his return to South Africa he taught at the University of the Witwatersrand in Johannesburg for three years. He was a poet, playwright, historian and cultural politician. His autobiography was published by David Philip in three volumes: *Karoo Morning* (1977), *Bursting World* (1983) and *A Local Habitation* (1991).

Natasha Distiller was, until recently, Associate Professor of English and Chief Research Officer at the Institute for the Humanities in Africa (HUMA) at the University of Cape Town. She remains a Research Associate of HUMA. She has published extensively. Her most recent book is *Shakespeare and the Coconuts: On Post-apartheid South African Culture* (Wits University Press, 2012). She lives in Berkeley, California.

Pier Paolo Frassinelli teaches literature and cultural studies at Monash University, South Africa campus, and is a Senior Research Associate in the Faculty of Humanities at the University of Johannesburg. He has published in the fields of cultural, postcolonial, translation and early modern studies.

Victor Houliston graduated from Magdalen College, Oxford, in 1986 and is now a Professor of English Literature at the University of the Witwatersrand, Johannesburg. For many years he has been writing about the early English Jesuit leader and controversialist, Robert Persons, and related topics in early modern religious culture. His monograph *Catholic Resistance in Elizabethan England* was published by Ashgate in 2007. He is currently head of an international team working on a multivolume, multilingual edition of the 'Correspondence and Unpublished Papers of Robert Persons'.

Brian Pearce completed his Ph.D. in Drama and Theatre Studies at Royal Holloway, University of London, in 1992. He is currently Associate Professor in Drama Studies at Durban University of Technology and a Member of the Institute of Systems Science. He is an Honorary Life Member of the Shakespeare Society of Southern Africa and edited *Shakespeare in Southern Africa* from 2000 to 2008. He has worked as a theatre director, both professionally and in an educational context, and has directed *Twelfth Night* (1993) and *The Tempest* (2003) in Durban. He has published articles, chapters, reviews and editorials relating to Shakespeare. He has also directed student productions of plays by Molière, Ibsen, Strindberg, Wilde, Shaw, Anouilh, Beckett and Soyinka.

David Schalkwyk is Academic Director of Global Shakespeare, a joint venture between Queen Mary, University of London, and the University of Warwick. He was formerly Director of Research at the Folger Shakespeare Library in Washington, DC, and editor of *Shakespeare Quarterly*. Before that he was Professor of English at the University of Cape Town, where he held the positions of Head of Department and Deputy Dean in the Faculty of Humanities. He is the author of *Speech and Performance in Shakespeare's Sonnets and Plays* (Cambridge, 2002), *Literature and the Touch of the Real* (Delaware, 2004) and *Shakespeare, Love and Service* (Cambridge, 2008). His most recent book is *Hamlet's Dreams: The Robben Island Shakespeare* (Bloomsbury, 2013). He is currently working on a monograph on love in Shakespeare.

Chris Thurman is Associate Professor in the Department of English at the University of the Witwatersrand, Johannesburg. He is the editor of the journal *Shakespeare in Southern Africa* and compiler of *Sport versus Art: A South African Contest* (Wits University Press, 2010) and *Text Bites* (Oxford University Press, 2009). His other books are *At Large: Reviewing the Arts in South Africa* (Common Ground, 2012) and *Guy Butler: Reassessing a South African Literary Life* (University of KwaZulu-Natal Press, 2010). He contributes to various publications as an arts critic and occasional political commentator.

Laurence Wright is HA Molteno Professor of English and Director of the Institute for the Study of English in Africa (ISEA) at Rhodes University. He is Honorary Life President of the Shakespeare Society of Southern Africa, Chairman of the Grahamstown Foundation and Vice President of the English Academy of Southern Africa. Recent work includes *South Africa's Education Crisis: Views from the Eastern Cape* (ISEA, 2012); 'Notes from a Rhenish Mission: The Sparse Code of a Great Song', in '*No Other World*': *Essays on the Life-work of Don Maclennan* (Print Matters, 2012); and 'Guy Butler's South Africanism: "Being present where you are"', in the *English Academy Review* 29.2 (2012).

Sandra Young is a Senior Lecturer in the Department of English at the University of Cape Town where she teaches early modern literature and thought, postcolonial and feminist theory, and African and South African literature. She was recently Helen Watson Buckner Memorial Research Fellow at Brown University while completing her book manuscript, 'Imagining Africa and the New World in the Sixteenth Century: Producing Colonial Difference as Scientific Knowledge', which reflects on the vocabularies and representational practices of early modern geographies and exploration narratives. She has published on Shakespearean drama, early American colonial literature, race and the public sphere in nineteenth-century New York (an award-winning co-authored essay in *American Literature*), women's prison writing under apartheid and the problematics of archive, memory and trauma in Truth and Reconciliation Commission (TRC) testimonies.

Acknowledgements

I wish to express my gratitude to the Research Office of the University of the Witwatersrand (Wits), the National Research Foundation of South Africa, the trustees of the Friedel Sellschop endowment and the Academic and Non-Fiction Authors' Association of South Africa (ANFASA) for their financial support of this project. As always, the staff at the National English Literary Museum – in particular, Cecilia Blight and Ann Torlesse – were tremendously helpful in facilitating archival research. Thanks also to Ciska Thurman, Lyndsay Hughes and Frances Ringwood for their help with transcription and formatting. Guy Butler's literary executors kindly agreed to the publication of his lectures and essays. The cover image (the 1490 Martellus map of the world) and the illustrations used in Butler's essay 'Shakespeare, Daniel and Augustus Caesar' are in the public domain (see List of Figures for details).

This book is dedicated to those Shakespeareans who – as teachers, performers, directors, critics, friends and colleagues – have deepened my understanding of how one might attempt an answer to the question: *Why Shakespeare?*

Chris Thurman
Johannesburg, January 2014

Foreword

David Schalkwyk

I recall walking down the corridors of the English Department of the University of Stellenbosch in the late 1970s, where I had just been appointed to my first teaching job – a temporary lectureship split down the middle with a colleague. I was on my way to see the head of department, to receive my teaching allocation for the year. I hoped that I wouldn't be asked to lecture on *Twelfth Night*: I couldn't imagine what I would say about the play.

Looking back on it now, I can't imagine I had absolutely nothing to say about it. I must have thought of the obvious things. But what *is* obvious about Shakespeare's greatest romantic comedy, possibly even his greatest play? In 1976, at Stellenbosch, the undergraduate experience of being discouraged from reading critics (let alone scholars) was deeply ingrained and carried over even to postgraduate responses and the frightening prospect of standing before a class, expected to illuminate a play that was alternately strangely beautiful and bewilderingly opaque. That one might try to relate *Twelfth Night* to South Africa, to the here and now of local conditions and concerns, was then as unthinkable as the notion that one might turn to history to fill in the blank the play must have represented for me.

How might one have related *Twelfth Night* to the South Africa of 1976, shortly after apartheid had been declared a crime against humanity by the United Nations, and just before the country was to explode in a wave of decisive, youthful resistance? When I was doing research for my book, *Hamlet's Dreams: The Robben Island Shakespeare*, written in Washington, DC, some 35 years later, I was struck by two things: Saths Cooper's statement, in an interview with Matthew Hahn, that he 'focused on more serious works rather than the comedies because this was a political prison' and Govan Mbeki's choice of the opening speech of *Twelfth Night*, Orsino's self-indulgent but poetically resonant 'If music be the food of love, play on; / Give me excess of it' (1.1.1–2).[1] Mbeki was generally known for his uncompromising, even Stalinist, positions on Robben Island. So, given all of Shakespeare to choose as his signature passage, in about 1976, this uncompromising Marxist choose a comedy – the very one that, at a roughly parallel moment only 40 or so kilometres away, had me stumped.

I was stumped for a variety of reasons, as I think about it now. A broadly Leavisite training in practical criticism and close reading had made me attentive to the 'words on the page' to a degree for which I remain extremely grateful today, but

---

[1] See David Schalkwyk, *Hamlet's Dreams: The Robben Island Shakespeare* (London: Bloomsbury, 2013), p. 36.

it froze those words in a limbo from which I believed, at this moment of personal and national crisis, I could not recover them for my students. This was before the theoretical turn in Shakespeare studies, which was to achieve its apotheosis 10 years later in the *annus mirabilis* of 1986, when some of the most transformative texts of the new theory were published, and certainly before the hegemonic hold of the New Historicism on the profession first in the United States and then in the United Kingdom.

This form of historicism never established itself in South Africa. The reasons are twofold. First, unless they had been trained in scholarly research and could use the physical resources of the British Library, the Bodleian or, more remotely, the Folger Shakespeare Library in Washington, DC, or the Huntington Library in Pasadena, South African academics and students had little or no access to the archive that was an absolutely necessary requirement for the new scholarship. Second, South African English departments did not, until much later, develop the new professional culture that, as described by Stanley Fish, needed a machine to reproduce itself, like the medieval guilds whose attenuated forms Shakespeare would have known well. Fish argued that the profession was an 'interpretive community' that set its own rules and protocols for admission and reproduction – its chief purpose was simply to reproduce itself through a variety of successive hurdles of the Ph.D., the tenure process, promotion and, for the happy few, international recognition and celebrity.

If this system needed a machine, the New Historicism provided the perfect apparatus – it had Greenblatt's analogical method, radically different from the causal model of materialist theory, coupled to an archive whose resources were virtually infinite. The combination of the analogy and historical (con)text enabled the profession to produce endless numbers of Ph.D.s, first and second books, to keep itself going. Only the economic crisis that hit the publishing industry in the late 1990s threatened the impetus of this apparatus – as fewer libraries could afford to buy the endless stream of monographs, and even fewer beneficiaries of the system had either the inclination or the finances to buy their colleagues' monographs at institutional prices of $100 per book, or more. The symbiosis of the academic publishing industry and universities in need of an 'objective' authority for the measure of excellence has, in effect, come to an end. The humanist academies in the United States and the United Kingdom are currently in crisis, and that crisis goes to the root of the profession itself, now increasingly transformed into an exploitative institution in which tenure is an increasingly remote promise and adjunct teaching at near-poverty wages an established reality. We have been looking for a replacement for the New Historicism for a long time. Very few candidates have presented themselves.

One of the concepts that *South African Essays on 'Universal' Shakespeare* puts under pressure is the 'we' in my sentence above. Rightly, some authors question the assumptions inherent in the unreflecting use of the first person plural, so that at this tiny point of grammar the very notion of the universal is undermined. What is intriguing is that it should still survive, in this book's title (despite the scare quotes), in the use of pronouns, and in the strenuous efforts to escape it. The graduate and undergraduate training I received assumed the universality of Shakespeare without a second thought. In my first year of graduate study (a BA Honours in South Africa's peculiar system), the teaching of the Shakespeare course was reserved for the most senior professor, whose field was in fact the nineteenth-century novel. The assumption that no scholarship was required to teach or study Shakespeare – that it was the privilege of age and authority – was underlined by the only twentieth-century text in the course that could be regarded as 'theoretical': the Leavis-Bateson debate that appeared in *Scrutiny* in 1953, just before that journal ceased publication.

I reread that debate in preparing to write this foreword and was struck by a number of things. The first is the displacement of the debate in the context of 1970s South Africa. Leavis titled his reply 'The Responsible Critic', incorporating as his subtitle a variation of Bateson's original: 'The Function of Criticism at *Any* Time'. Bateson's title was 'The Function of Criticism at the *Present* Time', taken directly from Matthew Arnold's great essay of 1864. Characteristically, Leavis's displacement of 'any' for 'present' moves the polemic into the realm of the universal, the unconditional, and away from the local or contextual. But curiously, by the time Leavis gets to his 'Rejoinder' to Bateson's response, he is located firmly in the present and the local: 'the "order of ideas" in which talent finds itself today is *not* one that favours maturation ... To make a show of energizing on behalf of the function of criticism while ignoring this situation is to be worse than futile.'[2]

The ironies abound. We were being expected to understand the function of criticism at *any* time through a debate about criticism and literature that was rooted in England two decades earlier, before I was born. Before we scoff, however, recall that Derrida has been dead for almost 10 years, Raymond Williams, 15, Foucault, 20, and Frantz Fanon, more than 50. So there is nothing inherently absurd asking graduates to read a 20-year-old polemic.

If we turn to the substance of the Bateson-Leavis polemic, in broad strokes it heralded developments to come, beyond the miseries of postwar Britain. The fundamental difference between the antagonists resides in their attitudes towards the role of the critic in relation to social context. Bateson offers the manifesto that the responsible critic must also be a scholar. Bateson is a strong contextualist: the critic's responsibility is to recover what the author could have meant from his 'social context'. Under no circumstances should he 'read everything written in English', as he accuses Leavis of doing, 'as if it were written yesterday'.[3] To this claim (or aim) Leavis responds in a way that points to a later, equally intense debate about the role of context in the determination of meaning:

---

2   F.R. Leavis, 'The Responsible Critic: The Function of Criticism at Any Time', in *A Selection from Scrutiny: Volume 2* (Cambridge: Cambridge University Press, 1968), p. 288.

3   F.W. Bateson, 'The Function of Criticism at the Present Time', in Leavis (ed.), ibid., p. 305.

How does one set to work to arrive at this final inclusive context, the establishment of which puts the poem back in 'its original historical setting', so that the human experience in it begins to be realized and re-enacted by the reader? Mr Bateson doesn't tell us, and doesn't begin to consider the problem. He merely follows up those plainly false assertions about the passage of Marvell and Pope with some random notes from his historical reading.

That is all he *could* do. And all he could do more would be to go on doing that more voluminously and industriously. For the 'total social context' that he postulates is an illusion ... there is nothing to correspond – nothing answering to Mr Bateson's 'social context' that can be set over against the poem, or induced to re-establish itself around it as a kind of framework or completion, and there never *was* such a thing.[4]

I will return to Leavis's pre-echo of Derrida in his equally intense polemic with John Searle.[5] It should be clear that Bateson represents a much more restricted, determinist, and idealised form of historicism – what, after Greenblatt and Louis Montrose, we now know as the 'old historicism'. That old historicist impulse is clearly recognised, if in attenuated forms, in the essays by Guy Butler included in this volume and in Laurence Wright's account of Butler's grand project on *King Lear*. Even Butler's discussion of imagery in *Antony and Cleopatra* and *Macbeth* echoes Rosamund Tuve and Bateson in its tendency to locate the origins of such imagery in the religious or emblematic tradition of historically situated context or tradition.[6] It is also striking that Butler's aim in providing his account of *King Lear* is the Arnoldian goal at the heart of the Leavis-Bateson debate: 'To see the object as in itself it really is.'[7] In the age in which theory no longer commands much attention, precisely because of its success, this aim seems quaint and hopelessly archaic: the delusions of idealism in the guise of empiricism. Just as, in the views of Leavis and Derrida, the 'total social context is an illusion', so the 'object as it actually is', we have been convinced, lies beyond the bounds of human perception and language.

Despite being the pre-eminent Shakespearean critic and scholar in South Africa at the time, Butler was hardly ever mentioned in the Stellenbosch English department. I recall responding in my wide-eyed innocence in conversation with the then-Head that one of the candidates for a new position in the department had a D.Phil. from Oxford: 'Wow, how could we not appoint him!' To which came

---

[4]   Leavis, 'The Responsible Critic', pp. 292–3.

[5]   That debate, with only a paraphrase of Searle's original *Glyph* essay, is collected in Jacques Derrida, *Limited Inc* (Evanston, IL: Northwestern University Press, 1988).

[6]   Rosamund Tuve's scholarly approach to Elizabethan and metaphysical poetry is singled out for attack at the opening of 'The Responsible Critic' (p. 281). See Rosemond Tuve, *Elizabethan and Metaphysical Imagery: Renaissance Poetic and Twentieth-century Critics* (Chicago: University of Chicago Press, 1968).

[7]   Matthew Arnold and Walter Pater, *The Function of Criticism at the Present Time and An Essay on Style* (New York: Macmillan, 1900), p. 13.

the response, 'We will probably not appoint him *because* he has a D.Phil. from Oxford.' F.W. Bateson was an Oxford man, although he did not have a doctorate (Leavis addresses him pointedly as *Mr* Bateson). Guy Butler returned to South Africa in 1947 having read English Honours at Brasenose College, Oxford – and, it is worth noting, he would subsequently express a strongly anti-Leavisian position on more than one occasion.[8]

To make Butler's work available in this collection of essays is, as Wright intimates, to reanimate a form of historicism that the profession of English has not recognised or taught for some 40 years, and in doing so, to return us to the terms of the debate between Leavis and Bateson in 1953. Do the essays other than Butler's take us beyond those terms?

To answer that, let us first dispose of the New Historicism. I have remarked that this movement and practice have never been especially strong in South African Shakespeare studies. Despite its Foucauldian lever on subversion and power, its archival demands (at least until the establishment of EEBO – Early English Books Online) were simply beyond the capacities of students, graduate or undergraduate, teachers and researchers in the far South. The New Historicism solved the issues of the 'object as it really is' and the 'total social context' by sidestepping both. The object is always seen in its posited relation to other objects (texts) and the 'total context' is turned into whatever variety of texts may be brought into relation with the textual object in any single act of critical scholarship. The crucial move is to replace the old quest for causal explanations that marked both old historicism and Marxist criticism with a perspectival practice in which the object is placed in relation to other texts, not in order to establish a causal explanatory relation between text and context but rather to bring about a change of aspect: the object is seen differently when placed in conjunction with any number of possible contemporary texts and images.[9] This can be a lot of fun, and it produces lots of Ph.D. dissertations, but it does not tell us why we should be teaching and performing Shakespeare in South Africa.

Deciding why we should do the latter returns us, strangely perhaps, to Leavis's decisive criticism of Bateson's historicism, and his devout commitment to the function of criticism *at any time*: evaluation. To be a critic, for Leavis, was to be engaged in a continuous process of unflinching *evaluation* of literature. The terms in which Leavis states this may now seem quaintly humanist and idealist: 'One judges a poem ... as one alone can, out of one's personal living ... The *utile*

---

[8] See Guy Butler, *A Local Habitation* (Johannesburg: David Philip, 1991), p. 6, and Chris Thurman, 'Lawrence, Leavis and Butler: Some Reflections on Appropriation, Influence, Association and "Redemption"', in Jim Phelps and Nigel Bell (eds), *D.H. Lawrence around the World: South African Perspectives* (Empangeni: Echoing Green Press), p. 270.

[9] For an account of this Wittgensteinian aspect of Greenblatt's work, which is derived from Clifford Geertz, see Chapter 5 of David Schalkwyk, *Literature and the Touch of the Real* (Newark: University of Delaware Press, 2004).

of criticism is to see that the created work fulfills its *raison d'etre*: that is, that it is read, understood and duly valued, and has the influence it should have in the contemporary sensibility.'[10] Much of this is irritatingly vague, but it does speak to the critic's engagement not only with literature but also with the demands of the society in which she lives and works. One of the simultaneously exhilarating and exhausting things about being a South African literary critic is that one's 'personal experience', no matter how far one has transferred oneself to the metropole, imposes this need for finding (or denying) value and for determining the influence of literature in one's society. For literature, read Shakespeare. Of necessity we (I know ...) need to keep answering the question of the value and influence of Shakespeare in our social and political context. This is, strangely, a responsibility called for by a critic who has, in the South African context, been excoriated for giving rise to the worst forms of cultural complacency and political irresponsibility.

When, in her contribution to this book, Natasha Distiller seeks to find in cognitive theory an explanation for Shakespeare's renewal of the human through *form*, she is implicitly engaged in a fundamental kind of (re)evaluation. Sandra Young finds value in Shakespeare's capacity for displacement, caught uneasily between the potential of these 'inherited' texts to be the forge for 'new interpretations and new meanings' in the murky politics of post-apartheid South Africa and a global world unmoored from its fixation and dependence on the northern metropole. Pier Paolo Frassinelli is also concerned with the 'decentring and displacement of Shakespeare's texts', to make them 'resonate with and speak to the new local and global habitations into which they are reinserted'. His focus on Shakespeare's fecund translatability finds the value of Distiller's transformative form in 'the multilingual and creolised character of Shakespeare's own language, and therefore the multicultural dimension that Shakespeare's texts embody'. Victor Houliston's essay comes closest to the historicisms I have been discussing, but even here there is a closing call to the recognition of Shakespeare's value as someone able to transform substance and form into the values of a living community: 'To interpret *1 Henry IV* as a plea for religious toleration, putting local obligations before ideology, is not to depoliticise Shakespeare. It is to restore to the term "political" its primary meaning: consideration of life in community.'

The underlying compulsion with evaluating Shakespeare that I have claimed is especially characteristic of South African (and ex–South African) Shakespeareans is simultaneously the source of immense anxiety. We keep asking and being asked, 'Why Shakespeare?' American and British Shakespeareans do not feel the need to justify, in social or aesthetic terms, what they teach and research, although increasingly they are under pressure to justify the humanities as such. How does one do that? The problems involved in justifying the humanities are very similar to those encapsulated by justifying Shakespeare. In a recent presentation to members of the US Congress, Alexa (Alex) Huang attempted to justify the humanities through Shakespeare. The response, as Huang put it to me, was an alarming

---

[10]   Leavis, 'The Responsible Critic', pp. 295–7.

enthusiasm for 'weaponizing' Shakespeare as one more instrument in the war on terror. The very form of the question 'Why Shakespeare?' leads to an instrumental argument. Perhaps that is why Chris Thurman, in his essay, suggests that we stop taking ourselves and the question so seriously, and '[treat] our understandable anxiety about Shakespeare ironically'.

The essays in this collection that address (if only implicitly) the question 'Why Shakespeare?' are understandably haunted by the spectre of universality that lurks in our title. Most react to the word as if it were a puffadder. If we know *one* thing about Shakespeare, it is that he is *not* universal! We are right to flinch at the word, but not because of what the word means or can be made to mean. Asked for evidence of Shakespeare's universality, universalists point to the fact that after 450 years, his stature and influence in global terms is growing. Anti-universalists respond that that's because of a particular kind of historical, political and cultural violence that entrenched him within a colonised world, and that that process is being extended and strengthened by the unstoppable reach of global capital. No refutation of this argument is possible; but that does not mean that it is true, only that it is futile.

The notion of Shakespeare's universality is nowadays implicitly held in tension with the global, which, though not universally endorsed, is more readily accepted. What's the difference? One answer might be that the notion of universality is a product of a particular moment in (Western) history: the enlightenment notions of 'taste' in Kant, for instance, or universal human rights. That matrix has been subjected to a complex critique, especially by postcolonial theory, not least because it is a local intellectual formation that passes itself off as a universal, disinterested one in its diguised pursuit of violent discrimination and exploitation. Shakespeare has been attacked precisely for being part of this occlusion of local desire in the form of supposedly universal truth.

The global, on the other hand, once it has been removed from the neo-liberal notion of 'globalisation' as the mere extension of enlightenment universality, offers what the essays in this collection celebrate as more fluid, plural, flexible and mutually enhancing possibilities, in which a Shakespeare that is no longer the product or the property of a single nation or language may be the vehicle for the meeting of local sensibilities, values and transformation: Young's 'lateral Shakespeare'.

The reason we want to flinch at the notion of the universal is not because it claims too much but rather because it is vacuous. It offers neither a conceptual nor rhetorical hold on the issues that concern us. It is futile to try and convince a US congressman who wishes to cut funding to the National Endowment for the Humanities or a South African minister of education who is determined to excise Shakespeare from the syllabus that he is valuable because he is universal. To someone who has no notion of what the humanities are or might mean, no general or abstract argument can get any traction or hold. The same is true of someone who questions the worth of Shakespeare. One would have to engage that person in the experience of a Shakespeare text: showing at specific, local points, but also within the framework of the whole, why it is striking, valuable, worth preserving and sharing. This is hard work – it also renders the 'critic' vulnerable. But it is the only way in which it can be done. Such local encounters seek to engender an event that transforms the experience of the text and its place in the shared lives of the participants in unexpected and unpredictable ways. Such events are what we aim for (I hope) when we teach Shakespeare, and they are always limited, local, dialogical; they cannot appeal to the universal as a starting point.

There is a recent movement in Shakespeare criticism that (as far as I know) has had little influence in South Africa and is so far relatively marginal in the United States and Britain. Following writers like Alain Badiou, Shakespeareans have begun to ponder a new version of the universal based especially on a conception of St Paul's negation of difference, in Galatians 3:28, through the messianic event of Christ's life and death: 'There is neither Jew nor Gentile, neither slave nor free, nor is there male and female, for you are all one in Christ Jesus.'[11] Badiou's writing is maddeningly opaque, but, in contrast to Levinas's ethics of openness to the Other, which depends upon difference, Badiou extolls the 'event' as that which, like Christ's coming, constitutes a transformative rupture in the continuity of history, and in an utterly unhistoricist, un-Hegelian way, gives rise to a new form of subjectivity:

> Against these trifling descriptions (of a reality that is both obvious and inconsistent in itself), genuine thought should affirm the following principle: since differences are what there is, and since every truth is the coming-to-be of that which is not yet, so differences are then precisely what truths depose, or render insignificant. No light is shed on any concrete situation by the notion of the 'recognition of the other'. Every modern collective configuration involves people from everywhere, who have their different ways of eating and speaking, who wear different sorts of headgear, follow different religions, have complex and varied relations to sexuality, prefer authority or disorder, and such is the way of the world.[12]

In a review, Adrian Johnston glosses this in the following way:

> 'Difference' as such isn't worthy of the labor of thinking, being what is most obvious and immediately given in today's globalized living spaces. Instead, the challenge to 'think the same', to grasp what is true for all and thus what

---

[11]   New International Version, 2011. See Alain Badiou, *Saint Paul: The Foundation of Universalism*, trans. Ray Brassier (Palo Alto: Stanford University Press, 2003). A reasonably clear lecture on the event as creative novelty may be found on the European Graduate School website at: egs.edu/index.php?id=344471&part=4.

[12]   Alain Badiou, *Ethics: An Essay on the Understanding of Evil*, trans. Peter Hallward (London: Verso, 2001), p. 27.

should be dignified as universal, is increasingly more relevant and pressing in contemporary socio-political contexts.[13]

Would following Badiou's challenge simply restore old ideas about Shakespeare's 'universality' and ignore the respect for difference upon which the very concept of South Africa as the 'Rainbow Nation' has depended? I think not, for two reasons. The 'event' as Badiou thinks of it is necessarily something completely new and transformative, unpredictable from within the conditions out of which it arises and which it changes; and that event, just as Christ brought into being a new form of Christian subjectivity, also by definition produces forms of subjectivity that we are yet to know, yet to inhabit. Moving away from a geographical, political and cultural obeisance to our historical allegiances – allies for whom our difference will always be a quaint kind of Shakespeare tourism – to what is now called the 'global South' may enable the kind of event that Badiou urges, in which the universality of Shakespeare will mean such a thing as dreams are made on. One never knows. It's worth a try.

---

[13] Adrian Johnstone, 'Review: Alain Badiou', *Metapsychology: Online Reviews* (2002). Available online at: metapsychology.mentalhelp.net/poc/view_doc. php?type=book&id=1278.

Introduction
Generation S:
'Southern' Shakespeares
across Time and Space

Chris Thurman

In their recent book *Theory from the South: Or, How Euro-America Is Evolving Toward Africa* (2012), anthropologists Jean and John Comaroff express a growing dissatisfaction amongst scholars internationally (from disciplines across the arts, humanities and social sciences) with various prevailing assumptions about the relationship between the 'global north' and the 'global south' in assessments of modernity. They ask, 'What if we posit that, in the present moment, it is the global south that affords privileged insight into the workings of the world at large?':

> To the degree that the making of modernity has been a world-historical process, it can as well be narrated from its undersides as it can from its self-proclaimed centers – like those maps that, as a cosmic joke, invert planet Earth to place the south on top, the north below ... because the history of the present reveals itself more starkly in the antipodes, it challenges us to make sense of it, empirically and theoretically, from that distinct advantage.[1]

What might this mean for the field of Shakespeare studies, whose historical and geographical scope expands from early modern Europe to a contemporary 'postmodern' globe?

The image on the cover of this book is one form of the cartographical inversion that the Comaroffs describe: an upside-down version of the world map produced by Henricus Martellus (Heinrich Hammer) towards the end of the fifteenth century. The map famously, or infamously, extends and expands the length of the southern African landmass, making it look much more difficult to access the Indian Ocean and east Asia from Europe by rounding the Cape of Good Hope. It has been suggested that this distortion was encouraged either by Christopher Columbus (to strengthen his case for a westward passage to China) or by King Joao II of Portugal (to 'discourage competitors' after the success of Bartholomew

---

[1]   Jean and John Comaroff, *Theory from the South: Or, How Euro-America Is Evolving Toward Africa* (London: Paradigm, 2012), pp. 1–7.

Dias's voyage in 1488).[2] Significantly, Martellus had to break the frame painted around the map in order to accommodate the southern African extrusion: 'To show Africa breaking the map frame is a symbolic statement that the continent is not confined to the *oikumene* [inhabited/civilised world], but it also suggests that Dias' voyage is a kind of transgression whose implications are not yet understood.'[3] By inverting Martellus's map on the cover, I do not seek simply to 'turn the story upside down', which the Comaroffs warn is 'to leave intact the Manichean dualism that holds Euro-America and its others in the same, fixed embrace'. Rather, I want to emphasise a breaking of the frame – both to disrupt the frameworks within which 'South African Shakespeare' has been placed and to suggest that doing so has the potential to challenge some of the conceptual frameworks applied to Shakespeare studies more generally.

In a country like South Africa, Shakespeare is both a marginal concern and a prominent presence; while only a handful of his plays are performed professionally each year, and while few academics would claim Shakespeare as a primary research interest, the man from Stratford remains a significant figure in educational syllabi and a familiar symbol (whether loved or hated) in popular discourse. To apply the Comaroffs' paradigm, thinking about Shakespeare from a 'southern' / South African point of view may offer numerous insights into Shakespearean phenomena, not only in what they call 'Euro-America' but worldwide. The present collection addresses certain nuances of Shakespearean production and reception across time and space. Each essay is inflected by a South African connection: in some cases, simply because of the author's nationality, birthplace or institutional affiliation; in others, there is a more explicit engagement with what Shakespeare means, or has meant, in South Africa. By considering continuities and 'generation gaps' in South African Shakespeare studies, I suggest, the book presents new possibilities for understanding and assessing shifting manifestations of Shakespeare's work in major Shakespearean 'centres' such as Britain and the United States, as well as across the global north and south.

***

Over the last few decades, there have been a number of book-length studies of Shakespeare in/and South Africa. Martin Orkin's *Shakespeare against Apartheid* (1987) was followed, in the early years of the country's transition to democracy, by David Johnson's *Shakespeare and South Africa* (1996) and by *Post-Colonial*

---

2   Anthony Parr, 'Inventions of Africa', in *T'kama-Adamastor: Inventions of Africa in a South African Painting*, ed. Ivan Vladislavic (Johannesburg: University of the Witwatersrand, 2000), p. 107. Parr provides a useful overview of the conflicting theories about the map's provenance and relates it to other key documents in the history of European-African cartography.

3   Ibid., p. 109. Parr is careful to note that 'the Martellus map is not merely idiosyncratic in this respect': previous maps of Europe had breached the margin to take in Scandinavian trade routes, and subsequent world maps would also include a 'frame-breaking Cape'.

Shakespeares (1998), edited by Orkin and Ania Loomba, which contains numerous essays on 'SA Shakespeare'. Rohan Quince's *Shakespeare in South Africa* (2000) is a study of stage productions during the apartheid era. In 2005, Natasha Distiller's *South Africa, Shakespeare and Post-Colonial Culture* and Orkin's *Local Shakespeares: Proximations and Power* took up the theme once more, emphasising the point made above about the relationship between South Africa (as an admittedly problematic 'representative' of aspects of postmodernity/postcoloniality) and 'global' Shakespeare studies. *The Shakespeare International Yearbook 2009* contained a special section on 'South African Shakespeare in the Twentieth Century' (edited by Laurence Wright). 2012 saw the publication of Distiller's *Shakespeare and the Coconuts: On Post-apartheid South African Culture* and Ashwin Desai's *Reading Revolution: Shakespeare on Robben Island*. David Schalkwyk's *Hamlet's Dreams*, which also treats of the so-called Robben Island Bible (a copy of the *Complete Works* circulated amongst political prisoners) along with South African prison memoirs, appeared early in 2013. The annual journal *Shakespeare in Southern Africa* has, in recent volumes, published articles that stretch back to the nineteenth century (on early engagement with Shakespeare by black South Africans as well as on 'settler' Shakespeareans in the Eastern Cape)[4] and reviews that are directly concerned with contemporary South African appropriations of Shakespeare. The field is thus well established and continues to grow. Insofar as the essays collected here constitute an extension of this field, that is a felicitous outcome – but it is not the book's primary concern. Rather, what binds these essays together is a broader interest in the ways in which 'Shakespeare' (that is, not only Shakespeare's work but also Shakespeare-as-symbol: the idea of Shakespeare, as it were) has been and continues to be transported across time and space.

It is notable that what emerge in these pages as matters of concern to South Africans teaching and writing on Shakespeare are matters with which Shakespeareans across the globe in the twenty-first century must grapple: multilingualism and the hegemony of English; Shakespeare as metonym for the 'canonical' and his contested place in educational curricula; the relationship between page and stage/screen, between text and performance; Shakespeare and empire or neo-imperialism; Shakespeare and race or ethnicity. Admittedly, some of them have historical inflections specific to South Africa, such as the apartheid government's 'Bantu Education' policies, or the privilege of 'white liberals', or Shakespeare's co-option as a means of black oppression. Race, of course, is an acute concern – to the point, for instance, that some South African readers may (rightly) find it discomfiting that all of the contributors to this volume are white. Yet

---

[4]   See Brian Willan, 'Whose Shakespeare? Early Black South African Engagement with Shakespeare', *Shakespeare in Southern Africa* 24 (2012): pp. 3–18; and Laurence Wright, 'Cultivating Grahamstown: Nathaniel Merriman, Shakespeare and Books', *Shakespeare in Southern Africa* 20 (2008): pp. 25–38, along with Merriman's lectures reproduced in volumes 20 (2008): pp. 39–62, and 21 (2009): pp. 1–22.

the book also demonstrates that any narrative of South African 'exceptionalism' (and such narratives are widely accepted) is flawed and inadequate, for it cannot explain South Africa's position in the global economy, in the cultural fluidity of a world defined by transmission and migration and exchange, or even in intersecting geopolitical networks. Reciprocally, it demonstrates that narratives of implicit or explicit 'exclusion' are no longer tenable; South African Shakespeare scholars are, *wille we nelle we*, part of the global community of Shakespeare scholarship.

***

The title of my introduction alludes to generational differences and similarities. Some 60 years separate the birth dates of the 'oldest' contributor to this book (the late Guy Butler – more on whom below) and the younger authors. Brian Pearce's essay takes us a couple of generations further back, to the era of G. Wilson Knight and E.M.W. Tillyard and John Dover Wilson, the scholarship inherited by South African Shakespeareans as much as by the Anglo-American academy. One might thus track shifts in ideological positioning: from an early-mid-twentieth-century perspective – in which the dominance of 'Englishness', of Shakespeare in exported English culture, of early modern Europe as intrinsically significant to that culture, and of Shakespeare in the 'high art' establishment, remains self-evident and unchallenged – to a post-apartheid perspective, ever-anxious about Shakespeare's place in the global south in the twenty-first century, driven by a desire both to justify and to critique that place in terms of relevance or applicability or complicity. One might also track stylistic and methodological shifts, which run more or less in parallel with the changing styles and methodologies of literary scholarship over the last hundred years: from an essayistic (perhaps occasionally even belletristic) approach to a rigorously, self-consciously scientist or 'research-based' one; or from historicism to New Criticism to high theory to New Historicism and now, in Terry Eagleton's formulation, the challenge of writing 'after theory'.[5]

Yet I anticipate – indeed, I hope – that readers of this book, encountering 'Generation S', will also find such generalised trajectories inaccurate. The 'rise and fall of the man of letters' is a narrative that has been convincingly elucidated by John Gross[6] and others, taking in the effect of the formalisation of literary studies at universities and the subsequent social or institutional pressures that shaped the development of disciplines like English/Literary Studies and Drama. Nonetheless, any Shakespearean reading decades- or even centuries-old works of criticism on the plays, sonnets and narrative poems is likely to discern a sense of critical kinship (of shared reading experience and shared affective or intellectual responses to Shakespeare) with the authors of such works – alongside, and despite, any manifest political or cultural distance from them.

---

[5]   See Terry Eagleton, *After Theory* (London: Allen Lane, 2003).

[6]   See John Gross, *The Rise and Fall of the Man of Letters: Aspects of English Literary Life since 1880* (London: Penguin, 1991).

How, then, can this phenomenon be discussed without recourse to claims of universality? Is it possible to problematise the Jonsonian dictum that Shakespeare was 'not of an age, but for all time' (a declaration that has subsequently been echoed in various forms: not of a country, but for all countries; not of a language, but for all languages) without dismissing its transnational, transcultural or atemporal claims? What are the uses, and limits, of a humanism that ostensibly seeks to disregard difference – and the institutionalised hierarchies of power based on differentiation – but that in fact typically reinforces difference-as-inequality?

These are the questions that Natasha Distiller, Sandra Young and Pier Paolo Frassinelli address in the first section of this book. Distiller's answers take her into the heady terrain of neuroscience and cognitive literary studies as she seeks to escape 'the tiresome binary construction which continually sets essentialism against deconstruction as polar opposites, when they have never been as utterly philosophically different as they have sometimes been made to seem – although they can be politically at odds'. Young takes Jonson as her starting point but engages with geopolitical, rather than temporal, 'universality'; she, too, suggests an alternative to 'vacillating between ... two poles' (in this case, of resistance and appropriation) through the recognition that 'Shakespeare has become wonderfully, productively, unhinged'. Frassinelli considers 'the confluence of the translational and the transnational', working on the premise that Shakespeare's works are always-already translated by time – or, more specifically, history – before additional processes of linguistic transformation are undertaken.

The second section in the book contains a few examples of how Shakespeare's work has been further 'mediated': processes of mediation that have both facilitated the 'universal spread' of Shakespeare and have reinscribed our separation from him. Victor Houliston's essay elucidates the connections between Sir John Oldcastle and Shakespeare's Falstaff, demonstrating the Catholic-Protestant tensions that informed and were informed by Shakespeare's work, but also affirming that 'The more we know about the actual circumstances of early modern English people, the less confident we should be about the drawing of party lines.' My own reflections on 'mediation' concern the medium of film and its (perhaps inevitable) aggravation of national rivalries over the 'ownership' of Shakespeare-as-cultural-capital, using Al Pacino's playfulness in *Looking for Richard* as instance and football/soccer as analogue. Brian Pearce's survey of critical approaches – both literary and theatrical – to Shakespeare's late plays in the early decades of the twentieth century not only explains the renewed interest in these plays but also provides a useful overview of the development of differing 'schools' in Shakespearean criticism during this period.

Pearce's essay helps us to understand the 'apolitical' Shakespearean tradition that was reproduced by South African English academics (despite the fact that groundbreaking translations and adaptations of Shakespeare's plays were being undertaken by Sol Plaatje during precisely the period Pearce describes, establishing a parallel 'black' South African tradition of responding to Shakespeare that would, during the course of the twentieth century, become increasingly politicised). It was noted above that names such as Wilson Knight and Tillyard and Dover Wilson, and of course the ubiquitous A.C. Bradley, dominated Shakespearean criticism into the middle decades of the century. During the 1960s and 1970s, of course, scholars in the Anglo-American academy began to turn away from this critical canon to embrace the 'radical' possibilities of literary theory and, later, cultural materialism. Yet in countries like South Africa, this shift only occurred some 10 or 20 years later – and even then, it was attenuated by a kind of conservatism on the part of literary scholars generally and Shakespeareans in particular.

One might attribute this inertia to the country's isolation or to the anachronism that often results from a 'colonial cringe', especially amongst English-speakers in former English colonies. It is telling that there were no South African (or South Africa–based) Shakespeareans in the 1950s, 1960s and 1970s whose work had global scholarly impact. Yet this was not matched by a dearth of Shakespeare-related activity in South Africa during these years. There was lots of Shakespeare in classrooms and theatres, but less in locally published academic journals and books, and very little indeed from South Africans in internationally published journals and books. Instead, there were conferences, public lectures, Shakespeare festivals – events that have for the most part been forgotten. This book posits the enigmatic (and often controversial) figure of Guy Butler as a representative of these previous generations of South African Shakespeare teachers, theatre-makers and scholars. Butler was considered by many to be the country's foremost Shakespearean, yet his published output as a Shakespeare scholar was comparatively slim – and mostly appeared in the 1980s and 1990s, the latter part of his career, by which stage his theoretical, methodological and ideological approaches were decidedly 'old-fashioned'. The third section of the book thus seeks to present, and to engage with, some of Butler's previously unpublished work.

***

Insofar as there was substantially less Shakespeare scholarship published than produced in South Africa or by South Africans for much of the twentieth century, this arguably reflects an acute instance of a broader 'English studies' pattern in the country. Although Shakespeare-related essays, articles and reviews appeared in various local literary or scholarly journals that flourished and withered in the decades after World War II – years of increasing isolation as the apartheid state became an international pariah – it was only in 1987 that the journal *Shakespeare in Southern Africa* was established.[7] Prior to this, much of the material published

---

[7]   A publication such as volume 20 (1977) of the journal *English Studies in Africa* provides an insight into the state of Shakespeare scholarship in South Africa at the time. There was enough research and writing activity in the field to justify two semi-themed issues of the journal – much of the space is dedicated to articles and essays on Shakespeare (although none of them, it must be said, directly engages with the question of Shakespeare-in-South-Africa). Yet Shakespeare studies could not fill both issues of volume 20; the

on Shakespeare was oriented towards teachers and teaching;[8] moreover, the 'public lecture' remained as prestigious a forum for disseminating ideas as the published article.

The material collected under the heading 'Butler's Shakespeare Reconsidered' is one means of representing this only partly documented scholarly activity. Instead of Samuel Butler (Victorian polymath and author of *Shakespeare's Sonnets Reconsidered*), we have Guy Butler: a much-contested but important figure in South African literary history. I have previously written about Butler as poet, essayist, dramatist, historian, memoirist and cultural politician – offering, in *Guy Butler: Reassessing a South African Literary Life* (2010), this apology: 'I have not engaged with Butler's research into and writing on Shakespeare in the depth that these indubitably merit. Indeed, an entire volume could and ought to be dedicated to the subject, but much of it is beyond the scope of this book.'[9] That claim may have been something of an overstatement, but the final section of the present volume is, at least, a partial response to it.

In various ways, Butler's scholarship is dated. Critics such as Orkin and Distiller have, in fact, suggested that Butler's version of Shakespeare was a conservative and reactionary one even when it was 'current'. In other ways, however, his essays remain astute and pertinent. This tension – which reflects the fact that good literary criticism does not become moribund, even though it becomes perceived as outmoded, or *is* in fact outmoded – is part of the impetus behind the 'Generation S' notion. Laurence Wright's essay on Butler's *Lear* offers a number of insights into Butler-as-Shakespearean more generally, applying these to the tidal ebb and flow of early modern studies, of literary studies and of other related disciplines. As Wright notes, Butler was 'no fan' of New Historicist and Cultural Materialist 'presentism', nor of their precursors; if Maynard Mack's seminal work was *King Lear in Our Time* (1965), Butler's magnum opus was to be titled *King Lear in Shakespeare's Time*. Butler frequently expounded upon the need to 'remove our twentieth century spectacles and reach for an Elizabethan pair'.[10] His was a broadly historicist approach – emphasising context and background, sources and influences – with a focus on performance and Elizabethan/Jacobean reception. This is all fair enough, but what are we to make of the dismissive tone that marks the opening paragraphs of his 'Shakespeare's Dramatic Vision'?

Shakespearean material sits alongside two articles on Herman Charles Bosman and Pauline Smith, a conjunction that gives some idea of the success of the 'SA Eng. Lit.' campaign (spearheaded by Butler among others) that perhaps reached its apex in the 1970s.

[8]   See Malcolm Hacksley's bibliography of Shakespeare articles in *CRUX – A Journal on the Teaching of English* as an example of a rich but 'overlooked resource'. 'Shakespeare in *CRUX*, 1967–1991: An Overlooked Resource for Teachers of Shakespeare?', *Occasional Papers and Reviews* (Shakespeare Society of Southern Africa) 7.1 (1992): pp. 14–20.

[9]   Chris Thurman, *Guy Butler: Reassessing a South African Literary Life* (Scottsville: University of KwaZulu-Natal Press, 2010), p. 4.

[10]   Guy Butler, 'Jacobean Psychiatry: Edgar's Curative Stratagems', *Shakespeare in Southern Africa* 2 (1988): p. 21.

The generation of [Walter] Clyde-Curry and Tillyard could still assume that most readers knew the elements of the Christian doctrine of man, so that no explication of this seemed necessary. Judging from some recent critical works, however, and from the muddled paganism of many of my students, this assumption can no longer be made. Enlightened post-Christians, who still believe that the great works of the European past are worth studying, all need to be reminded of this Christian scheme from time to time – particularly when writers like Jan Kott believe that they are doing Shakespeare some sort of a favour by calling him our contemporary – as if it were a great honour to be dragged from the pinnacle of the English Renaissance to paddle with us in the 'filthy modern tide'.

I believe that it can be demonstrated that Shakespeare accepted, with improved Renaissance amplifications, the great medieval synthesis or myth. For all our achievements since, we have not managed to replace it. We live in a fragmenting cosmos.[11]

There are two important observations to be made in response to this curmudgeonly complaint. The first is that Butler's claim here – along with his aside about the theological ignorance of his students – is entirely at odds with his practice as a teacher, which was constantly to relate Shakespeare to affairs of the day. Wright emphasises this point in his essay, echoing the recollection of another former student (later a colleague and friend), Paul Walters:

With a quick turn of phrase or a passing topical reference to matters of the day, [Butler] could suddenly collapse the centuries between Shakespeare and ourselves or illuminate some difficulty of the text while simultaneously passing a challenging, penetrating comment on some sacred cow or unquestioned assumption of our own time.[12]

One might argue in mitigation of Butler's relentless historicism – of his insistence on the inadequate historical knowledge of most people who read or view Shakespeare's plays – that focusing on how far removed the Elizabethan past was from the global post–World War II present allowed Butler to critique that present: the increasingly hollow ideological conflict of the Cold War, the absurdly tragic policy of apartheid, or the self-congratulatory rhetoric that denied the abuses of the twentieth century in order to affirm some pseudo-Hegelian vision of 'progress'. A sympathetic reading of Butler's editorial in the inaugural volume (1987) of *Shakespeare in Southern Africa* would see its conclusion as an affirmation of such a notion:

Some may believe this is neither the time nor the place to be founding a society to encourage the appreciation of a dramatist who was born in a foreign land

---

[11]   See Jan Kott, *Shakespeare Our Contemporary* (London: Methuen, 1967). 'Filthy modern tide' is from W.B. Yeats's poem 'The Statues'.

[12]   Letter from Walters to Butler, 8 June 1983. Courtesy South African National English Literary Museum.

over four hundred years ago, and whose works are written in an archaic form of English. South Africa has more urgent matters to attend to. It certainly has; but that does not mean that long-term interests must be neglected. There are occasions when urgent matters may properly benefit from our attending to matters of permanent importance.[13]

The cover of the journal – showing John Kani and Joanna Weinberg in Janet Suzman's then-scandalous production of *Othello* – would seem to reinforce the point: Shakespeare's play, the prominence of the image implied, could speak directly to (and could inform, elucidate or protest against) a society in which love 'across the colour bar' was illegal. Orkin and Distiller, however, are among those who do not accept the editorial's closing declaration as evidence that Butler's historicism was the grounds of a radical challenge to the present; rather, Orkin suggested at the time, the journal and the Shakespeare Society that published it reinscribed 'the assimilationist and colonialist discourse so favoured amongst the South African ruling classes of earlier decades'.[14] Butler's editorial, Orkin argued, 'by means of a patronising version of dreams of a democratic millennium, sidesteps the central problem of the way in which the Shakespeare text is *presently* put to use within South Africa.'[15] David Johnson has noted that the practice of 'defending long-term interests' which Butler seemed to be promoting 'involved in the first issues of the journal a continuing investment in traditional English Shakespeare critics, with names like Dover Wilson, Muir, and Knights appearing most frequently in the endnotes'.[16]

Yet if, in the late 1980s, attention to the present and anticipation of the future meant, to many South African Shakespeareans, 'looking backward', a different kind of 'looking back' is afforded to the twenty-first-century observer – the hindsight made possible by 25 years during which the country both achieved the 'dream of a democratic millennium' and realised that the 'urgent matter' of opposing apartheid would be followed by a stream of other 'urgent matters' in the post-apartheid state: a growing wealth-poverty gap, HIV/AIDS, crime, ongoing racism and xenophobia, widespread corruption and occasional threats of a return to a police state. Some of these issues have indeed found their way into the pages of *Shakespeare in Southern Africa* over the last two decades (I make this observation as the journal's current editor), but there are also undoubtedly readers who would find evidence of 'the "relentlessly apolitical" stance of many Renaissance literary scholars' in the country.[17]

---

13 Butler, 'Editorial', *Shakespeare in Southern Africa* 1 (1987): p. v.

14 Orkin, *Drama and the South African State* (Manchester: Manchester University Press, 1991), p. 243.

15 Ibid., p. 242.

16 Johnson, *Shakespeare in South Africa* (Oxford: Oxford University Press, 1996), p. 208.

17 Thurman, 'Editorial', *Shakespeare in Southern Africa* 21 (2009): p. iii.

Irrespective of how one interprets his position as inaugural editor of *Shakespeare in Southern Africa* or his 'historicity' (which Wright distinguishes from 'supine thraldom to various *historicisms*'), it does seem fair to assert that Butler was more conservative as a Shakespearean than he was in any of his other literary-cultural roles. Whereas his poetry, drama and prose often challenge orthodoxies – religious, sociopolitical and otherwise – his Shakespeare scholarship tends to stress narrative resolution, to embrace Renaissance conceptions of cosmic harmony and divine providence. Perhaps one might apply, to Butler, Victor Kiernan's description of Shakespeare himself not as a 'conservative' but a 'conservator' – one who tries to 'recapture' a sense of something 'whole' even while living in a 'divided society'.[18] This can in turn be related to Wright's comments about the differences between Butler's mode of Shakespeare scholarship and that which has been adopted by, or forced upon, subsequent generations of academics, who 'find themselves trapped in the toils of a mechanical Nietzschean perspectivism' (some readers may take issue with this depiction):

> The whole [work] stays forever beyond the horizon, because the academic publishing system requires only the unique angle, and this necessitates marginalising what is already known, however adequate or compelling it might be ... Butler wrote his study of *Lear* not only out of a sense of awe and amazement that such a work exists, but because to a remarkable extent he identified with the play.
>
> This is absolutely not the way today's university-trained academics approach works of art, except perhaps in unguarded moments before an undergraduate audience ... [They fulfil] their managed role as distanced spectators caught up in the intellectual simulacra created by our culture's predicament of late literacy. No longer are they independently questing participants sharing life-changing artistic and intellectual experiences in one amazing circumambient universe.

More acutely, however, Kiernan's invocation of 'wholeness' resonates with the second point to which the earlier quotation from 'Shakespeare's Dramatic Vision' gives rise: Butler's misgivings about the centuries-long project of modernity are voiced, in his Shakespeare scholarship, in a manner that regrets modernity's 'fragmenting cosmos' (or its fragmenting view of the cosmos). Thus the vexed intellectual and affective wrestling with the contradictions and paradoxes of Christian theology, particularly prominent in Butler's poetry, is not discernible in his writing on Shakespeare – even though his much-loved *King Lear*, of all Shakespeare's plays, most urgently addresses questions of divine benevolence, fairness, indifference, malice or simple absence. The affirmation that 'The Gods are just, and of our pleasant vices / Make instruments to plague us' (5.3.169–70) is countered by the claim that, 'As flies to wanton boys, so are we to th'Gods; / They kill us for their sport' (4.1.36–7) and ample evidence to support Edmund's argument that 'heavenly compulsion' or 'a divine thrusting on' has, in fact, nothing to do with 'all that we are evil [or good] in' (1.2.119–23). Yet, as Wright notes,

---

[18]   Victor Kiernan, *Shakespeare: Poet and Citizen* (London: Verso, 1993), pp. 14–15.

Butler's *Lear* opus offers a 'profoundly Christian reading of the play'. Indeed, in a shorter article on '*Jacobean Psychiatry*' and *King Lear*, Butler concludes with a notion 'very dear to some Elizabethans': 'Men in their ignorance ascribe to the stars or to Fortune actions and events which are, in fact, the workings of God through Providence. Men think they are calling the tune, but the initiative has passed into someone else's hands in a way which is later seen to be providential.'[19]

How seriously can we take such claims about an assured world or cosmic view informing all of Shakespeare's work? In this case, Butler's focus is on Edgar foiling Gloucester's attempted suicide – deceiving his father in order to save him from despair. He alludes to instances in other plays (*The Two Noble Kinsmen* and *The Winter's Tale*) that demonstrate the principle of 'justified deception', but neglects to mention two of the most memorable manifestations of this idea in the Shakespearean oeuvre: the bed-tricks in *All's Well That Ends Well* and *Measure for Measure*.[20] The Duke in *Measure*, arranging a bed-trick to rectify the villainy of Angelo, declares that 'the doubleness of the benefit defends the deceit from reproof' (3.1.258–9); likewise, when Helena is forced into a similar contrivance in *All's Well*, she insists that it is 'wicked meaning in a lawful deed, / And lawful meaning in a wicked act' (3.7.45–6). Moreover, Helena's affirmation that 'Our remedies oft in ourselves do lie / Which we ascribe to heaven' echoes Edmund's dismissal of dependence on the divine or supernatural. These lines directly undermine Butler's argument that in Shakespeare's plays we see the working-out of the Elizabethan view that men (and women) are wrong if they 'think they are calling the tune'.

Nonetheless, this emphasis in Butler's Shakespeare scholarship resonates in a different key with that multivalent, contested word: 'universal'. When assessed in light of the Jonsonian formula ('not of an age, but for all time'), Butler's approach to Shakespeare appears contradictory – or, at least, ambiguous. On the one hand, if studying Shakespeare is a matter of 'permanent importance', then the man from Stratford *is* 'for all time'. On the other hand, Butler challenged the credo of Shakespeare's universality by persistently situating him in 'an age', demonstrating how he was bound by or embedded in history, in a time and place with its own beliefs, preoccupations, anxieties and customs. This contradiction is at least partly reconciled by Butler's focus on the cosmic dimensions of 'universality' – literally, Shakespeare's conception of the universe and his theological assumptions about the Creator of that universe.

***

A few more observations about Butler-as-Shakespearean are apposite when discussing the 'generation gaps' in Shakespeare scholarship, not just in South Africa but in various corners of the global academy. It is instructive to revisit those

---

[19] Butler, 'Jacobean Psychiatry', pp. 29–30.

[20] It is worth noting that Butler also chooses not to discuss the (ab)use of early modern psychiatric practices by Feste, Toby et al. to tormet the 'mad' Malvolio in *Twelfth Night*.

articles and papers (published and delivered late in his career) in which Butler most explicitly attempts to position Shakespeare studies as 'local', 'relevant' or 'postcolonial', in light of Sandra Young's contribution to this book. In 'Notes on Seeing and Hearing Shakespeare's Plays in South Africa' (1991), for instance, Butler affirms:

> Africans are generally more aware than Europeans that death is not a dead-end, but a change in status into a shade or ancestor. They have far less difficulty with Shakespeare's ghosts than we do. They are altogether more aware of the numinous, the unearthly, the sacral.
>
> This equips them ... for a more spontaneous response to certain elements in, for instance, *Macbeth* and *The Tempest* than the products of industrial secularisation.[21]

There is much to take issue with here – the terminology of 'African' and 'European', of 'we' and 'they', never mind the reductive essentialising of an African, and for that matter a European, culture and worldview – but what Butler is trying to argue is that black South Africans may in fact be better placed than their white compatriots, or 'Westerners' generally, to respond to Shakespeare's plays in ways that Shakespeare himself 'intended' (again the historicist leaning is discernible). Is this a valid way of assessing Shakespeare's relevance in a country like South Africa? Let us consider another example: 'The Fair Queen Who Liked Blacks' (1994), in which Butler considers the role of Queen Anne in increasing the prominence and status of 'blackamoors' at the courts of King James. The 'sympathy' of the Danish-Scottish-English queen for black attendants, slaves, merchants and envoys was not, Butler argues, simply a matter of keeping 'fashionable items in her entourage'.[22] Rather, it extended to artistic enterprises (she commissioned Jonson to write his *Maske of Blackness*, in which she performed, 'challenging the rigid conventional equation of blackness and ugliness, of light and beauty') and, indeed, to Shakespeare's commentary on matters of love, race and state: according to Butler, both *Othello* and *Antony and Cleopatra* were influenced by Anne's unorthodox attitudes towards 'Moorish' Others in early modern Europe.[23] Once more, Butler's primary interest in the plays' conception, production and early reception is evident; ultimately, as the paper's title implies, the focus is on 'the fair queen' and not the 'blacks' she 'liked'. But what can we make of the focus on race? It is a common assumption that, as race is central to the South African story,

---

[21] Butler, 'Notes on Seeing and Hearing Shakespeare's Plays in South Africa', in *Guy Butler: Essays and Lectures 1949–1991*, ed. Stephen Watson (Cape Town: David Philip, 1994), pp. 223–4.

[22] Butler, 'The Fair Queen Who Liked Blacks', in *Shakespeare Across Cultures: Conference Papers* (Grahamstown: Shakespeare Society of Southern Africa, 1994), p. 19. Later published in *Shakespeare in Southern Africa* 9 (1996): pp. 1–21.

[23] Ibid., p. 43.

those of Shakespeare's plays (and sonnets) that directly address racial issues are of inherent interest to South Africans. As Young suggests, however,

> If it is to be meaningful as a critical paradigm, 'global Shakespeare' has to go further than adding superficial, race-based 'interest' to the early modern period. Its real value ... is to be found in its invitation to recognise with greater perspicacity the ideological dimensions of cultural and critical life and the fundamental asymmetries of power relations at work.

This going-further-than (or going-beyond) race speaks to another facet of the 'generation gap' between current South African – and 'global' – Shakespeare scholars and their predecessors. It is perhaps analogous, albeit not equivalent, to changing analyses of gender in the 'power relations at work' inside and outside Shakespeare's plays. Butler's ideas about 'the feminine principle', the maternal figure and the family structure in *King Lear* were rejected out of hand by Janet Adelman who, in 1985, castigated Butler for seeming to be 'wholly ignorant of a large body of feminist and psychoanalytic work' and for writing 'absolutely solipsistically', without citing critical material published more recently than 1966 (one wonders what the author of *Suffocating Mothers* would have made of Butler's treatment of the mother-figure and the nature/family/women versus law/city/men binary in *Coriolanus*).[24]

It is worth noting, in light of Adelman's condemnation, that while Butler was obviously widely read, his Shakespearean essays and lectures are comparatively bare of references to other scholars – and certainly to recent work in the field; Butler's generation, and those before him, were not as anxious as contemporary academics to be (or to be seen to be) 'up to speed'. In his lectures in particular, Butler makes frequent use of phrases such as 'critics have noted that' without feeling obliged to provide specific references. This is reminiscent of an older image of the 'professor' – the learned man, speaking with an authority that issues ex cathedra, who has no insecurities about corroboration. In his notes for a presentation on *Antony and Cleopatra*, Butler introduces a claim by remarking: 'Two professors of classics have assured me that ...' This kind of informal citation would not pass muster in a peer-reviewed publication, but is perhaps germane to the delivery of a public/popular lecture.

Mary-Helen Simpson observes a similar mismatch between the casual mode of quotation in a series of lectures on 'Destabilising Shakespeare', delivered by André Brink in 1994, and the expectations of bibliographical accuracy that readers may bring to Brink's *Destabilising Shakespeare*, published two years

---

[24] Janet Adelman, *Report on 'King Lear and the Feminine Principle' for PMLA* (Modern Language Association of America), 11 October 1985. Courtesy South African National English Literary Museum. See Butler, 'Soldier Heroes in Corrupt Societies: A Comparison of N.P. van Wyk Louw's Germanicus and Shakespeare's Coriolanus' (Booklet: N.P. van Wyk Louw lecture, Rand Afrikaans University, 13 September 1976).

later.[25] Simpson's complaint about referencing is not mere pedantry; cavalier allusions to Shakespeare's plays and to theoretical material, she implies, reinforce the ideological disjunctions manifested in Brink's habit of invoking 'literary and historical critics such as Wilson (1924), Rowse (1950) and Kott (1965) in close proximity to citations of Stallybrass (1991) or Dollimore and Sinfield (1985) as though they belong to the same order of critical methodology.' Perhaps this is an unfair objection. After all, one of the hypotheses tested in the present volume is that Shakespeare scholars whose methodologies and whose politics might differ substantially – largely as a result of their differing geographical, socio-cultural or temporal locations – may nonetheless be placed in productive dialogue.

Let us return to Adelman's frustration with Butler over the retrograde notion of the 'feminine principle', which is echoed in Simpson's suggestion that Brink (owing to 'a rather too ready acceptance of supposed Renaissance binarisms between masculine *virtus* and warrior behaviour and the "feminine" tendency he identifies in characters such as Richard II') frequently 'lapses into a rather essentialized Feminism'. Brink's 'attempts at destabilization', according to Simpson, 'seem somewhat belated' – coming, as they do, a decade or more after those seminal works with which a title like *Destabilising Shakespeare* seems to associate itself: Stephen Greenblatt's *Renaissance Self-fashioning* (1980), Jonathan Dollimore's *Radical Tragedy* (1984), John Drakakis's *Alternative Shakespeares* (1985) and Terry Eagleton's *William Shakespeare* (1986). By the mid-1990s, world political and economic developments had at least partially 'consigned' these texts to a discrete – past – historical moment. This brings into question the possibility (and the desirability) of any theoretical position remaining 'radical'. Even the feminist readings of Shakespeare so persuasively championed by a critic such as Adelman can be limiting. In her essay, Natasha Distiller endorses feminist critiques of 'universal Shakespeare' as well as of 'the evolution of science and biology as discursive fields'; but, echoing Judith Butler, she notes that the value of such critiques can be undermined if they become too deterministic:

> We all inherit structures: psychic, social, linguistic, which various theories from psychoanalysis to feminism to Marxism have worked so hard to point out. But if we are to avoid a dead-end determinism which in any event is patently inadequate in the face of many things human, from great art to the surprises of individual relationships, we have to acknowledge that there is something in what it is to be human which always exceeds its inherited categories or starting points.

The essays in this collection navigate a path between Marxism and humanism, between the 'universal' and the 'particular', between South Africa and 'the globe', between *then* and *now*. If the 'Generation S' concept seeks to identify strands of continuity, or indeed fault lines, running across the accumulating seams of Shakespeare scholarship, then it also (to extend an awkward geological metaphor)

---

[25] See Mary-Helen Simpson, 'Shakespeare on the Brink' (Review of André Brink, *Destabilising Shakespeare*), *Scrutiny2* 2.2 (1997): pp. 64–6.

acknowledges each layer of such scholarship to be inextricably embedded and, for better or worse, 'dated'. Butler related Coriolanus, the 'soldier hero in a corrupt society', to critiques of Afrikaner nationalism (with Volumnia as *volksmoeder*).[26] Twenty-first-century South Africans who know, courtesy of Mark Gevisser's biography of Thabo Mbeki, that *Coriolanus* is the former state president's favourite Shakespearean work are inclined to see a different application of the play to the country's sociopolitical problems.[27] No doubt later South African generations will find – and create – new 'local significance' in the play, requiring a self-revising process of *wirkungsgeschichte*.

***

In the months prior to the 2012 London Olympics, the Royal Shakespeare Company and the Globe Theatre put on 'the biggest celebration of Shakespeare ever staged': the World Shakespeare Festival (incorporating the Globe to Globe project), in which a host of international theatre companies performed in almost 70 productions across the city over the course of three months. While the extravaganza was still underway, Emer O'Toole penned this rather scathing response:

> We have reached the point where what's interesting about Shakespeare isn't Shakespeare at all – it's the themes and innovations that theatre artists bring to the texts. And yet, when asked why this year's World Shakespeare Festival looks so darned exciting, most people will spout euphoric praise of old Wills. All the world loves Shakespeare! His plays are universal!
>
> Universal my toe. Shakespeare is full of classism, sexism, racism and defunct social mores. *The Taming of the Shrew* (aka The Shaming of the Vagina-Bearer) is about as universally relevant as the chastity belt. I'm sick of directors tying themselves up in conceptual knots, trying to frame poor Katherina as some kind of feminist heroine. *The Merchant of Venice* (Or The Evil Jew) is about as universal as the Nuremberg laws. What's that? Shakespeare allows Shylock to express the progressive sentiment that Jews are people before confiscating his property and forcing him to convert to Christianity, therefore *Merchant* is actually a humanist text? Come off it, sister.
>
> So where has the idea that Shakespeare is 'universal' come from? Why do people the world over study and perform Shakespeare? Colonialism. That's where, and that's why. Shakespeare was a powerful tool of empire, transported to foreign climes along with the doctrine of European cultural superiority. Taught in schools and performed under the proscenium arches built where the British conquered, universal Shakespeare was both a beacon of the greatness of

---

[26] The figure of the *volksmoeder* (mother of the nation) was frequently invoked as a symbol of female identity under Afrikaner nationalism.

[27] See Mark Gevisser, *Thabo Mbeki: A Dream Deferred* (Johannesburg: Jonathan Ball, 2007). At the time of writing, David Johnson's chapter on 'Coriolanus in South Africa' is forthcoming in the *Cambridge Shakespeare Encyclopaedia*, vol. 2, *The World's Shakespeare*, ed. Andrew Murphy (Cambridge University Press).

European civilisation and a gateway into that greatness – to know the bard was to be civilised. True story.

Today, while the doctrine of European cultural superiority is disavowed by all but the crazies, the myth of Shakespeare's universality hangs tough. There's something uncomfortably colonial about this – if we can root Shakespeare's dominance in his universality, rather than in history, we can bask in the cosy knowledge that our culture is just a tad superior after all.[28]

Such critiques are familiar to contemporary Shakespeare scholars, most of whom would agree with the basic tenet: 'Why do people the world over study and perform Shakespeare? Colonialism.' But that is a reductive approach to the problem of 'universality'. We can accept that, whatever the merits of Shakespeare's plays – their 'appeal' – might be, they owe both their creation and their dissemination to a dense web of material circumstances. The question, then, is what do we make of them, given that they are mired in history? Might this inextricable intertwinement not make 'universal' Shakespeare *more* interesting because it/he is problematic, complex, 'tainted'?

It is tempting to vindicate this claim by invoking Jorge Luis Borges's wonderful story 'Pierre Menard, Author of the *Quixote*', in which a literary scholar tries to persuade readers that an exact reproduction of *Don Quixote* by a twentieth-century imitator is 'almost infinitely richer' precisely because of the four centuries that have passed since Cervantes wrote his novel (Menard's version is 'more ambiguous ... but ambiguity is richness').[29] Ultimately, however, Borges's ironic distance from the narrator suggests to us that this affirmation is itself somewhat simplistic. Perhaps a more appropriate model is Derrida's reinterpretation of Rousseau's concept of the 'supplement', according to which texts, authors and ideas that come *after* some pre-existing 'original' (or 'presence') establish a paradoxical relationship with it.[30] For Derrida, the supplement explains, completes or alters the presence; in this way, it actually points to some inadequacy or shortcoming in the presence. Yet the presence, no less than the supplement, remains an autonomous entity – they are reciprocal, mutually definitive, but they remain independent. South African Shakespeare scholarship today is another 'supplement' in this sense: self-contained, but in perpetual dialogue – with Shakespeare's work, with centuries of Shakespeare criticism, and with the notion of the 'universal' itself. Such an approach is interrogative and subversive even as it is celebratory, recognising the autonomy of the Shakespearean presence but making bold to explain, complete or alter it in fashioning a supplement to 'universal' Shakespeare.

---

[28]   Emer O'Toole, 'Shakespeare, Universal? No, It's Cultural Imperialism', *Guardian*, 21 May 2012, n.p., guardian.co.uk/commentisfree/2012/may/21/shakespeare-universal-cultural-imperialism.

[29]   Jorge Luis Borges, 'Pierre Menard, Author of the Quixote', in *Labyrinths* (Harmondsworth: Penguin, 1970), p. 69.

[30]   Jacques Derrida, *Of Grammatology* (Baltimore: Johns Hopkins University Press, 1976), pp. 140ff.

PART 1
'Universal' Will

Chapter 1
On Being Human

Natasha Distiller

> In teleology, they will come to say, that the final cause of the creation of the earth was Shakespeare.
>
> —Ralph Waldo Emerson[1]

In this essay, I want to make a positive claim for the relationship between Shakespeare and a notion of the human. I am exploring this idea, as will be seen, in full knowledge of the dangerous politics of the universal Shakespeare, and with no desire to reinscribe or justify those politics. Instead, I want to see what happens to the idea of the universal Shakespeare when we draw on the fact that there is a relation between form and content, through the rubric of recent interdisciplinary developments in the cognitive sciences and literary studies. Exploring the relation between form and content has always been one of the tasks of literary criticism. Can we link our disciplinary sense of the constitutive connection between aesthetics and meaning to information about the structure of the brain which is emerging in a current critical practice as foundational to what it means to be human? And can we establish a relation between post-structuralism's concentration on the constructed nature of human systems of meaning, and the vexed question of what makes us human, which cannot be reduced to inherited form, or a linguistic superstructure, or cultural determinants (and the answers to which literary criticism historically has laid some claim)? This may be one way out of the tiresome binary construction which continually sets essentialism against deconstruction as polar opposites, when they have never been as utterly philosophically different as they have sometimes been made to seem – although they can be politically at odds.[2]

By linking literary structure, linguistic structure and biological structure to Shakespeare's specific contributions to the canon, as I propose to do below, I hope to suggest a way to acknowledge why his work has been so consistently compelling for some readers, without disavowing the historical systems of class, race, gender and nationalist dominations which have helped to constitute 'him' as the universal voice of humanity. Shakespeare may not be *the* universal voice of humanity, but I want to explore how he may be said to be *a* voice that captures

---

[1]   Quoted by Marjorie Garber, *Shakespeare After All* (New York: Anchor Books, Random House, 2004), p. 33.

[2]   See Diana Fuss, *Essentially Speaking: Feminism, Nature and Difference* (New York and London: Routledge, 1989); Natasha Distiller, *Shakespeare, South Africa, and Post-Colonial Culture* (Lampeter: Edwin Mellen, 2005).

something which might be universally human. This suggestion may be one way out of the oppositional politics still at work in Shakespeare studies and elsewhere between liberal humanism and a more politically committed materialism. It may also offer a way forward in what appears to be a reformulated interest in the category of the human as an analytical possibility. What happens if we try to think humanism through together with a politically committed sensibility, to look for new ways of opening up the question of Shakespeare's relationship to the human content he so insistently seems to stand for in some quarters? In what follows I want first to outline an emerging scholarly approach to the question of being human, then to interrogate some of it (especially in the context of how it has been taken up by Shakespeare studies so far) and, finally, to turn to what may be Shakespeare's place in the renewed debate around what it means to be human.

***

As part of its development as a discipline, English literature was fundamentally concerned to find ways to identify and evaluate the highest, best expressions of what it means to be human. Whether the origins of the subject are considered to be in the emergence of the humanities from the study of rhetoric and from the European culture wars of the eighteenth century,[3] in Matthew Arnold's nineteenth-century educational interventions, in colonial education practices or in the professionalisation of the subject in the early twentieth century, 'Eng. Lit.' has been developed around a concern to identify and evaluate the 'best' written cultural expressions of human life, even if those criteria have since been radically expanded.

But, as a number of critics have pointed out, the project of developing a canon of the best literature in English was always implicated in a complex political field that it disavowed for a long time. For example, a collection of essays edited by Peter Widdowson sketched the discipline's various ideological and material constituting factors; Gauri Viswanathan has detailed the colonial politics behind the development of the formal study of Eng. Lit.; and Terry Eagleton has argued that its institutionalisation was informed by a nostalgic, conservative ideological programme, one deeply implicated in class and gender politics.[4] More recently, Neil Rhodes has also argued for the imbrications of gender and class politics in the development of English studies from as far back as the Renaissance.[5]

---

[3]   For elaboration on these alternative 'origins', see Neil Rhodes, *Shakespeare and the Origins of English* (Oxford: Oxford University Press, 2004); Matthew Arnold, *Culture and Anarchy* [1869], ed. Samuel Lipman (New Haven and London: Yale University Press, 1994); Gauri Viswanathan, *Masks of Conquest: Literary Study and British Rule in India* (New York: Columbia University Press, 1989); and Terry Eagleton, *Literary Theory: An Introduction*, 2nd edn (Oxford: Blackwell, 1996), respectively.

[4]   See Peter Widdowson (ed.), *Re-Reading English* (London and New York: Methuen, 1982), Viswanathan's *Masks of Conquest* and Eagleton's *Literary Theory*.

[5]   Neil Rhodes, *Shakespeare and the Origins of English*, p. 192.

In Shakespeare studies in particular, the universal Shakespeare that is one of the cornerstones of the discipline came under fire for being classed, raced and gendered. Furthermore, 'his' supposed apolitical universality was revealed to be ideologically complicit with the oppressive bourgeois practices of the state.[6] Shakespeare's putative universality was interrogated in material terms, and responsible historical accounts attempted to trace the process of the accretion of his reputation instead of assuming its self-perpetuating and self-evident nature.[7] Nevertheless, or perhaps because of this sustained undermining of Shakespeare's putative universality, defenses of Shakespeare's unique human genius continue to be produced, and in popular cultures around the globe Shakespeare's self-evident status remains commonsensical.[8] Marjorie Garber offers perhaps one of the most measured accounts of the imbrications of Shakespeare with modern Anglo-American culture, along with the recognition of the historical – that is, material and political – trajectory of the development of 'his' current, apparently transcendent and immutable, meanings.[9] In my own work, I have tried to account for Shakespeare's presence in South African literary and popular culture, in terms which acknowledge both the political and the affective power of the texts and the icon; indeed, which insist on their imbrication without diminishing what our writers have made of Shakespeare accordingly.[10] Nevertheless, the field remains broadly split between those who would continue to speak in the terms of a universal humanist tradition, and the now-dominant academic ethos which is highly suspicious of the politics of such claims. It is not surprising that the opening sentence of a recent article by John Lee in the journal *Shakespeare* which addresses

---

[6]   Catherine Belsey, *The Subject of Tragedy: Identity and Difference in Renaissance Drama* (London and New York: Methuen, 1985); Jonathan Dollimore and Alan Sinfield (eds), *Political Shakespeare: New Essays in Cultural Materialism* (Manchester and New York: Manchester University Press, 1985); Martin Orkin, *Shakespeare against Apartheid* (Craighall: Ad. Donker, 1987); Jonathan Dollimore, *Radical Tragedy*, 2nd edn (Hertfordshire: Harvester Wheatsheaf, 1989).

[7]   Gary Taylor, *Reinventing Shakespeare: A Cultural History from the Restoration to the Present* (Oxford: Oxford University Press, 1989); Michael Evans, *Signifying Nothing: Truth's True Contexts in Shakespeare's Texts*, 2nd edn (Hertfordshire: Harvester Wheatsheaf, 1989); Michael Bristol, *Shakespeare's America, America's Shakespeare* (London and New York: Routledge, 1990); Terence Hawkes, *Meaning by Shakespeare* (London and New York: Routledge, 1992).

[8]   For two informed, intelligent examples, see Jonathan Bate, *The Genius of Shakespeare* (London and Basingstoke: Picador, 1997); Catherine Belsey, *Why Shakespeare?* (Hampshire and New York: Palgrave Macmillan, 2007).

[9]   Garber, *Shakespeare After All*.

[10]   For example, Distiller, *Shakespeare, South Africa, and Post-Colonial Culture*; Natasha Distiller, 'Shakespeare and the Coconuts', *Shakespeare Survey* 62 (2009): pp. 211–21.

this theoretical situation begins, 'Human nature, in the world of English literary studies, has not had a good last thirty years or so.'[11] But this may be changing.

Lee's article was part of a special themed issue, rather provocatively (given the context outlined above) entitled 'Shakespeare and the Meaning of Life'. The editor of that issue, Andy Mousley, argues that despite the ongoing suspicion with which the idea of the human is viewed in the humanities, there is a 'return to the human subject, not only in literary studies but in a range of disciplines concerned with the possibility of a re-animated humanism'.[12] He speaks for a 'soft essentialism ... that asserts that human life unfolds within a definable number of possibilities'.[13] He also believes that Shakespeare can 'help us' to know why it matters to return to the notion of the human in literary studies, and to be able to conceptualise which notion of the human we should be concerned with. For me, questions immediately arise: Why do we need Shakespeare, specifically, to do this, outside of his position within the canon, which presents his texts as the obvious place to look in the first place? Why look for universalising terms within which to place 'him' outside of a kind of circular logic which self-evidently makes Shakespeare the place of the universally human? Is it to compensate for the insistent voices that assert 'his' embeddedness in ideological systems? Is it to use his iconic value to endorse a particular version of English studies that is authorised by its claim to offer a universal truth value, a sense that we can after all say something concrete about what it means to be human? While not addressing why we need a universal Shakespeare specifically, Mousley suggests that we need a version of the human in literary studies because without one, we cannot identify on a human level with, for example, 'Falstaff's fear of war as the body's natural fear of mortal danger'. Instead, through the prisms of the kinds of thinking that now dominate the field, the body becomes an object of alienated, intellectualised enquiry and 'the human face of history' is 'erased'.[14] Without a communal sense of the human, according to this argument, we cannot have literature, since literature acquires its purpose in the articulation of generally true, shared experiences.[15]

It has never been clear to me why pointing out the contingent and implicated nature of human relationships and experiences is dehumanising, or disabling of the power of well-written stories. But more to the point here, Mousley's

---

[11]   John Lee, 'Shakespeare, Human Nature, and English Literature', *Shakespeare* 5.1–4 (2009): pp. 176–89, 176.

[12]   Andy Mousley, 'Introduction: Shakespeare and the Meaning of Life', *Shakespeare* 5.1–4 (2009): pp. 134–43, 134.

[13]   Mousley, 'Introduction', p. 136.

[14]   Ibid., p. 137.

[15]   Mousley goes on to say that Shakespeare, particularly, can 'help us' with understanding the meaning of life because of 'the representation of experiential density in [his] work' (ibid., p. 139). As I will argue below, this says very little about the Shakespearean or early modern form in which this representation takes shape, and instead is a comment about what is valuable in good literature generally.

example wants to suggest that *1 Henry IV* loses its capacity to communicate a (putatively) universally shared human anxiety about death if we insist on working through a prism which acknowledges the differences that history makes to what a work of art can mean.[16] What I think this argument does, as do all attempts to justify Shakespeare's universal truth value through an appeal to the shared human emotions in his work, is to separate form from content – to believe that we can lose all that is actually Shakespearean about Shakespeare and still be left with an essential Shakespearean truth. By this logic, since all great literature is about humanity, there is nothing specifically Shakespearean about Shakespeare's universal messages, and we could just as easily learn about an apparently shared human fear of mortality in the same way from any other text deemed well written by a sufficient number of people with socioeconomic clout (Zakes Mda's *Ways of Dying*, perhaps, or Zadie Smith's *The Autograph Man*?). The logic, meant to legitimate and authorise Shakespeare specifically, works in the opposite manner, to strip him of any specificity. It also disingenuously denies the fact of an education in English as a specifically implicated commodity, such that Shakespeare's form, his language, his cultural references, the way he uses genres, are simply not equally available to everyone. Differences – historical, cultural, linguistic – do matter.[17] And I remain unconvinced that a critically engaged approach, which recognises this, is by definition an alienated or alienating one, or that respecting difference properly amounts to 'fetishizing' it.[18]

In the same issue of the journal, and somewhat more productively in my view, John Lee argues that the political Shakespeare criticisms which refused and refuted the putatively apolitical assertions of the universally human in Shakespeare studies could do so because they did not engage with intellectual developments in the cognitive and neurosciences.[19] Over the past 10 years or so, a radical convergence of the humanities (particularly in the study of literature) and these branches of the sciences seems to have been gathering momentum.[20] The emerging potential of what is sometimes called cognitive literary studies is beginning to be discussed

---

[16]   Ibid., p. 136.

[17]   For examples of how the politics of access to English has been played out in specific arenas, not specifically Shakespearean, see Modhumita Roy, 'Writers and Politics/ Writers in Politics', in *Ngugi wa Thiong'o: Texts and Contexts*, ed. Charles Cantalupo (Trenton, NJ: Africa World Press, 1985); Helen Tiffin, 'Plato's Cave: Educational and Critical Practices', in *New National and Post-Colonial Literatures: An Introduction*, ed. Bruce King (Oxford: Clarenden, 1996), pp. 143–63.

[18]   Mousley, 'Introduction', p. 141.

[19]   Lee, 'Shakespeare, Human Nature, and English Literature'.

[20]   Patrick Colm Hogan, *Cognitive Science, Literature, and the Arts*: *A Guide for Humanists* (New York and London: Routledge, 2003), p. 2. The editors of the *Shakespeare International Yearbook*'s special issue on 'Shakespeare Studies today' cite Mary Thomas Crane's *Shakespeare's Brain* (2000) as the 'first full-length "cognitive" study of Shakespeare' (Graham Bradshaw, Tom Bishop and Mark Turner (eds), *Shakespeare International Yearbook* 4 [Aldershot and Burlington: Ashgate, 2004], pp. ix–x).

amongst those literary theorists willing to take the intellectual risk of re-engaging with a notion of the human, and with a scientific approach, which has also tended to prove extremely problematic for literary studies.[21]

One of the practitioners within this field, F. Elizabeth Hart, defines cognitive literary studies as follows:

> An interest in the cognitive, from a literary perspective, is an interest in exploring how both the architecture and the contents of the human brain/mind – both in terms of its on-line processing of information and its evolutionary history – may contribute structurally to the writing, reading, and interpretation of texts ... a cognitive literary exploration becomes, as well, a venture into the territory of epistemology, in which the presence of the brain/mind as a tool – a process-facilitator – must be cross-fertilized into all our accounts of what constitutes literary knowledge and knowing.[22]

In addition to changing the way we think about how and what we know, this work may enable new ways of understanding how we change what we think and know:

> There is also an opening for what might be called a 'neural historicism', which would explore how the peculiar structure and workings of the human brain may enable cultural innovation over time and offer revisionary accounts of the representation of mind and mental processes in literary-cultural history along new lines suggested by the frameworks and models emerging from the cognitive neurosciences.[23]

The implications, for what we have come to accept as received post-structuralist wisdom about how meaning is made, are profound. As Hart puts it elsewhere, the problem with the idea that language precedes and creates the human subject (as I would put it in the context of this argument, the idea that form determines content) is that it is 'an inescapably top-down and formalist declaration even while it aims to support a nonidealist method'.[24] She suggests, essentially, that none of the political approaches have been able to account for agency because none of them can account for the material, biological aspect of language. In seeing language as

---

[21]   For overviews of the suspicions of literary scholars, as well as with literary practices and engagements with cognitive sciences, see Tony Jackson, 'Questioning Interdisciplinarity: Cognitive Science, Evolutionary Psychology, and Literary Criticism,' *Poetics Today* 21 (2000): pp. 319–47; Alan Richardson, 'Cognitive Science and the Future of Literary Studies', *Philosophy and Literature* 23 (1999): pp. 157–73; Mary Thomas Crane and Alan Richardson, 'Literary Studies and Cognitive Science: Toward a New Interdisciplinarity', *Mosaic* 32 (1999): pp. 123–40.

[22]   F. Elizabeth Hart, 'The Epistemology of Cognitive Literary Studies', *Philosophy and Literature* 25.2 (2001): pp. 314–34, 319.

[23]   Crane and Richardson, 'Literary Studies and Cognitive Science', n.p.

[24]   F. Elizabeth Hart, 'Matter, System, and Early Modern Studies: Outlines for a Materialist Linguistics', *Configurations* 6.3 (1998): pp. 311–43, 322.

the producer of the subject, even as they historicise and account for ideological change and operations, they cannot provide an account of linguistic innovation that makes sense, since language always precedes the ideology they seek to account for. She calls for a literary theory that is capable of 'giving the production of linguistic structure a cause-and-effect-schema that operate[s] from a material – indeed, a biological – base toward an increasingly abstract superstructure'. In this way she seeks an account of creativity, 'of language users' capacity to produce and comprehend an infinite number of new utterances through the use of finite resources'.[25] As her vocabulary suggests, she is marrying a Marxist-originated historical materialism with a cognitive, scientific and theoretical linguistic approach:

> A materialist theory begins ... on the assumption that linguistic forms emerge from their situated, historical contexts, and that no analysis with claims to explanatory power may be attempted without factoring in the contingencies of the language speaker's social and physical situatedness – determinants, in other words, of human subjectivity. Forms emerge from the subject's material conditions through the mediating presence of a semantic system, a system whose rootedness in the material cognitive system closes the formalist gaps between content and structure, subject and system.[26]

Hart hopes to accommodate the fact of cultural change, understood in terms of human evolution, and which links evolution to 'essential identity'. Her project provides some sense of how this new thinking is going about its business, and how it can help to break what those proponents of a productive interdisciplinarity between literary studies and the cognitive sciences often begin by invoking: the current deadlock between post-structuralist readings, which are typically denoted 'constructionist' or 'relativist', and 'realist' or 'essentialist' readings. Taking the materialism of the brain seriously helps us to understand that culture and biology do not exist in a binary relation; in fact, they co-constitute, since the physical development of the brain depends on the infant's initial intersubjective experiences in the first place, and then on the life experiences which follow.[27] This is a new way to account for the unknowable, the uncontrollable, in what post-structuralist theories would call the development of the subject. In earlier work, I tried to account for this potential to exceed our starting points, our material terms, by invoking 'the place of the human' in an attempt to theorise what South African writers made of Shakespeare in the context of an oppressive and violent history.

---

[25] Hart, 'Matter, System, and Early Modern Studies', p. 327.

[26] Ibid., p. 328.

[27] Sue Gerhardt, *Why Love Matters: How Affection Shapes a Baby's Brain* (London and New York: Routledge, 2008); Regina Pally, *The Mind-Brain Relationship* (London and New York: Karnac, 2000); Mark Solms and Oliver Turnbull, *The Brain and the Inner World: An Introduction to the Neuroscience of Subjective Experience* (London and New York: Karnac, 2006).

I wanted to take seriously their creativity, their literary productions, as well as their capacities for resistance in a system of which they were simultaneously the products and in which they were often complicit, in Mark Saunders's terms.[28] If we dismiss the possibility of agency, of the unexpected response against and within constitutive systems, we erase whole histories of subaltern expression, for one thing, amongst other implications for what it might mean to be human. Cognitive literary studies may offer another way to frame the idea that who and what we are, and how and what we know, is tied up in where we come from while simultaneously allowing for the human capacity to exceed these starting points while still taking them with us.

Initially, the most obvious point of connection between a cognitive scientific approach and Shakespeare studies was via cognitive accounts of how metaphor works. This was the entire focus of an issue of the *Shakespeare International Yearbook* that had a special section on 'Shakespeare in the Age of Cognitive Science'.[29] So, for example, in a discussion of the metaphor of the suburb in Portia's speech to Brutus in *Julius Caesar* 2.1, Eve Sweetser finds that Shakespeare's writing 'evokes extremely basic shared aspects of our cognitive structure'.[30] This 'our', meant to refer to all humanity, relies (once more) on a specific culture which silently expands to become the model for all cultures. Sweetser continues,

> and yet [Shakespeare] constantly shows us how deeply ambiguous are the ways they [aspects of our cognitive structure] play out in the broader contexts of our culture-specific worlds. His work thus 'catches' a modern audience partly because it is built on artistic use of image structures and metaphors which they share with the original audience – some of this shared structure being due to historical cultural continuity, and some to shared human embodiment and neural structure.

The audience Sweeter has in mind, which catches the resonances of what is universal in Shakespeare because of what it shares with his contemporaries, is clearly Western, or at least Western-influenced. The 'shared human embodiment and neural structure' which, to take the cognitive scientific point about the relation between form and content, results in part from 'historical cultural continuity', is defined by the formative cultural histories and neurological structures of Western people. This is important because Sweetser and others want to connect 'modern'

---

[28] Mark Saunders, *Complicities: The Intellectual and Apartheid* (Pietermaritzburg: University of Natal Press, 2002); Distiller, *Shakespeare, South Africa, and Post-Colonial Culture*.

[29] Bradshaw, Bishop and Turner (eds), *Shakespeare International Yearbook*.

[30] Eve Sweetser, '"The Suburbs of Your Good Pleasure": Cognition, Culture and the Bases of Metaphoric Structure', *Shakespeare International Yearbook* 4, ed. Graham Bradshaw, Tom Bishop and Mark Turner (Aldershot and Burlington: Ashgate, 2004), pp. 24–51, 24.

audiences with Elizabethans in order to strengthen the claim for the shared humanity Shakespeare can be seen to be instantiating, as I will discuss shortly.

Shakespeare studies has moved beyond the use of metaphor, to make more of what neuroscience is teaching us about the relation between the structure of the brain and the thoughts, emotions and responses that structure makes possible and is made by. But the importance of linking today's (implicitly Western) audiences with Shakespeare's remains an important weapon in the universalists' arsenal.

In his defence of human nature, and its place in Shakespeare's texts, Lee suggests that the new cognitive literary work is the way to answer the problem of agency for theories of culture-and-politics, or culture-as-politics, which refuse the notion of a universal human nature. He also suggests it is a way to connect early modern subjectivity with our own, and so to reclaim an experience of the universal human that Shakespeare can then be seen to be expressing. This last suggestion, the fact of the shared structure of the human brain across history as the basis for interpretive claims, enables not only a claim for a human nature but a specific historical connectivity between ourselves and Shakespeare which answers the barriers to universality thrown up by the now-dominant historicist insistence that we acknowledge what we cannot recognise, or run the risk of mis-recognising, in Shakespeare's early modern texts. It is possible to hear in this claim also a weariness with the insistence on respecting Elizabethan difference which has been so much a part of the turn to historicism in the field, and which the current move towards presentism is also articulating.[31] Indeed, while no one to my knowledge has yet made this connection, cognitive literary studies may offer an interesting perspective to presentist critics – provided that an approach seeking to connect modern audiences to the Elizabethans can deal with the Eurocentrism which seems to be reinscribing itself in these attempts in Shakespeare studies so far, so that the colonising politics of the old liberal humanism risks being reanimated here.

Perhaps the most sustained application of this incarnation of the argument is Arthur Kinney's. He begins his book *Shakespeare and Cognition* with the assertion: 'Our brains work just as those of the Elizabethans worked, genetically, experientially, and culturally.'[32] Relying on neuroscientific understandings of the processes of how we see and interpret what we see, Kinney stresses the importance of sight to the experience of watching and understanding a Renaissance play. 'Knowing how the brains of Shakespeare's playgoers functioned', Kinney says, 'can help to recapture how the plays were received in his own time and how variously they might have been interpreted.'[33] Ultimately, this argument is evidence for what is universal in Shakespeare's work, allowing us to share an experience with Shakespeare's original audiences. If, as the cognitive sciences are

---

[31] See Evelyn Gajowski (ed.), *Presentism, Gender, and Sexuality in Shakespeare* (Basingstoke, Hampshire: Palgrave Macmillan, 2009).

[32] Arthur F. Kinney, *Shakespeare and Cognition: Aristotle's Legacy and Shakespearean Drama* (New York and London: Routledge, 2006), p. xv.

[33] Ibid., p. 24.

demonstrating, what we think we see depends on previous experiences because of the ways the brain's hardwiring develops in response, the possibilities of seeing and knowing are at once shared across time and place *and* culturally determined: 'Cognition is not, finally, what we see but what we think.'[34] Shakespeare's genius, the capacity in his work to speak across times and places – the universally human element, we might say – lies, suggests Kinney, in his ability to invoke the indeterminate possibility of what is knowable in 'certain key moments' in his plays:

> Shakespeare's legacy is that he seizes upon the complexity of thought, of objects seen and imagined, as they are processed by a brain that already has certain well-worn genetic, experiential and cultural responses, and, making use of their essential plurisignificance and ambiguity ... [Shakespeare] writes his plays in such a way ... that there is only indeterminacy at the heart of the most lasting drama.[35]

This neuroscientifically endorsed universal Shakespeare is less convincing to me than is the point, which emerges here, that what makes Shakespeare compelling has less to do with his famous indeterminacy than with his use of form.[36] This point, to which I will return in the section below, seems to me much more productive than a focus on Shakespeare's content, the universal appeal of his stories, whether due to his masterful use of ambiguity or not, which can be extracted from their linguistic and cultural specificity (so, for example, in teaching Shakespeare, schoolteachers work with a modernised text and a transposed storyline – *King Lear* approached via a discussion about the modern relationships between fathers and adolescent daughters, for example, taking the early modern language and cultural referents out of the play, but still teaching 'Shakespeare').[37] As I have suggested, such an argument only poses the question of what in fact is universal about Shakespeare that cannot be said to be universal about all good literature, which will consist of a convincing exploration of some form of human emotion.

But there may well be something in the connection of the early modern and the modern via biology as well as culture. Lee suggests another reason Shakespeare in particular fits the universal bill, a reason which also connects Elizabethan cultural understandings and those that are emerging in economically dominant cultural

---

[34]   Ibid., p. 130.

[35]   Ibid., p. 132.

[36]   It must be said, too, that Kinney's 'us' is once again silently universalised; if culture helps to shape biology as much as vice versa, then the universally human brain structure presented here, in these terms, is Anglo-American: 'we' might share the same brain structure as Shakespeare's Elizabethans, creating a cultural continuity that is also biological, but 'we' are also clearly not participating in other, non-Western, cultural histories with whatever implications they might have for brain structuring.

[37]   See Distiller, *Shakespeare, South Africa, and Post-Colonial Culture*, p. 231.

forms now.[38] He argues that the cognitive sciences have made it clear that the feeling of being an individual, the experience of unique selfhood that comprises what it means to be a person, is an automatic and biological process; it is a function of the way the brain works.[39] Lee points out that such scientific discoveries necessitate 'non-humanist ... understandings of our natures', in that the feeling of uniqueness we understand as our experiences of our inner selves is 'not our own [but rather] a much more automatic affair than we have ... thought'. We now have 'a conception of identity that looks a lot more "what"-centred than it does "who"-centred', with the recognition that what makes us feel uniquely ourselves is the product of a biochemical process.[40] In this, Lee suggests, we are becoming more and more like the Elizabethans and their belief in the humours as shaping of human personality and response. Indeed, humoural theory has been posited as the first theory of the unconscious, dependent as it is on the conceptualisation of the human psyche as being made up of a combination of biologically based, inherited attributes and the conscious mind.[41] It is apposite, then, that the application of cognitive literary theory might be currently most successfully practised within early modern studies: cognitive literary theory may approximate an Elizabethan understanding of what it means to be human.[42]

But Lee also points out the ways in which Shakespeare, particularly, refuses this construction of human subjectivity as biologically driven, the ways in which his plays take seriously the feelings and processes of being constituted as a unique subject. Shakespeare works with and through the feeling our brains cause that we are something more than just brains. That is why, Lee says, 'However overly optimistic Shakespeare's narratives of identity might prove to be, we are likely to continue to value and to believe in them, as they give particularly rich expression to our experience of our sense of identity.'[43] Shakespeare, as Joel Fineman argued from a different perspective, speaks to us with the intensity he does because he articulates something intrinsically modern about subjectivity.[44]

Again, one could perhaps churlishly question the deployment of Lee's 'we', and point out that there have been very different ways that Shakespeare's narratives

---

[38] For more on the connections between early modern and modern cultural formations, see Robert Weimann, *Author's Pen and Actor's Voice: Playing and Writing in Shakespeare's Time* (Cambridge: Cambridge University Press, 2000).

[39] Lee, 'Shakespeare, Human Nature, and English Literature', pp. 179, 182.

[40] Ibid., p. 183; see also Crane and Richardson, 'Literary Studies and Cognitive Science', n.p.

[41] James S. Uleman, 'Introduction: Becoming Aware of the New Unconscious', in *The New Unconscious*, ed. Ran R. Hassin, James S. Uleman and John A. Bargh (Oxford: Oxford University Press, 2005), pp. 3–15, 3.

[42] Richardson, 'Cognitive Science and the Future of Literary Studies', pp. 170–71.

[43] Lee, 'Shakespeare, Human Nature, and English Literature', p. 183.

[44] Joel Fineman, *Shakespeare's Perjured Eye: The Invention of Poetic Subjectivity in the Sonnets* (Berkeley: University of California Press, 1986).

of identity have been read; for example, the ways in which the Sophiatown writers of the 1950s in South Africa made use of what they constructed as an expression of urban African experience in Shakespeare's representations of life. In this example, the invocation of a common 'we' reverberates with power dynamics in the context of a specific history. Lee's account, again in a typically liberal humanist way – that is, in the liberal humanist way objected to by the materialist criticisms whose conclusions about the centrality of culture he is refuting – lifts the experience of being human out of history and so overwrites or denies precisely the apartheid experiences the Sophiatown writers were using a universal Shakespeare to articulate and to protest against. All of this is to point out the difficulties of asserting a common humanity in terms that do not render themselves problematic in the very face of the historical and cultural specificities they want to transcend. But I also mean to take seriously Lee's suggestion that there may be something in Shakespeare which can be seen to resonate with something fundamental to human nature, something which articulates an awareness of what it means to be human. This something, I want to suggest, has to be understood to operate at the level of form, not content. After all, part of what I have been suggesting is that the relation between the brain and culture should not be seen as binary, that the two make each other in complex ways. This might be seen as similar to the aesthetic relation between form and content, which is also a political relation, where each is made by the possibilities of the other, and shaped and enabled and limited accordingly.

It seems to me that the most fruitful lesson of the cognitive sciences, the mutual inter-reliance of 'culture' and 'nature' or 'biology', can be overlooked by a cognitive literary theory which uses it to reinscribe a universal Shakespeare via recourse, at last, to the fact of a biologically universal humanity which underlies (and so, in some way, trumps) cultural specificity. For example, the most recent argument of this kind, Lee's, cannot take the constitutive complexity of the relation between the brain and its embodied context into account: in his terms, we are still in the realm of a culture/nature binary, where nature is being brought back into the picture as and through science, to counter the claims of a cultural materialism which sees all humanity as always-already (and only) formulated and shaped by and in history: 'Far from being an empty stage across which cultural forces play, the brain is now emerging ... as the protagonist in its own play.'[45] Lee is after a way to assert '[t]he power of human thought independent of culture to transform and reveal'.[46] This relies yet again on a notion of nature, or science, or biology, which is outside of culture and history. As the vast and growing literature by feminist historians of science illustrates, however, as disciplines these arenas themselves are implicated in human history and in the contested gender, class and race relations which comprise European cultures.[47] None of the advocates for the application of

---

[45]   Lee, 'Shakespeare, Human Nature, and English Literature', p. 183.

[46]   Ibid., p. 181.

[47]   For example, see Donna Haraway, *Primate Visions: Gender, Race and Nature in the World of Modern Science* (London and New York: Routledge, 1989); Londa Schiebinger,

cognitive scientific insights to literature that I have read begin to deal with this fact, concerned as they are to make peace between the humanities and the sciences, in the face particularly of the former's critique of the latter's claims to objectivity. Along the way, the dominant thinking in the humanities is often charged with reducing everything to discourse and/or culture. The reductive presentation of 'post-structuralism' and/or materialist criticisms concerned with the functioning of ideologies, the implicit assumption that the attempt to be political (or politically responsible) is somehow incommensurate with or opposite to a sensible, rational, grounding in the real, is part of the problem of the ideological fields staked out by these commentators even as they argue that these fields need to interpenetrate. The lurking investment in a universal Shakespeare *über alles* recurs in a constant underlying hostility of some degree or another to the materialist criticisms that have dominated the field in recent decades. So the editors of the special issue of the *Shakespeare International Yearbook* to which I have referred suggest that the reason Shakespeare studies was not on the cognitive ball until recently was the turn to New Historicism and the 'political' theoretical focus it demanded; as they put it, the situation can be summed up in the fact that *Metaphors We Live By* came out in the same year as *Renaissance Self-Fashioning*. Implicitly, they are suggesting that the latter grabbed all the attention and set the new agenda at the expense of the former, as though it were in the end always a competition between mutually exclusive positions.[48]

I find myself remaining sceptical, in precisely the terms detailed by those speaking for an opening of the literary theoretical mind, about the wholesale embracing of the idea that we should submit to the lessons of science. I am too aware of and convinced by the histories of the evolution of science and biology as discursive fields fundamentally implicated in gendered and raced formations, out of which their positions of knowledge and putative objectivity are constituted. When the neuroscientific literature, in its idiots' guides or introductions to brain science for non-scientists,[49] talks without comment about the primitive, ancestral or lizard brain, for example, I cannot help but baulk at the hierarchical assumptions about higher-level functioning, and the potential encoding of justifications for 'primitive' behaviour, most usually in a gendered context. More worryingly, the 'scientific' approach virtually always seems to endorse heterosexuality and the gender system it insists upon: describing how the brain's task is to mediate between and regulate internal and external systems, Solms and Turnbull write, 'the same applies to sexual needs – though sexual "consummation" is necessary

---

The Mind Has No Sex? Women in the Origins of Modern Science (Cambridge, MA, and London: Harvard University Press, 1989); Londa Schiebinger, *Nature's Body: Gender in the Making of Modern Science* (New Brunswick, NJ: Rutgers University Press, 2004).

48   Bradshaw, Bishop and Turner (eds), *Shakespeare International Yearbook*, pp. x–xi.

49   For example, Pally, *The Mind-Brain Relationship*.

for the survival of our species as a whole.'[50] But it seems to me there may be a very fruitful point to be made here about materiality and structure, which can indeed offer new ways of thinking about very old problems in post-structuralism – and, in the process, say something about Shakespeare and the discourse of universal humanity that clings to him.

***

Biological form is crucially enabling to the way the brain operates, making it clear that 'Structures define the relations into which [cognitive] processes and contents can enter. Indeed, they allow processes and contents to exist at all.'[51] That form always matters – that it sets the terms for how something can be said or known and therefore for what can be said or known – is a truism in literary studies. But this is not to suggest that form is the a priori, as Judith Butler's work on the discursive nature of sex long ago made clear (that is, not that sex does not exist, but that the experience of sex will always be already gendered).[52] As I have been suggesting, what the new interdisciplinary relation between cognitive studies and literary studies may enable is a move away from a binary model that sees constructionist/relativist approaches set against and in opposition to essentialist or realist approaches. The two are seen instead to exist in a relation of continuum and mutual implication.[53] Of course, this relies on not succumbing to the privileged status that 'science' occupies as a reliable and infallible marker of reality in popular discourse. Without falling back onto the final authority of science, I would now like to apply the idea that biology might allow us to see how an embodied and imperative experience of form could be constituted as the mark of the human.[54] The mark of the human is that which sets the terms for who 'we' are, as individuals and groups, without also rising above the human histories, cultures and individual experiences that constitute the differing content of who 'we' might be. Shakespeare, I suggest, may have been particularly good at working with inherited form and pushing it, mutating it, making something new out of the existing constitutive possibilities. In this way, the processes of his artistic production could be seen to speak to what may be the human tendency to exceed the forms that also mark the starting points of what it means to be human.

---

[50]   Solms and Turnbull, *The Brain and the Inner World*, p. 19. See also Simon LeVay, *The Sexual Brain* (Cambridge, MA, and London: MIT Press, 1994), and the critique in Natasha Distiller, *Fixing Gender: Lesbian Mothers and the Oedipus Complex* (Madison, NJ: Fairleigh Dickinson University Press, 2011).

[51]   Colm Hogan, *Cognitive Science, Literature, and the Arts*, p. 30.

[52]   Judith Butler, *Gender Trouble: Feminism and the Subversion of Identity* (London and New York: Routledge, 1999 [1990]).

[53]   Hart, 'The Epistemology of Cognitive Literary Studies', pp. 320–21.

[54]   Lacan's notion of the real speaks to this biological 'reality' in terms which acknowledge its existence outside of signification without invoking the discursive history of biology as a discipline or a concept.

This ability for hardware to be altered in unexpected and sometimes unique ways by the software which it allows to run may be the elusive work of agency – may be that which makes us human, and not linguistic automata.

I move now to two brief examples of how, in literary terms, Shakespeare exceeds what he inherits. In so doing, he may be seen to be modelling with literature the elusive humanity he is so often seen to be expressing. But this aspect of the power of his work lies not in his content – not in his characterisation or his metaphor or his storylines, all of which are tied to his cultural specificity and hence are not universally accessible, as countless generations of students and an entire editing industry can attest. Rather, if there is a way Shakespeare's texts are indeed exemplary of a shared humanity, it is in their formal work.[55]

Titus Andronicus and the sonnets are both controversial texts precisely because they cannot be contained within the parameters of traditional English literature and the kind of humanist individual it assumes, the kind which is invisibly classed, raced and gendered, and which is in control of its own fate. In the case of the sonnets, Shakespeare's mastery of Petrarchism is manifest in the poems' ability to both contain and exceed the rules of the genre, simultaneously concluding the tradition and inventing a new one.[56] Many academics have been concerned to articulate and explore the enormous complexity of the relationship between the poet and his young man, let alone its implications for the love poetry tradition of which it makes strategic use. For example, David Schalkwyk has recently detailed the ways in which the poet invokes the language of service in order to express the complexities of love and the obligations both love and service should assert over the youth.[57] At the same time, the sonnets' authenticity of tone and emotion have caused no end of homophobic trouble,[58] and have consistently rendered an account of their poetic power necessary.[59] In their irresistibly compelling presentation of emotional and sexual relationships, the sonnets both are and are not perfectly Petrarchan: their homoeroticism extends the genre's usually heterosexual logic and casts in a new way its masculine self-concerns; their misogyny hurls the idealised mistress from her pedestal while revealing the dark underside of the poetics of

---

[55]   This can be put in cognitive scientific terms, in terms of theories of how creativity works with first, the artist learning continuity, and then varying on that schema to innovate – the vocabulary is from Colm Hogan's summary of Howard Gardner's account of achieving mastery of a field, and his accounting for extraordinary creativity through the notion of remote associations (Colm Hogan, *Cognitive Science, Literature, and the Arts*, pp. 63–4).

[56]   Heather Dubrow, *Echoes of Desire: English Petrarchism and Its Counter-discourses* (Ithaca, NY, and London: Cornell University Press, 1995); Fineman, *Shakespeare's Perjured Eye*.

[57]   David Schalkwyk, *Shakespeare, Love and Service* (Cambridge: Cambridge University Press, 2008).

[58]   See Joseph Pequigney, *Such Is My Love: A Study of Shakespeare's Sonnets* (Chicago and London: University of Chicago Press, 1985).

[59]   Helen Vendler, *The Art of Shakespeare's Sonnets* (Cambridge, MA: Harvard University Press, 1997).

praise addressed to a woman, its uncompromisable terms and conditions of sexual unavailability. Shakespeare's sonnets are so good because they manage to take a form and, using it, make it into something else. They at once rely on Petrarchism and all its constituent discourses of love, life and subjectivity, and alter and exceed them. They do not make full sense, their mastery of their genre cannot be properly appreciated, without grounding them in the tradition they both need and subvert, invert and refuse.

The easiest, most recognisable and least complex example of this (given that it takes book-length works to draw out the full inter- and intra- and para-textuality of the sonnets) is Sonnet 130, perhaps the most familiar of the poems:

> My mistress' eyes are nothing like the sun;
> Coral is far more red than her lips' red;
> If snow be white, why then her breasts are dun;
> If hairs be wires, black wires grow on her head;
> I have seen roses damasked, red and white,
> But no such roses see I in her cheeks;
> And in some perfume is there more delight
> Than in the breath that from my mistress reeks.
> I love to hear her speak, yet well I know
> That music hath a far more pleasing sound;
> I grant I never saw a goddess go;
> My mistress when she walks treads on the ground.
> And yet, by heaven, I think my love as rare
> As any she belied with false compare.[60]

Traditionally this sonnet is read as a declaration of true love: she may not be perfect, but I adore her anyway. In fact, it is a radical interrogation of the terms of Petrarchism, a questioning of the ability to say anything at all about love. Relying on the love sonnet tradition, it places that entire tradition under erasure. In a sonnet about the perfect mistress's perfect imperfections, the mistress herself is described in order to render the possibility of her description impossible. Beginning with the contingent 'ifs' of the first quatrain, the poet offers an account of the mistress's breasts and hairs that makes sense only if one accepts the Petrarchan proposition that snow is perfectly white or that hairs are golden wires. Since these descriptions are metaphors, and patently not literally true, the terms in which the sonnet mistress can be understood exist only to call themselves into question: since hairs are not golden wires, what exactly grows on the mistress's head? This language of praise cannot describe the beloved in the very terms in which it comes into being. Far from having a 'realistic' portrait of a 'real' woman, evidence of the poet's 'real' love, we have an account of the impossibility of knowing what it is that the language of love can ever actually say about its object. This is at once a comment

---

[60]   This version of the sonnet is from Katherine Duncan-Jones's 1997 Arden edition (Croatia: Thimas Nelson and Sons).

on the reductive and idealising tendencies of Petrarchism and an extension of Petrarchism's engagement with the limitations of language to adequately capture the mistress's beauty or the poet's emotion. It both extends and refuses, by undermining, Petrarchism's problems with its own tradition.

The radical contingency of the couplet, too, leaves us ultimately with the knowledge that we are being presented with the impossibility of the Petrarchan position – which is, of course, perfectly Petrarchan, since the poet has constantly to assert the authenticity of his emotion in the context of a thoroughly overdetermined generic imperative to do just that. At the same time, however, the couplet refuses the very terms it also relies upon. 'And yet, by heaven, I think my love as rare / As any she belied with false compare': how rare, how exceptional, is a love which can be compared to loves which have been belied with false compare? This love is at least as rare as those loves based on the lie of the artificial and unlikely comparisons of Petrarchan praise. It may, by extension, be equally as worthless or unreal. Or it may exceed them. It is impossible to know. The nature of the poet's love cannot be declared. This makes it exceptional in Petrarchan terms, since it recognises it cannot ring true in those terms. It is also extraordinarily typical in Petrarchan terms, since Shakespeare's poet is aware that by the time he is writing, no Petrarchan declaration can ring true in Petrarchan terms. The poet's statement of love is both potentially void and also therefore utterly genuine in ways not containable within the language on which it relies. This sonnet both is and is not the incarnation of the Petrarchan problem of true praise. It both is and is not a declaration of love. It relies on the tradition it simultaneously invokes and refuses, exhausts and extends.

Titus Andronicus, too, works by exceeding what it needs in order to make sense. The play transgresses boundaries both formally and thematically, making it a remarkable feat of innovation. I suspect its radical eclecticism is partly responsible for its checkered critical reception, and is one of the reasons it is so difficult to stage convincingly. The play offers an exemplar of the relation between form and content, from its opening mélange of history and politics: the Roman system it begins by performing, the aggressive clash of rulership options which sets the play in motion, contains bits of all the Roman and Elizabethan systems presented at once. Far from this being a flaw in the writing of a young man (as is sometimes suggested), it signals the modus operandi of the play. *Titus* enacts boundary violations on every level: of classical precedent, of bodily integrity, of its exploration of the effects of inadequate state structures unable to deliver justice, of the line between madness and sanity in a world where injustice is uncontainable by either human or divine structures. Concerns with the uncontainability of violence, and with trauma's ability to seep from generation to generation, are echoed throughout the work. The *Metamorphoses*, literally presented on stage as well as invoked thematically and linguistically, mark the play's interest in physical and psychic change – in shifts of outlines – as well as in the Ovidian tradition which it, again, invokes to exceed. Time and again, critics point to the ways in which this play mixes different elements together, unexpectedly, with excessive results. Of its bloody, irreverent use of classical form, its most recent editors Jonathan Bate and Eric Rasmussen comment,

> The brilliance of *Titus* is that it is suffused with the language of the Elizabethan classroom – words like 'tutor', 'instruct', 'lesson' – yet it uses classical literature as 'pattern and precedent' not for virtue but for high crime and misdemeanour ... Again, the lesson of classical literature was that tragedy should be kept apart from comedy, high art from low.[61]

The play questions the relation of justice to revenge, casting the boundaries of both in doubt. In the process, especially for modern audiences who do not have the devilish associations with black characters and sexually independent women to cue their responses to Aaron and Tamora as the automatic villains of the piece, the play calls into question the apparent distinction between, or easy understanding of, good and evil, hero and villain. It is Titus's dedication to Rome's 'cruel, irreligious piety' (1.1.130) in his insistence on sacrificing Tamora's eldest son which sets the violence in motion, along the way raising the question of the distinction between religious sacrifice and murder, and so between the apparent heroism of the war the characters have just returned from fighting and nationalist butchery. Tamora's plea for clemency (1.1.104–20) raises all these issues, and from the mouth of the one who first vows revenge, in this revenge tragedy which calls itself into question in all the ways mentioned above. Titus, the eponymous hero, by the end of the first act, is as tainted and morally blurred as any of the villains, and his words and actions call into question the limits of the stoic virtues. Titus's ambiguous status as a revenge hero relates to the play's exceeding of generic form in a much more overt way than his later incarnation, Hamlet. While mimicking perfectly the excessive relation of human agency to inherited form, *Titus* also flatly refuses the traditional Eng. Lit. humanist resolution outlined by Dollimore in *Radical Tragedy*.[62] The play starts with contentions over burial rites and rights, and ends with more violated burials. There is no resolution, no moving forward, no cleaning up of the human mess parents bequeath so bloodily to their children in this play.

Thus *Titus* is an excessive play in every way, not just in its notorious violence. Its excess, I am suggesting, speaks to what it is in Shakespeare's work that earns it the appellation of the universally human. We all inherit structures: psychic, social, linguistic, which various theories from psychoanalysis to feminism to Marxism have worked so hard to point out. But if we are to avoid a dead-end determinism which in any event is patently inadequate in the face of many things human, from great art to the surprises of individual relationships, we have to acknowledge that

---

[61]   Jonathan Bate and Eric Rasmussen (eds), *The RSC Shakespeare: Complete Works* (Basingstoke: Macmillan/Random House Modern Library, 2007), p. 1618.

[62]   Dollimore, *Radical Tragedy*.

there is something in what it is to be human which always exceeds its inherited categories or starting points.[63]

There are other Shakespeare texts which perform this work (although Shakespeare is not the only artist ever to offer examples, his oeuvre may be particularly rich in them). Looking at *Othello* or *The Merchant of Venice* through the lens presented here, for example, enables another way to account for the problematics of race these plays present. Is Othello challenging or confirming the Elizabethan stereotype of the violent, jealous Moor? Is Shylock more human than his original audiences would have expected, or typically venal and damned? Similarly, does *The Taming of the Shrew* critique or endorse a particularly violent brand of gender and class relations? Shakespeare is using the forms at his disposal and pushing them in new ways, into new territory. What he produces are works at once terribly familiar and exhilaratingly innovative. This is one reason why his work continues to fascinate particular, and particularly educated, modern audiences. It helps to explain how Shakespeare's texts seem to at least accommodate, and at most reflect or account for, the changes that modernity and postmodernity have wrought on the inheritances of early modernity.

As a specifically located writer, in his literary and historical context, Shakespeare exceeds the terms he inherits. This is what it means to be human and where the uncontrollable in humanity and human response resides – where agency manifests. Of course, Shakespeare is not the only writer to exceed the terms he inherits, to extend form and genre and push language into new expressions. This is exactly what great writers do. But because of a specific material, political and ideological history, he is the most well known, as well as possibly the best, English example we have. His reputation should not be extricated from the colonial history in which it is bound up, but it should not be reduced to that history either. By 'we', I mean we citizens of the world, those of us across places and languages and cultures with the means to read and to be educated to whatever degree, for most of whom Shakespeare will signify something to do with literature and thus with the great expression of what it means to be human. This is an argument based on materialism, not an invocation of a transcendent humanism. It also cannot be the last word in the expression of the human, but only one example of how literature (as a specific cultural form, in a specific cultural context) might offer a politically responsible humanist theory to a diverse world.

---

[63] Judith Butler has expressed this same point via psychoanalysis and literature in *Antigone's Claim: Kinship between Life and Death* (New York: Columbia University Press, 2000).

Chapter 2
Shakespeare without Borders

Sandra Young

Introduction

When Ben Jonson declared that Shakespeare was 'not for an age, but for all time', the effect would have been less powerful – because less plausible – had he chosen to declare his contemporary's universal appeal in geopolitical rather than temporal terms.[1] More obviously open to question, an exaggerated claim that Shakespeare's work would resonate as much in Surinam, Ethiopia or Beijing as it could be assumed to resonate for audiences in London or Stratford, might have receded from view rather more quickly. Temporality's imagined continuity doesn't seem to hold for the diversity of sociopolitical spaces named for their geographical location; this was the case even during the early seventeenth century, when geographers and natural historians were anxious to be able to account for the 'whole world' in their compilations.[2] But as Franco Moretti's surprising work on the mapping of literature has shown, a geographical register may enable new insights into the connectedness of peoples and histories, while acknowledging infinite plurality. For Moretti, the map is a powerful representational and analytical tool in 'bringing to light connections that would otherwise remain hidden'.[3]

As it turned out, the dissemination of Shakespeare's work and cultural resonance across the globe has been absorbed into social imaginaries more widely and more intimately than even Jonson might have cared to imagine. Given the incalculable and wildly diverse cultural appropriations of Shakespeare, the unity of the singular authorial identifier, 'Shakespeare', has been rendered irrecoverably multiple, forever changed and changing.[4] This is not simply an effect of time

---

[1]   See Jonson's preface to the First Folio of 1623.

[2]   See, for example, George Abbot's brief but purportedly compendious volume from 1599, *A briefe description of the whole worlde wherein are particularly described all the monarchies, empires, and kingdomes of the same, with their seuerall titles and situations thereunto adioyning.*

[3]   Franco Moretti, *Atlas of the European Novel, 1800–1900* (New York: Verso, 1998), p. 3.

[4]   For some recent examples of scholarship that concerns itself with the surprising reach of Shakespeare's drama and local appropriations of his work, see, for example, Sonia Massai's collection, *World-wide Shakespeares: Local Appropriations in Film and Performance* (New York: Routledge, 2005), *Native Shakespeares: Indigenous*

passing. It is also a function of global cultural entanglement. Dispersed in this way, 'Shakespeare' is irrevocably transformed.

Recent critical interest in transnationalism has invited scholars to think about the geopolitical not as the unchanging ground beneath our feet but as a site of exchange and negotiation, and as an ever-shifting element within a more fluid and complex web of meaning-making. The challenge of transnationalism is not to abandon an alertness to place and time but rather to recognise the currents of movement, the shifts and the interconnectedness of the elements that help to constitute 'place' in the production of meaning. In his review of Susan Stanford Friedman's *Mappings: Feminism and the Cultural Geographies of Encounter*, for example, Richard Pearce acknowledges the surprising usefulness of spatially inflected thought for complex questions of culture and identity: 'Geopolitical thinking requires careful consideration of the local, regional, national, and transnational issues that inflect all individual, cultural, and collective identities.'[5]

To complicate the 'national' (inherent in the notion of the transnational) is not necessarily to abandon it as an element of analysis; rather, we must understand its ambit both as exceeding the porous borders of cultural identifications and as necessarily contingent and unstable. What might that mean for Shakespeare studies as it is practised in South Africa? In particular, what fresh insights might the transnational offer to postcolonial Shakespeare, a field that has grown complacent and overly secure with the now-normative confrontations of postcolonial critiques? What does it do to Shakespeare to imagine 'him' circulating across borders, and back, transformed by encounters with that which cannot be anticipated? Might a more global perspective on Shakespeare help us to think differently about the epistemological and cultural category 'South African Shakespeare'?

Isabel Hofmeyr foregrounds a set of terms and preoccupations for understanding anew the relationship between literature, identity and geography, preoccupations that may have productive application for Shakespeare studies in South Africa. For Hofmeyr, oceanic studies offer a means of thinking about the movement between geopolitical spaces from the vantage point of the marginalised, or at least in ways that avoid the Eurocentrism of an earlier mode of literary historiography. Meg Samuelson articulates a similar methodological innovation as an invitation to reflect on Africa from the vantage point of 'the ship' in the hope of reimagining 'the continent as a series of exits and entrances', and 'as a space criss-crossed' and 'deeply entangled in a world of movement and trade', making it impossible to fall back into essentialisms or to reproduce predictable dichotomies.[6]

Appropriations on a Global Scale (Aldershot: Ashgate, 2008) and *Chinese Shakespeares: Two Centuries of Cultural Exchange* (New York: Columbia University Press, 2009).

[5]   Richard Pearce, 'Geography Lessons', *NOVEL: A Forum on Fiction* 32.3 (Spring 1999): p. 450.

[6]   Meg Samuelson, 'Oceanic Africa: Thinking from the Cape' (Seminar paper, 'Thinking Africa and the African Diaspora Differently Workshop', hosted by the Centre for African Studies, University of Cape Town, 14 December 2011), n.p. See Samuelson

In making a case for Indian Ocean studies as a rich opportunity for new thinking about tired theoretical models, Hofmeyr argues that the 'Indian Ocean obliges us to extend our axes of investigation' for it 'complicates [familiar] binaries, moving us away from the simplicities of the resistant local and the dominating global and toward a historically deep archive of competing universalisms'.[7] Hofmeyr is careful not to overstate the value of the transnational, as though it were a panacea for the shortcomings of a more invested or predictable postcolonialism, as if it weren't capable of 'its own forms of exclusion'.[8] She argues that 'it is critical to engage with debates on transnationalism in the global south' and suggests that 'we look quite literally at our location in southern Africa – between two oceans – and see what analytical purchase that may provide'.[9] What would an 'attunement' to our location (at the tip of Africa, between two oceans) mean for Shakespeare studies in southern Africa? How might we 'set our familiar hermeneutics adrift', as Samuelson puts it, in the hope of generating new perspectives on the ways Shakespeare resonates in this place?

The challenge of contemporary literary scholarship is surely to deploy analytical paradigms not for their own sake but for their value in helping to illuminate the politics of literary production today. It may be that the paradigm of postcolonialism and its categories of analysis have become self-reproducing and normative within an academy that is all too detached from the anti-colonial imperatives that first gave postcolonialism life.[10] The temporal paradigm that allows 'postcolonialism' to announce prematurely a break from colonial power relations and the limitation of its self-generating categories of analysis have been acknowledged for some years now, even as they yield critical insights. As we try to understand the impact of Shakespeare and his place in South Africa, the imperative before us is to attend to the politics of each new instance of representation, each new deployment of theory, and to endeavour to trouble the familiar categories of thought that have emerged within the field of postcolonial Shakespeare within South Africa. To begin with, the delineation of the field itself warrants reconsideration.

(2010) for an example of her deployment of oceanic methodologies in her reading of Zoë Wicomb's fiction.

[7] Isabel Hofmeyr, 'Universalizing the Indian Ocean', *PMLA* 125.3 (May 2010): p. 722.

[8] Hofmeyr, 'The Black Atlantic Meets the Indian Ocean: Forging New Paradigms of Transnationalism for the Global South – Literary and Cultural Perspectives', *Social Dynamics* 33.2 (2007): p. 6.

[9] Ibid., p. 4.

[10] Anthony Bogues articulated a similar critique of postcolonialism at a workshop on 'Thinking Africa and the African Diaspora Differently', held at the Centre for African Studies at the University of Cape Town, December 2011.

'Shakespeare in South Africa'

The notion of a 'South African Shakespeare' – whether thought of as an existing field of scholarship and analysis or as an object worth trying to define – is undoubtedly useful, not only in securing a place for distinctive scholarship within an Africa-centric academy but also in naming a position from which to forge new interpretations and breathe new meanings into an inherited Shakespeare. However, it inevitably carries limitations as a delineating description of a cultural field. One may well ask how it serves scholarship and theatre-making in South Africa to define a field in this way, using such clear geopolitical boundaries? To be sure, the clarity of the shoreline and the banks of the Limpopo and Orange Rivers makes for a comforting national delineation, as does the identifiable political entity, if not the unity, that undergirds a recognisably 'South African' cultural life.[11] But though this delineation has undoubtedly nurtured and enabled Shakespeare studies in South Africa, it has equally closed off ways of thinking about cultural practice, feeding norms and stereotypes, and made it difficult to see the ways South African cultural and intellectual life is entangled with worlds beyond the country's borders.

It is instructive to think about how scholars working with contemporary literature in South Africa have conceived of a South African literary field. Leon de Kock describes, with wry humour, a discernible pattern in scholars' attempts to set out the field of South African literature: it is a process, he argues, that seems to induce anxiety and the compulsion to apologise, despite the imperative to go ahead with the delineation regardless.[12] So why the imperative, one might ask, to set out – as a field identified under a fixed sign – literature produced in or about South Africa? Is it not time to abandon the idea of a 'South African Literature' and, equally, 'South African Shakespeare'? Could we find a way to speak of creative practice in South Africa, and the literature and scholarship it nurtures, in terms that acknowledge the connections and mutually constitutive pathways of influence and adaptation in a more complex, interconnected global circulation of ideas and cultural production?

---

[11]   See Meg Samuelson, 'Oceanic Africa'.

[12]   Stefan Helgesson is therefore all the more perplexed that De Kock himself feels the need to press ahead with an attempt at such a restrictive delineation of the field of South African literature himself: 'When rereading [De Kock's] essay from 2001, I am once again struck by its richly textured reasoning; it is perhaps the most trenchant critique of South African literary historiography to date. What puzzles me, however, is De Kock's apparent need to restrict this inquiry into South African literary studies specifically to South Africa – despite everything. He is well aware that he is yet again staging "the impossibility of origin and unity" (p. 277), a compulsively South African theme, but prefers to repeat it (at the highest conceptual level) rather than reconfigure the question in a comparative and transnational framework. (Which is even more striking considering that the essay purports to deal with "South Africa in the Global Imaginary".)' See Helgesson, 'Provincialising English: Rethinking Literature', *English Studies in Africa* 51.1 (2008): p. 127.

Though it might be a useful shorthand for establishing a set of identifications, a designation that derives its terms from a geographical or political space is not just inadequate but also positively misleading in a context as complex as South Africa – a place, even two decades after transition, of 'largely *unresolved* difference'.[13] It may thus be more productive to deploy terms that enable an 'opening out' rather than those that are definitive. Hedley Twidle has remarked that the subtle but significant shift in orientation signalled in the change from 'South African literature' to 'Literature *in* South Africa' allows for a much wider, more open conceptualisation of literary activity in the country.[14] 'Literature in South Africa' acknowledges the points of connection between cultural life in South Africa and other parts of Africa and beyond, and therefore produces a very different object of study to the category of 'South African literature'. It allows for the multiple layerings and textures of a cultural context that is far more nuanced than even a complex historical account might convey.

The notion of 'South African Shakespeare', similarly, is regrettably limiting and perhaps even disingenuous – given Shakespeare's entanglement with the country's colonial history, in the first instance, and, in the second, his availability as a resource for African writers and activists (for example, in the vibrant life of Sophiatown, as Natasha Distiller has convincingly argued).[15] Who is to say what, or who, 'Shakespeare' is in South Africa, given the complexity of Shakespeare's cultural and political legacy in this country? While Shakespeare may be thought of as synonymous with colonialism, since 1994 in particular, as Laurence Wright has argued, scholars have worked hard to debunk the monolithic Shakespeare, disentangling him from his association with conservative and bigoted politics and claiming him as a resource for confrontation with cultural norms. Published soon after 1994, for example, André Brink's *Destabilising Shakespeare* claims Shakespeare for liberatory politics by demonstrating the many 'strategies and devices ... through which some of the apparent "constants" of the Elizabethan/ Jacobean world are challenged or subverted: kingship, power, identity, gender.'[16]

The scholarship that emerged in the 1990s as South African academics engaged with postcolonial studies seemed to bring new perspectives to international scholarship at a time when the world was particularly attentive to things South African and the country was self-consciously caught up with

---

[13] Leon de Kock, 'South Africa in the Global Imaginary: An Introduction', *Poetics Today* 22.2 (2001): p. 264.

[14] 'The Perils of the Archive: Peter D. McDonald and Hedley Twidle in conversation' (Joint Seminar on Apartheid Censorship and its Consequences). University of Cape Town, 14 April 2011.

[15] Natasha Distiller, 'South African Shakespeare: A Model for Understanding Cultural Transformation?', *Shakespeare in Southern Africa* 15 (2003): pp. 21–7.

[16] André Brink, *Destabilising Shakespeare* (Grahamstown: Shakespeare Society of Southern Africa, 1996), p. i.

its own new coming-into-being after apartheid.[17] Shakespeare studies was also revitalised by the opportunity to consider anew the place of Shakespeare within the educational, cultural and political life of the South African 'post colony'. Post-apartheid innovations in the field have established a place for seemingly marginal Shakespeares, within both criticism and theatre practice, and have dislodged the simplistic association of Shakespeare with orthodoxy and conservatism. They have helped us to recognise the ways in which Shakespeare has been a resource for a more critical politics, pre- and post-1994. And yet, even reconceived in this way, the notion of 'South African Shakespeare' remains awkwardly tethered to its disciplinary location and to the two monolithic but overlapping categories by which it is identified. The assertion of a nation-based delineation in this form produces a certain defensiveness in relation to rest of the world, particularly when the first term, 'South African', appears only as a qualifying adjective to the dominant term in the partnership, the noun, 'Shakespeare', whose canonicity seems unimpeachable. Given the disciplinary stature of Shakespeare studies, it is hard to come at it sideways, as it were – to ask new questions of a field which announces itself so formally, both to its interlocutors and to those who might prefer to remain on the fringes.

Travelling Shakespeare

The nature of cultural translocation will mean, necessarily, that Shakespeare in South Africa is 'a thing apart', necessarily transformed from what might be thought of as its place of origin. Edward Said's reflections on 'traveling theory' offer a set of terms with which to conceptualise the ways in which theories – and metropolitan literary forms, to extend Said's argument – are accommodated, appropriated, unhinged and transformed in new contexts. The difficulty with Said's model, if read too literally, is that it seems to reinforce a model of influence that moves from the centre to the periphery. In fact his position is more radical and invites an acknowledgement of influence in the opposite direction.[18] New spaces and modes of self-writing potentially have an irrevocably transformative influence on canonical forms. If Said is right, this would be felt not only *outside* what might

---

[17]   Of particular significance was the international conference held in Johannesburg in 1996, 'Shakespeare–Post-coloniality–Johannesburg, 1996', followed by Martin Orkin and Ania Loomba's collection, *Post-colonial Shakespeares* (1998). Since then, scholarship by Natasha Distiller, David Johnson, Deborah Seddon and Laurence Wright has broken new ground in developing a language with which to discuss the particular cultural resonances of Shakespeare in South Africa. For a rich account of the history of Shakespeare scholarship in South Africa, see Laurence Wright's introduction to his special edition of *The Shakespearean International Yearbook*, 'South African Shakespeare in the Twentieth Century' (2009).

[18]   As argued by Harry Garuba in his position paper at the workshop on 'Thinking Africa and the African Diaspora Differently' held at the Centre for African Studies at the University of Cape Town, December 2011.

have counted as the 'origin' but also at what might seem its centre, in a relationship of mutual influence that Said refers to, with emphasis, as '*affiliation*': 'To speak here only of borrowing and adaptation is not adequate. There is in particular an intellectual, and perhaps moral, community of a remarkable kind, *affiliation* in the deepest and most interesting sense of the word.'[19]

It is worth taking a moment to consider how Said reaches this affirmation before returning to Shakespeare. Said would also have us recognise the possibility that a new locale may create the conditions for a rekindling of provocations and resistances. Through a careful exposition of Fanon's *Wretched of the Earth* and its response to the Marxism of Lukács, Said shows how the Lukácsian subject-object dialectic, when translocated to colonial Algeria, cannot find fulfilment and resolution after revolution, but must be extended and transformed by the race-based nationalism of the colony.[20] Said concludes that

> when Fanon dramatized the colonial struggle in the language of the manifestly European subject-object dialectic, we think of them not simply as coming after Lukács, using him at a belated second degree, so to speak, but rather as pulling him from one sphere or region into another. This movement suggests the possibility of actively different locales, sites, situations for theory, without facile universalism or over-general totalizing.

The usefulness of Lukács in Algeria is not a sign of his extraordinary universalism and remarkable relevance for a locale outside his own; instead, as Said understands it, Fanon's engagement with Lukács serves both to extend and to challenge his thought beyond its European preserve, and 'reignite' its most potent 'core'. For Said, 'the exercise involved in figuring out where the theory went and how in getting there its fiery core was reignited is invigorating – and is also another voyage, one that is central to intellectual life in the late twentieth century.'

The implication for Shakespeare studies is striking. The vividness of South African interpretations of Shakespeare do not affirm, simplistically, his supposed universalism. Rather, they contribute to the reinvigoration of his work which, having crossed over multiple borders in time and space, is transformed and set aglow in a process of mutual enlivening. The invitation to scholars is to trace this process of invigoration and reflect on its resonances.

Stefan Helgesson reminds us that to create a literature that is 'properly "one's own"' is not so much a break from the inherited tradition of romantic literature, but its ideal: 'The high premium that is placed on nurturing/discovering/studying

---

[19] Edward Said, 'Traveling Theory Reconsidered', in *Reflections on Exile and Other Essays* (Cambridge, MA: Harvard University Press, 2002), p. 452.

[20] For Said, Fanon's introduction of the 'new complication' of nationalism (p. 448) does more than add texture and detail to the model of revolution he derives from Lukács. Rather, it demonstrates the limitation of the oppositional model, where the overthrow of one dominating 'nation' by another is imagined as a route to liberation. For Fanon, one set of bureaucrats and authority figures, formed under colonialism, will simply replace another.

a literature that is properly "one's own" and not "derivative" is in itself the most visible sign of the Romantic legacy.'[21] A more radical assertion acknowledges that literature that has travelled (from what might be thought of as its point of 'origin') and has been shaped by the resonances of a new space and moment is itself transformative, in an ongoing cycle of becoming. To be sure, the notion of 'origins', as Said acknowledges even as he deploys the term, is misleading in a world rendered more complex by global circuits of exchange. The key is to recognise that any literature is necessarily in conversation with different traditions and constituted in infinite difference.

What Might the 'Global' Offer Shakespeare Studies in South Africa?

Various possibilities for scholarship emerge through what has been described as the 'global turn' in Shakespeare studies. 'Global Shakespeare' situates 'Shakespeare' – then and now – within a global system of meaning-making and within complex networks of cultural production, so that it may offer an opportunity to render more complex Shakespeare's world, and our own.

Approaching the material with a heightened awareness of the global dimensions both of the context within which the works were produced and, now, the contexts within which they are performed, taught and researched, is not new. Yet the appearance relatively recently of field-defining collections that explore the global dimensions of early modern cultural production (such as Blackwell's 2009 *Companion to the Global Renaissance*, edited by Jyotsna Singh), the launch by Palgrave Macmillan of a book series devoted to 'Global Shakespeares' and the standard inclusion at major Shakespeare conferences of seminar panels dealing with 'the global' (for instance, at the British Shakespeare Association conference in 2009, the International Shakespeare Association conference in Prague in 2011 and the Shakespeare Association of America conference in 2012) suggest that this has become a compelling or at least productive rubric with which to approach a more open study of Shakespeare – particularly when it remains alert to the many local(s) within the global.

Reading Shakespeare with an increased awareness of global contexts of exchange promises to bring into view, as Singh would have it, the dark side of the Renaissance. It offers a language and an analytical framework that reveals early modern global cultural and economic entanglements. By definition, almost, the global perspective calls into question the idea of discrete, self-contained and authentic national identifications and draws attention instead to the production of power within global systems of exchange. For example, when the production both of wealth and nationhood are seen to emerge out of the pursuit of colonisation and slavery's economic interlocking of Europe, Africa and the 'New World', the construction of 'Englishness' becomes contingent, fluid and provisional.

---

[21]   Helgesson, 'Provincialising English', p. 124.

It allows us, too, to acknowledge the complexity of Shakespeare's own cultural and political moment, and the cross currents of the 'enlarged' world to which his drama addresses itself. The possibility that he might have just read John Pory's 1600 translation of Leo Africanus and been inspired to create *Othello* (first performed in 1603), or that he might have read accounts of New World discoveries and shipwrecks, the Bermuda and others, and had his imagination enlivened to place Prospero on Caliban's island, is significant – but not in the way that an earlier moment of 'source' criticism would have us believe, that is to say, significant for giving us a clue as to what Shakespeare was *really* thinking or, worse, what his drama *really* means. Rather, the possibility that Shakespeare is likely to have read these accounts suggests that his own historical moment is much more 'plugged into' global circuits than would have been apparent in later, more nationalistic periods, when Shakespeare was marshalled in the service of England and its colonial endeavours.

'Global Shakespeare' situates 'Shakespeare' – then and now – within a global system of meaning-making and within complex networks of cultural production, rendering Shakespeare's world more complex (as well as our own). The turn to the 'global' is, however, equally vulnerable to the reductiveness that has at times robbed postcolonialism of its critical acuity. Just as postcolonial theory seemed to offer a new language with which to think about culture's implication in relations of power, and just as it seemed to decentre European dominance by accounting for the discursive and epistemological processes which produced categories of difference, it was also susceptible to uncritical reproduction – what Ania Loomba has dismissed as the 'simplistic "all is hybrid and multicultural" argument'.[22] For example, when Indian Ocean studies avoids the history of slavery while alluding euphemistically to the 'cultural entanglement' of the peoples of the Indian Ocean world, this seems to me a missed opportunity to think in more nuanced terms about labour and compulsion.[23] The view across the Indian Ocean does not render talk of slavery unnecessary but, rather, complicates the absolute terms in which slavery has been understood, as a result of the dominance of 'Atlantic readings of slavery where the boundary between enslaved and free is unequivocally demarcated and racialized', as Isabel Hofmeyr has argued.[24]

If it is to be meaningful as a critical paradigm, 'global Shakespeare' has to go further than adding superficial, race-based 'interest' to the early modern

---

[22] Ania Loomba, Review of *Remapping the Mediterranean World in Early Modern English Writings* and *Speaking of the Moor: From 'Alcazar' to 'Othello'*, *Shakespeare Studies* 38 (2010): pp. 269–70.

[23] I was struck by this explicit avoidance of slavery at an otherwise compelling seminar I attended at the International Shakespeare Association conference in Prague in 2011. In reflecting on the way the 'Ocean' figures in early modern culture, the seminar sought to look East, across the Indian Ocean, rather than across the Atlantic – and therefore would not be confronted with the issue of slavery, we were told.

[24] Hofmeyr, 'Universalizing the Indian Ocean', p. 722.

period. Its real value, to my mind, is to be found in its invitation to recognise with greater perspicacity the ideological dimensions of cultural and critical life and the fundamental asymmetries of power relations at work, whether in the early modern period or in post-apartheid South Africa. In this, it is not unlike 'postcolonialism' or, in the context of South Africa, a new attention to 'Africanisation'. The rigour doesn't inhere in bringing into focus cultural diversity alone, but in a willingness to recognise exploitative power structures and racist inequities, even as the more complex relationships of exchange come into view. It is well to recognise, too, that the 'global' does not necessarily counteract insularity or a provincialism assuming that the part speaks for the whole. Critical sensitivity to the impact of the 'global' calls for *more* careful historicism, not less. Without an attentiveness to the myriad of 'locals' within the global, it may have the effect of universalising what is culturally dominant.

Invigoration of the study and performance of Shakespeare this many years into democracy in South Africa depends on an openness both to the immediacy of what is here – the local and familiar – and the ways it is in conversation with worlds beyond the immediate – our elsewhere. Dislodged from its embeddedness within an earlier incarnation of colonialism, Shakespeare in South Africa today has ceased to be (exclusively) English and is 'at liberty'.

Innovative Theatre-Making and the 'Africanisation' of Shakespeare

The invigoration of Shakespeare in South Africa is dependent on the practice of theatre-making, not just on scholarship, and may require an on-the-ground shift or at least an opening up of the theatre scene to new and diverse audiences and innovative stagings. The power dynamics at work within South African theatre remain a barrier to innovation. Cape Town–based actor/director Guy de Lancey has challenged theatre-makers and academics 'to find a new voice for Shakespeare in South Africa'.[25] He complains that there is 'too much reverence in theatre in Cape Town in general' and that the 'politics of producing Shakespeare', in particular, is constraining: 'one is constantly needing to seek permission' and the weight of convention 'militates against thinking too much'.[26] One may well ask, who gets to make theatre? To whom is it performed – which audiences, which critics, which funders, are imagined at the scene of creative theatre-making? Given recessionary economic constraints and the difficulty of attracting viable audiences,

---

[25]   In a devastating critique of the culture of South African Shakespeare, De Lancey calls for a revision of the 'conceptual architecture of the work of Shakespeare that challenges flaccid preconceived "arts council" notions, sclerotic Cape Town academic ones, the reflex exclusions of post modern "institutes of performing and creative arts" and their tenured yawning board members, and engages an audience from beginning to end' (available online at: theatreofcruelty.wordpress.com/2012/12/16/things-tighten-things-fall-apart-we-are-walking-without-walking-a-site-specific-report).

[26]   Guy de Lancey, interview with the author (January 2011), n.p.

conservative imperatives govern theatre production. This is not necessarily a matter of funding – at least, not exclusively. The self-funded Cape Town theatre group, The Mechanicals, for example, and their thought-provoking, self-conscious productions,[27] suggest to me that the greatest hope of unsettling the disturbing association of Shakespeare with colonial apologetics is to be found away from traditional theatre-making establishments which seem to have bought into an old-fashioned association of Shakespeare with literary elevation, without recognising the very particular cultural and political model we in South Africa inherited along with a British colonial education system. There *is* innovative, 'gutsy' theatre on offer in South Africa, but independent directors and actors indicate that it is poorly funded, and the runs are often short and poorly supported because it is unable to secure an association with mainstream Shakespeare. It seems to me that, if we hope to work within an invigorated field, we need to pay attention to the contexts of theatre-making and do more, as theatre critics and academics, to support independent practitioners doing innovative work.[28]

If the theatre-making and criticism that emerge from this context are to be taken seriously locally and internationally, within the academy and without, and if these are to draw postgraduate students and yield new and challenging approaches, they will need the latitude to forge new interpretations and new stagings. While the notional 'Africanisation' of Shakespeare appeared to do just this in the Royal Shakespeare Company/Baxter production of *The Tempest* in 2009, in truth the invocation of a generalised 'African' aesthetic (and the affective milieu of a post-TRC 'new' South Africa) worked only to lend colour, interest and legitimacy to a version of 'Shakespeare' that is aligned with privilege.[29] In a review of this production, I argued that an

---

[27] The Mechanicals articulate their approach to Shakespeare (in materials relating to their 2012 production of *King Lear*) in this way: 'Inverting received notions of the inaccessibility of Shakespearean text, The Mechanicals strive to demystify the nostalgic reverence for the language, while at the same time steering away from a popularized send-up of the complexities of the material' (available online at: guydelancey.com/king-lear.html).

[28] Veteran theatre reviewer Peter Tromp describes The Mechanicals' staging of *A Midsummer Night's Dream* as 'one of the most enjoyable, inventive and strangest Shakespeare productions I have ever seen' ('Mechanicals return to form in boisterous fashion', *The Next 48 Hours*, 18 March 2011; available online at: 48hours.co.za/archive/old/18march2011/stories/11march/story03.html). See my comparison of this production of *A Midsummer Night's Dream* with the more troubling, mainstream Maynardville production of *The Taming of the Shrew* running concurrently in 'A Charming, Troubling Circus: Roy Sargeant's *Taming of the Shrew*' in *Shakespeare in Southern Africa* 23 (2011): pp. 81–3.

[29] See my review article (2010) for a fuller account of my misgivings about this particular staging of an 'Africanised' *Tempest* and the troubling effects of its racialised logic in seeking to translate 'Shakespeare' into an 'Africa' that, on the one hand, lives by a rule of primal violence and, on the other, responds to imperialist abuses of power with TRC-style forgiveness.

African *Tempest* that engages the discourse of forgiveness allows 'Shakespeare' to share in the sociality invoked by *ubuntu*. Post-apartheid theatre would do better to resist a post–Truth and Reconciliation Commission hope of transcendence and an iconic 'Shakespeare'. However, it may take great boldness to claim the latitude with which to trespass beyond an apparently familiar 'Africa' and an uninterrogated 'Shakespeare'.

The boundary-breaking irreverence of my fantasy would require theatre-practitioners to resist the glib and feel-good reproduction of a 'rainbow' Africa whose task it is to provide colour and reconciliatory affect for consumption by a privileged audience. Irreverence, both towards Shakespeare and towards 'Africa', might be especially invigorating to the field, introducing surprising interpretations and adaptations and new critical perspectives. As long as Shakespeare continues to be held up as 'our guru' (as Nadine Gordimer put it recently), nothing more can be said.[30] His work becomes fixed, authoritative, untouchable – and considerably less interesting – and his interlocutors within contemporary public and creative life are sidelined. Fortunately, the alternative is already at play: as Guy de Lancey puts it, 'that irreverance is there, in the text.'[31] But a tricky paradox emerges in this vision of an enlivened and transformed Shakespeare in South Africa: Shakespeare will need to occupy a place alongside other works, other cultural expressions, and relinquish the persistent claim to exceptionalism if it/he is to flourish.[32]

It would be a mistake for scholars trying to define the field of 'South African literature' to succumb to the silent imperative to apologise in advance for the effects of translocation. The tic in many South African responses to Shakespeare is the need to claim him as extraordinary, as prophetic, as universal – and not necessarily while engaging with his work but rather as a precursor to this engagement, in an authorising gesture that appears before real arguments can be staged. This keeps Shakespeare at a chilly remove, mars the potential for more robust and innovative treatments of Shakespeare and overwhelms any new and surprising perspectives, reducing them to further evidence still of Shakespeare's exceptionalism and transcendence. In what can only be a bilateral engagement – Shakespeare and his others – 'Shakespeare' is always already the privileged partner and the 'global' in 'global Shakespeare' functions as the colourful affirmation of Shakespeare's pre-eminence and universal relevance. Colette Gordon points out that this relationship is dependent on a performance of authenticity on the part of the 'foreign': 'Shakespeare doesn't have to be authentic, but the foreign in

---

[30] Gordimer was answering a question from the floor at the launch of her collection of essays, *Telling Times*, at the Centre for the Book in Cape Town (hosted by the Centre for Violence and Reconciliation), 2 August 2011.

[31] De Lancey, interview with the author, n.p.

[32] For a fuller example of this kind of argument, see Barbara Bowen, 'Beyond Shakespearean Exceptionalism', in Lloyd Davis (ed.), *Shakespeare Matters: History, Teaching, Performance* (Newark: University of Delaware Press, 2003).

"foreign Shakespeare" does.'[33] There is tremendous scope in theatre practice and in scholarship to unsettle this hierarchy.

Much Shakespearean theatre and criticism subscribes to a reverence that Shakespeare would probably have found perplexing. Even within postcolonial Shakespeare studies, there is a need to avoid the temptation to view Shakespeare as the 'privileged site for thinking about non-Western subjectivities' as Harry Garuba put it in an otherwise positive review of the 1998 collection *Post-colonial Shakespeares*.[34] When Garuba stresses the definitive article in quoting the editors ('Shakespeare provides *the* language for expressing racial difference and human sameness as well as colonial hybridities'), Shakespeare is rendered uniquely prescient in a way the editors may not have intended. Even so, Garuba's caution is well taken: Shakespeare's availability for contemporary engagement is paradoxically enhanced by creative and critical latitude. Only when he ceases to be 'our guru', *the* privileged site of meaning-making and humanist affirmation, apparently neutral – and only when he becomes one of many potentially rich experiences of literature from exciting new writers and theatre-makers – might the field of Shakespeare studies undergo renewal.

The Lateral View

The insoluble contest between canonical Shakespeare, tethered to a racist colonial educational heritage, and a more irreverent or satirical Shakespeare, an ally in the critique of power, is perhaps a symptom of the view northwards – a view in which 'Africa' will inevitably figure as the less empowered partner, and Shakespeare will always belong elsewhere. A more open view, one that acknowledges cultural engagement as always in flux, always becoming, regardless of the 'distance' (in time and place and context) it has travelled, is more promising.

As long as the primary view is to the north, postcolonial South African Shakespeare studies is likely to remain stuck in a regrettable polarisation, always inevitably the lesser partner, on the periphery. But what if relationships, conversations, were imagined with different interlocutors; what if we were to engage with other nontraditional centres of Shakespeare practice? What kinds of questions might emerge, when the conversation anticipates neither affirmation nor resistance but proceeds with a more open orientation? The sense of marginalisation in Shakespeare studies in South Africa derives from the persistence of the view

---

[33] Colette Gordon, 'What's Hecuba to Him, or "Kupenga" to Them? Syncretic Theatre, Global Shakespeare' (Seminar paper, 'Global Shakespeares', World Shakespeare Conference, Prague, July 2011), p. 12. See also '*Hamlet* in England, *Hamlet* in Exile: What's Hecuba to Him, or *Kupenga* to Them?', *Shakespeare in Southern Africa* 23 (2011): pp. 64–9.

[34] Harry Garuba, 'Review of Post-Colonial Shakespeares', *Research in African Literatures* 33.1 (2002): pp. 218–20.

northwards. In truth, there is so much more to Shakespeare, as we would discover if we entered new conversations across the Atlantic and Indian Oceans.[35]

Instead of vacillating between the two poles of resistance and appropriation, our engagement with multiple 'Shakespeares' may open up new avenues of thought and offer new registers within which to explore human experience from this location, recognising that having travelled this far, Shakespeare has become wonderfully, productively, unhinged. If, in our scholarship, we are able to look sideways – askance and in unpredictable directions, towards other centres of culture in the global south – we may be surprised at what emerges beyond the border of the familiar.

---

[35] In articulating it thus, I acknowledge an inspiring conversation with David Schalkwyk.

Chapter 3
'Many in One':
On Shakespeare, Language and Translation

Pier Paolo Frassinelli

Is it justifiable to assume that the source language in which the original text makes sense is different and distinct from the target language into which the translator renders the text as faithfully as possible? Are these languages countable? In other words, is it possible to isolate and juxtapose them as individual units, like apples, for example, and unlike water? By what measures is it possible to distinguish one from the other and endow it with a unity or body?

—Naoki Sakai, 'Translation'

thy speaking of my tongue, and I thine, most truly-falsely, must needs be granted to be much at one.

—William Shakespeare, *Henry V*

Therefore, you clown, abandon – which is in the vulgar, leave – the society – which in the boorish is company – of this female – which in the common is woman; which together is, abandon the society of this female, or, clown, thou perishest; or, to thy better understanding, diest; or, to wit, I kill thee, make thee away, translate thy life into death, thy liberty into bondage. I will deal in poison with thee, or in bastinado, or in steel. I will bandy with thee in faction, I will o'errun thee with policy. I will kill thee a hundred and fifty ways. Therefore tremble, and depart.

—William Shakespeare, *As You Like It*

You know I say nothing to him, for he understands not me, nor I him. He hath neither Latin, French, nor Italian, and you will come into the court and swear that I have a poor penny-worth in the English. He is a proper man's picture, but alas, who can converse with a dumb show?

—William Shakespeare, *The Merchant of Venice*

Shakespeare and/in Translation

Shakespeare comes to us inextricably intertwined with the problem of translation. He does so for a number of reasons: because his works are translated, published and performed in more languages all over the world than those of any other literary author. Many or indeed most readers and audiences today access Shakespeare's plays and poems in translation, in languages other than English. And they also experience Shakespeare in new media – from movies to songs and comic strips to downloadable clips – that perform their own translations of his works into new aesthetic and cultural forms. All of which is in turn translated into new academic approaches produced and reproduced in the classroom and in books and papers on Shakespeare and the translation and adaptation of his works into different national or linguistic contexts and media: postcolonial Shakespeares, native Shakespeares, national Shakespeares, Shakespeare and popular culture, Shakespeare and film, music, soap operas, Las Vegas.[1] The list goes on and on, producing an endless textual and semiotic proliferation, a play of difference and a displacement and deconstruction of meaning that are indeed what Jacques Derrida said translation is all about.[2]

But this is not the only way in which Shakespeare's works come to us as translated – or, at the opposite end of the spectrum, untranslatable – texts. In fact, Shakespeare doesn't need to be in another language or new medium to be in translation. Even if we just read one of the various editions of the English version of the texts ascribed to his name – and even without taking into account the textual interventions, which can be said to be a type of translation,[3] by the various editors who assembled these texts and, as a matter of course, modernised their spelling – the words come to us in translation. 'Time', as David Schalkwyk has nicely put it, is 'the primary betrayer of the text: it is its primary translator, and it acknowledges no ethical duty to preserve any of its meanings.' As the text

---

[1]   See, for instance, David Johnson, *Shakespeare and South Africa* (Oxford: Clarendon Press, 1996); John J. Joughin (ed.), *Shakespeare and National Culture* (Manchester and New York: Manchester University Press, 1997); Ania Loomba and Martin Orkin (eds), *Post-colonial Shakespeares* (London and New York: Routledge, 1998); Martin Orkin (ed.), *Local Shakespeares: Proximations and Power* (London and New York: Routledge, 2005); Sonia Massai (ed.), *World-Wide Shakespeares: Local Appropriations in Film and Performance* (London and New York: Routledge, 2005); Craig Dionne and Parmita Kapadia (eds), *Native Shakespeares: Indigenous Appropriations on a Global Stage* (Aldershot: Ashgate, 2008); and Natasha Distiller, *Shakespeare and the Coconuts: On Post-apartheid South African Culture* (Johannesburg: Wits University Press, 2012). As I refer to the multiplicity of textual and cultural interventions that are related to the afterlives of Shakespeare's texts and their transcultural circulation, here I deliberately blur the boundaries between 'translation proper' – to use Roman Jakobson's definition ('On Linguistic Aspects of Translation', in Lawrence Venuti [ed.], *The Translation Studies Reader* [London and New York: Routledge, 2000], pp. 113–18) – and what is usually meant by concepts such as adaptation or appropriation. For a critical discussion of the manifold uses of the term 'translation' in contemporary Shakespeare studies, see Ton Hoenselaars's introduction to *Shakespeare and the Languages of Translation* (London: Thomson, 2004), pp. 1–30 and his 'Translation Futures: Shakespearians and the Foreign Text', *Shakespeare Survey* 62 (2009): pp. 273–82.

[2]   See Jacques Derrida, 'Des Tours de Babel', trans. Joseph F. Graham, in Rainer Schulte and John Biguenet (eds), *Theories of Translation: An Anthology of Essays from Dryden to Derrida* (Chicago and London: University of Chicago Press, 1992), pp. 218–28.

[3]   In *After Babel*, George Steiner writes that 'Reader, actor, editor are translators out of time' (New York and London: Oxford University Press, 1975), p. 28.

travels from then to now, 'its iterations across time bring inevitable alterations and transformations', including the 'slow attenuation' or even 'loss of significance, as meanings that were alive for its original audience and readers become so obscure through historical change that they cease to act as part of the living experience of those engaging with the text'.[4] Think of jokes that are no longer funny, or the way the early modern dramatic text often incorporates references to then-current political events of which most readers and theatre audiences today have little or no knowledge. Hence the critical apparatus and extensive footnotes; hence, also, the paradox of translation, which keeps the text alive by 'refreshing it for new generations of readers and audiences';[5] and hence – another apparent paradox – the advantage 'those who read the plays in foreign translation' have over English-speaking readers, 'in that part of the work of comprehension has been done for them by the translator'.[6] Indeed, the very designation 'English' here testifies to the slipperiness of the signifier that stands for what Naoki Sakai calls the unity or body of a language, which, Sakai argues, is historically rooted in imaginary affiliations 'with nation and national culture and tradition'.[7] For it is not just in languages other than English that Shakespeare's texts can said to be 'foreign'. As Ton Hoenselaars, the editor of *Shakespeare and the Language of Translation*, has remarked, for the English-speaking world Shakespeare's works are also written in what is 'really a foreign language, in need, like all other languages, of translation'.[8]

Translation – including the translation of Shakespeare into modern English[9] – is responsible for turning old texts into our contemporaries. In Walter Benjamin's famous words, each new translation marks a stage in the text's 'continued life'.[10] Anticipating the more recent focus on translation as a creative process, in 'The Task of the Translator' (1923), Benjamin argued that translation is a rewriting of the original text, a textual intervention through which the 'life of the original attains ... its ever-renewed latest and most abundant flowering'.[11] It is, however, the text itself that is ultimately responsible for producing its own translations,

---

[4]   David Schalkwyk, 'Shakespeare's Untranslatability', *Shakespeare in Southern Africa* 18 (2006): pp. 38–9.

[5]   Ibid., p. 39.

[6]   Stanley Wells, 'Preface', in David and Ben Crystal (eds), *Shakespeare's Words: A Glossary and Language Companion* (London: Penguin, 2002), n.p.

[7]   Naoki Sakai, 'Translation and the Figure of the Border: Toward the Apprehension of Translation as Social Action', *Profession* (2010): p. 31.

[8]   See Hoenselaars's introduction to *Shakespeare and the Languages of Translation*, p. 21.

[9]   The proposal of translating Shakespeare into contemporary English, which was put forward in the 1990s by Susan Bassnett and Stanley Wells, found strenuous opposition precisely from those who argued that this kind of translation would have broken the links to the English national heritage (ibid., pp. 19–20).

[10]   Walter Benjamin, 'The Task of the Translator', 1923, trans. Harry Zohn, in Venuti (ed.), *The Translation Studies Reader*, p. 16.

[11]   Ibid., p. 17.

which bear witness to the reputation achieved by the original and 'come into being when in the course of its survival a work has reached the age of its fame'.[12] Thus reconceived, translation also constitutes an essential element of David Damrosch's more recent definition of world literature: 'I take world literature to encompass all literary works that circulate beyond their culture of origin, either in translation or in their original language ... a work only has an *effective* life as world literature whenever, and wherever, it is actively present within a literary system beyond that of its original culture.'[13] World literature, Damrosch argues, is (inter alia) '*writing that gains in translation*': that is, writing that can not only withstand being uprooted from its original context and language, but that in fact gains in translation by expanding 'in depth' as it increases 'its range'.[14] To achieve the status of world literature a text needs to leave home – its home culture and home language – and, as the global circulation of Shakespeare illustrates, some texts and authors clearly travel better than others.

In Shakespeare's case, these travels are the subject of a large and still growing body of scholarship dealing with the afterlives of his plays and poems and their global dissemination. This branch of Shakespeare studies looks at how his texts have been carried across from their place of origin, brought over to new shores, and repositioned within new languages and cultures. The result is a decentring and displacement of Shakespeare's works, which are made to resonate with and speak to new local and global habitations. Typically, in this context the proper noun Shakespeare (or Shakespeares, to underscore the multiplicity of conflicting interpretations and appropriations that make up the reception history of his works) is prefixed by qualifiers that recall various scenes of reading, rewriting and translation or is followed by prepositions that indicate his presence *in* particular places and times or, alternatively, invite us to think about the relations between Shakespeare's works *and* a specific context or medium. In each case, translation is identified with the transformative space inhabited by the text in its afterlives, when Shakespeare *becomes* a translated author – including in his national and linguistic

---

[12]   The main thrust of Benjamin's argument is that the task of the translator is not to reproduce the original in a different language, but to represent the hidden kinship of all languages by giving expression to a pre-Babelian 'pure language' (*reine Sprache*) that pre-exists and is expressed by the original. The task of the translator is therefore not to 'communicate' – as Benjamin puts it, 'any translation which intends to perform a transmitting function cannot transmit anything but information – hence, something inessential. The hallmark of bad translation' (p. 15) – but rather to fulfill the original's inherent translatability, 'an essential feature of certain works', by attempting to capture elements of the pure language to which both the original and its translation give expression. But – and here is the dialectical twist in Benjamin's argument – this pure language does not exist in form of a representable or reproducible object; it is, more elusively, the condition of possibility of translation.

[13]   David Damrosch, *What Is World Literature?* (Princeton and Oxford: Princeton University Press, 2003), p. 4. Emphasis in the original.

[14]   Ibid., pp. 288–9.

home, where, as studies such as Michael Dobson's *The Making of the National Poet* remind us, it was also through a long process of cultural appropriation that in the eighteenth century Shakespeare was translated into 'both symbol and exemplar of British national identity'.[15]

In the discussion that follows I want to take a different path. Focusing on what Sakai calls 'many in one' – that is, the presence of many languages in one – I am going to propose a revision of the established use of the language of appropriation and translation in Shakespeare studies, which as we have seen is usually deployed to designate how Shakespeare's works have been appropriated and translated in different geographical, cultural and historical contexts: a revision that reminds us once more of how, even at his most 'native', Shakespeare comes to us already translated. In short, my argument (which I will only be able to illustrate by way of a brief discussion of the three excerpts from Shakespeare that I use as epigraphs) is that by using the trope, as well as the properly linguistic aspect, of translation, the project of decentring Shakespeare with respect to his putative language and country of origin could also begin by taking into consideration the multilingual and creolised character of Shakespeare's own language, and therefore the multicultural dimension that Shakespeare's texts embody.[16] As Crystal Bartolovich argues in her essay 'Shakespeare's Globe?', close attention to the materials that went into the making of Shakespeare's plays – which 'were cobbled together from orts and fragments of other texts, many from places other than England, from continental and classic stories, the work of colleagues and other plays' – brings into view 'the extravagant syncretism of the cultural matrix we call "Shakespeare" ... and the language in which "he" wrote'.[17] Taken as a metonym for English(ness) – as is routinely done when it comes to underscoring his canonical status – Shakespeare can thus be approached as an exemplary instance of what Robert Stockammer describes as 'Babel in the second degree': that is, a reconfiguration of languages not as separate and discrete entities, but in terms of a constant transgression of linguistic and cultural boundaries that calls for a 'new concept of the translational' based on the recognition that 'People, peoples, and texts are ... multilingual in themselves.'[18]

---

[15] Michael Dobson, *The Making of the National Poet: Shakespeare, Adaptation, and Authorship, 1660–1769* (Oxford: Clarendon Press, 1992), p. 185.

[16] Jacques Derrida argues a related case about translation studies in general in *The Ear of the Other: Otobiography, Transference, Translation* (New York: Schocken Books, 1985), pp. 98–9, where he suggests that theories of translation do not sufficiently consider the possibility of multiple languages to be implicated in a text. The example provided by Derrida is James Joyce's *Finnegans Wake*, whose untranslatability, Derrida argues, derives from the multilingualism within the original text – for even the most successful translation in another language cannot render the multiplicity of languages present in the original.

[17] Crystal Bartolovich, 'Shakespeare's Globe?', in Jean Howard and Scott Cutler Shershow (eds), *Marxist Shakespeares* (London and New York: Routledge, 2001), p. 200.

[18] Robert Stockammer, 'COsMoPoLITerature' (available online at: komparatistik. uni-muenchen.de/personen/professoren/stockhammer/cosmopoliterature1.pdf). For further

Shakespeare: Already Translated

I want to restart with language. As Bill Ashcroft writes in *Caliban's Voice* with reference to the postcolonial world, 'Language itself is transformative, a space of translation. Translation no longer negotiates between languages, for language itself is the site of ceaseless translation.'[19] In the transcultural and polyglot space of the postcolony, where languages are constantly creolised through processes of appropriation and contamination, linguistic production reveals in a particularly stark way the fluid nature of language as such: translation is not a specific kind of linguistic intervention, something we do with language when we transfer meaning from one language to another. Rather, it is the substance of language itself.

This point has been most eloquently made in recent years by Naoki Sakai, who invites us to 'comprehend language from the viewpoint of translation', which is best done by reversing the 'conventional comprehension of translation that always presumes the unity of a language'.[20] The 'conventional' understanding of the unity of a language is of course the very condition of possibility of translation; how can you translate from one language to another without a notion of 'what is included or excluded in the database of a language, what is linguistic or extralinguistic, and what is proper to a particular language or not ... what we must avoid as heterogeneous to our language and reject as improper to it'?[21] The very possibility of translation is premised on the epistemic and strategic necessity of this notion of unity. We therefore understand languages as distinct, separate, countable entities. We commonly think of a language, Sakai writes, 'like an apple or orange, and unlike water'. For Sakai this notion of the 'unity of a language' is something akin to what Immanuel Kant called a 'regulative idea': that is to say, a rule or convention that 'organizes knowledge but is not empirically verifiable'.[22] Without this regulative idea, without the notion of the unity of a language, which is always in relation to the unity of another language, translation would clearly be impossible, or at the very least it would not be possible to determine what constitutes a good or a bad translation. And yet there is a paradox here:

> If the foreign is unambiguously incomprehensible, unknowable, and unfamiliar, it is impossible to talk about translation, because translation simply cannot be done. If, on the other hand, the foreign is comprehensible, knowable, and

---

discussion of Shakespeare's texts as discursive sites of translation, see Liz Oakley-Brown (ed.), *Shakespeare and the Translation of Identity in Early Modern England* (London and New York: Continuum, 2011).

[19]   Bill Ashcroft, *Caliban's Voice: The Transformation of English in Postcolonial Literatures* (London: Routledge, 2009), p. 161.

[20]   Sakai, 'Translation and the Figure of the Border', p. 26.

[21]   Ibid., p. 28.

[22]   Ibid., p. 27.

familiar, it is unnecessary to call for translation. Thus the status of the foreign in translation must always be ambiguous.[23]

Another way of expressing this ambiguity is to suggest that in a multilingual world, all languages are dialogic, heteroglossic, shot through and constituted by their relations with other languages. Edward Said pointed out on many occasions that 'the history of all cultures is the history of cultural borrowings': 'Culture is never just a matter of ownership, of borrowing and lending with absolute debtors and creditors, but rather of appropriations, common experiences, and interdependences of all kinds among different cultures. This is the universal norm.'[24] The same applies to languages, which are also the products of endless borrowings and exchanges.

This was, in fact, the perception shared by many early modern English authors, for whom English was a relatively new linguistic medium that they were helping to fashion – and none more so than Shakespeare, who in the first edition of the *Oxford English Dictionary* (1884–1928) was credited with having coined more than 2,000 words. The literary language they were forging was the product of countless lexical, morphological and rhetorical borrowings, the import of loan words and the adaptation of both vernacular forms and specialised idiolects.[25] Like early modern English itself, it was 'not a fixed linguistic system so much as a linguistic crossroads, a field where many languages – foreign tongues, local dialects, Latin and Greek – intersected': a 'strange tongue', both foreign and local, to be refined, transformed and adapted for one's own needs, in short 'a space of translation'.[26] Consider, for instance, the following passage from Thomas Heywood's *Apology for Actors* (1612), which praises contemporary playwrights for their contribution to turning the 'English tongue' from a 'harsh, uneven, and broken' assemblage of loan words into a proper 'language':

> our *English* tongue, which has been the most harsh, uneven, and broken language of the world, part *Dutch*, part *Irish*, *Saxon*, *Scotch*, *Welsh*, and indeed a gallimaffry of many, but perfect in none, is now by this secondary means of playing, continually refined, every writer striving in himselfe to add a new florish unto it; so that in processe, from the most rude and unpolisht tongue, it is grown to a most perfect and composed language, and many excellent workes,

---

[23]   Ibid., p. 32.

[24]   Edward Said, *Culture and Imperialism* (New York: Knopf, 1993), p. 213.

[25]   See Vanna Gentili, 'A National Idiom and Other Languages: Notes on Elizabethan Ambivalence with Examples from Shakespeare', in Michele Marrapodi and Giorgio Melchiori (eds), *Italian Studies in Shakespeare and His Contemporaries* (Newark: University of Delaware Press, 1999), pp. 187–205.

[26]   Steven Mullaney, 'Strange Things, Gross Terms, Curious Customs: The Rehearsal of Cultures in the Late Renaissance', *Representations* 3 (1983): p. 55.

and elaborate Poems writ in the same, that many Nations grow inamored of our tongue (before despised).[27]

A gallimaufry of many languages in one – and Heywood still left out French, Italian and Latin, as we are reminded by the dedicatory epistle prefacing Edmund Spenser's *The Shepherd's Calendar* (1579), signed by 'E.K.', which, contrary to Heywood's praise of linguistic innovation, commends the author for having 'laboured to restore, as to theyr rightfull heritage such good and naturall English words, as have ben long time out of use': a preferable option, according to 'E.K.', to what he laments as the current habit of patching up 'the holes with peces and rags of other languages, borrowing here of the French, there of the Italian, every where of the Latin' so as to 'have made our English tongue, a gallimaufray or hodgepodge of al other speches'.[28] Their different takes on the development of English notwithstanding, both commentators were pointing to the state of linguistic instability and interlingual contamination typical of European vernaculars during the Renaissance. As Steven Mullaney summarises,

> The medieval world had been structured around a dual language hierarchy: on the one hand, a stable and monolithic Latin for learned and official society, and on the other, the metamorphic, plural, and largely oral vernacular, a plethora of local dialects, idioms, and jargons that was the province of popular culture. As that hierarchy broke down, however, the linguistic worlds that had formerly been held apart, as distinct and separate entities, came into increasing contact with one another. The European vernaculars came to inhabit the boundaries of other languages, to import values, concepts, and ideologies from strange tongues both foreign and domestic.[29]

Within this historical constellation – behind which lurks the emergence of the modern nation-state and the identification of language and nation[30] – the

---

[27]   Thomas Heywood, *An Apology for Actors* (London, 1612), sig. F3r.

[28]   Edmund Spenser, *The Shepeards Calender* (London, 1579), sig. iv.

[29]   Mullaney, 'Strange Things', p. 56. The linguistic creolisation of English of course didn't end in the early modern period. As the reading of any food magazine or guide to literary theory would quickly make clear, its role as a global lingua franca notwithstanding – or in fact because of it – the English language is still importing loan words at a steady pace. The English spell check in the word programme I am using, for instance, accepts terms such as haute cuisine, Camembert and deconstruction as correct English – although *différance* and *weltliteratur* do admittedly still get underlined in red.

[30]   See Sakai's example of eighteenth-century Japan. He refers, in particular, to the intervention of the exponents of the *Kokugakusha* (National Studies scholars), who 'invented the Japanese language as an object in idea of systematic knowledge': 'The intellectual and literary maneuvers by the *Kokugakusha* inaugurated the modern prescription of the national imaginary. We cannot fail to recognize the aura of modernity in National Studies precisely because, generally speaking and even beyond the context of Japan's history, the imaginary affiliation with nation and national culture and tradition is modern. To the extent

descriptions of early modern English by Heywood and 'E.K.' as a mongrel or creole language work well to illustrate Naoki Sakai's definition of languages as 'many in one', in relation to which translation can be reconfigured as a social act that simultaneously involves drawing a border that indexes differentialist forms of identification along ethnic or national lines, and the crossing of that same border.[31]

This brings me to my second epigraph, which is excerpted from what is arguably the most famous scene of translation in the Shakespearean canon: the final dialogue between King Harry and Catherine[32] in *Henry V* – a scene that has the two characters speaking a 'broken' version of each other's tongue. What makes this scene, and more broadly *Henry V*, stand out in Shakespeare's oeuvre is the foregrounding of interlinguistic difference, which Shakespeare and other Elizabethan playwrights normally neutralised through linguistic homogenisation.[33] Although Shakespeare undoubtedly had a cosmopolitan outlook and, with the exception of the histories, set the majority of his plays outside of England, for the most part he hid from view the linguistic difference involved in his choice of settings and dramatis personae by turning, with the significant exception of people and place names, the language into English. As Dirk Delabastita has shown in his survey of the instances where Shakespeare's plays present 'cross-language situations', interlingual translation does not feature prominently among the dramatic devices he used to represent and negotiate cultural and national difference.[34] When it is present at all, the performance of translation is for the most part used for comic effect, as in the Latin grammar lesson that Shakespeare

---

that we take the modern regimes of reading, writing, reciting, translating, and so forth for granted, however, we tend to assume the modus operandi sustained by these regimes to be universally valid' ('Translation and the Figure of the Border', p. 31).

[31]   Ibid., p. 33.

[32]   This is the spelling in the Norton Shakespeare edition. In the Arden edition her name is anglicised as Katherine, while Harry is listed as King Henry, which, conversely, is closer to the French Henri, derived from the Latin Henricus.

[33]   This choice was of course dictated by the requirements of theatrical practice: Shakespeare and his colleagues were producing plays for a largely monolingual audience.

[34]   Dirk Delabastita, '"If I Know the letters and the Language": Translation as a Dramatic Device in Shakespeare's Plays', in Hoenselaars (ed.), *Shakespeare and the Languages of Translation*, p. 47. The failure of communication between different linguistic communities is, however, presented as an issue. It is, for instance, the subject of Portia's exchange with Nerissa regarding her English suitor in my final epigraph and of the dialogue between Caska and Cassius in *Julius Caesar*, which conflates intra- and interlinguistic language barriers:

CASSIUS: Did Cicero say anything?
CASKA: Ay, he spoke Greek.
CASSIUS: To what effect?
CASKA: [...] those that understood him smiled at one another, and shook their heads. But for mine own part, it was Greek to me. (1.2.274–80)

inserted into *The Merry Wives of Windsor*, where the already farcical dialogue between the Welsh-accented teacher and slow-witted pupil is disrupted by Mistress Quickly's grotesque sexual allusions and mistranslations: 'You do ill teach the child such words. He teaches him to hick and to hack, which they'll do fast enough of themselves, and to call "whorum". Fie upon you' (*The Merry Wives of Windsor*, 4.1.56–8).[35]

In *Henry V*, though, translation is an altogether more serious issue. Even in those scenes in which the play is supposed to derive comic energy from linguistic difference, such as when Catherine's mispronunciation of English words turns them into obscene puns – most famously in her '*De foot* et *de cown?*' (*Henry V*, 3.4.47), where the first, less obvious, pun is generated by the homophonic resemblance to the French *foutre* (to fuck) – this is undercut by our awareness that this difference is ultimately no laughing matter. It is the same with the bilingual exchange between Pistol and the French soldier at the end of the brutal battle of Agincourt (4.4.1–65). Linguistic difference here stands for the political and military opposition between France and England:

> two mighty monarchies,
> Whose high uprearèd and abutting fronts
> The perilous narrow ocean parts asunder.
> (Prologue, 20–22)

This physical barrier divides two nations at war with each other, whose (re)union is performed through the act of violent incorporation represented by the English invasion of France – an invasion that is also portrayed as an act of linguistic appropriation and that, in Stephen Greenblatt's words, is 'graphically figured as rape'.[36] This representation of violent political annexation as linguistic and physical violation is prefigured as such precisely when Catherine, in the language lesson imparted on her immediately after the English army has conquered the French city of Harfleur, prepares to surrender to Harry by learning the English terms for the various parts of her body, 'translating it into the conqueror's tongue'.[37] This first scene of translation is thus directly linked to the pivotal exchange between Harry and Catherine, where Harry claims possession of both France and the French

---

[35]   In his introduction to the New Arden edition, Giorgio Melchiori notes, 'The word-play, mostly with marked sexual innuendos, on the terminology of grammar and on (mis)translation is by no means limited to this scene, but runs through the play like a hidden linguistic thread that links together all or most of the characters.' Giorgio Melchiori (ed.), William Shakespeare, *The Merry Wives of Windsor* (Surrey: Nelson, 2000), p. 7. See also Patricia Parker, *Shakespeare from the Margins: Language, Culture, Context* (Chicago and London: University of Chicago Press, 1996), p. 48 and p. 116.

[36]   Stephan Greenblatt, *Shakespearean Negotiations: The Circulation of Social Energy in Renaissance England* (Berkeley: University of California Press, 1988), p. 59.

[37]   Michael Neill, *Putting History to the Question: Power, Politics, and Society in Renaissance Drama* (New York: Columbia University Press, 2000), p. 405.

king's daughter, whose subjection to his will is underscored by the act of linguistic appropriation performed through the translation of her name into Kate:

CATHERINE: Is it possible dat I should love de *ennemi* of France?

KING HARRY: No, it is not possible you should love the enemy of France, Kate. But in loving me, you should love the friend of France, for I love France so well that I will not part with a village of it. I will have it all mine; and Kate, when France is mine, and I am yours, then yours is France, and you are mine.

CATHERINE: I cannot tell vat is dat.

KING HARRY: No, Kate? I will tell thee in French – which I am sure will hang upon my tongue like a new-married wife about her husband's neck, hardly to be shook off. *Je quand suis le possesseur de France, et quand vous avez le possession de moi* – let me see, what then? Saint Denis be my speed! – *donc vôtre est France, et vous êtes mienne*. It is as easy for me, Kate, to conquer the kingdom as to speak so much more French. I shall never move thee in French, unless it be to laugh at me.

CATHERINE: *Sauf votre honneur, le français que vous parlez, il est meilleur que l'anglais lequel je parle.*

KING HARRY: No faith, it's not, Kate. But thy speaking of my tongue, and I thine, most truly-falsely, must needs be granted to be much at one. But Kate, dost thou understand thus much English? 'Canst thou love me?'

CATHERINE: I cannot tell.

(*Henry V*, 5.2.162–84)

Critics have argued that this is 'quite explicitly a scene of enforcement' in which Harry translates Catherine 'to his own purposes', and in which 'rape is sanctioned ... civilly, ceremoniously' in a crescendo that culminates when Catherine's mouth 'is conclusively "stopped" by the kiss of possession which signals the end of her speaking part'.[38]

There is indeed no doubt that Catherine's surrender to Harry's inscription of her body into an act of linguistic and territorial invasion materially and symbolically underscores the power dynamics represented in the scene. Yet, if we look at the exchange again from the perspective of translation, something else emerges – for the dialogue also brings into view the fragility of the linguistic boundaries that separate the two speakers and their national idioms. As Crystal Bartolovich has noted, 'Henry's protest in the final line betrays more than he is aware of, since, in a sense he clearly does not see, Katherine's observation (as well as his own) is quite insightful: their "speaking" *is* "much at one".'[39] French is

---

[38]   Ibid., p. 361. See also Greenblatt, *Shakespearean Negotiations*, pp. 59–60.

[39]   Bartolovich, 'Shakespeare's Globe', p. 185.

not the radically unfamiliar and alien language that, at first blush, the scene seems to suggest it is: 'much of Henry's *English*, after all, *is* "French". To give just a short list from the above exchange: "possible," "enemy," "village," are all – as the metropolitan linguists like to call them – "loan words" from the French, as are, even more significantly, both "conquer" and "possession".' The point here is not that Shakespeare is making an argument about etymology, but if our reading is informed by an awareness of the play of identity and difference between the two languages, it undermines Harry's politics of assimilation and the assertion of linguistic difference that underwrites it: 'How secure can the English "possession" of the "English" language be, if it is so evidently indebted?'[40] From this point of view, power relations are in the long run not just reinflected but arguably reverted, for the influx of French words into English sends us back to the Norman Conquest, which was responsible for removing the native ruling class, replacing it with a French-speaking monarchy and radically transforming the English language itself.

As my next epigraph illustrates, not only had loan words from French found their place in the English language, but they had become, in a further inversion of the power relations represented in the exchange between King Harry and Catherine, a marker of social prestige and cultural distinction. This is what Touchstone, the clown in *As You Like It*, plays with in his intralingual translation, which constitutes an act of simultaneous linguistic othering and refamiliarisation, bordering and border-crossing. Touchstone plays, in particular, with the cultural hierarchy of English words that (although ostensibly equivalent at the level of meaning) correspond to alternative, socially and culturally defined linguistic spaces – the Latin- and romance-derived terms of elevated speech and the plainer and more common Anglo-Saxon semantic equivalents – thus foregrounding the internal divisions and interlexicality of early modern English. In this act of linguistic bullying, Touchstone parades the power attached to the superior cultural and social position he inhabits, and uses his mastery of an elevated version of the English language and the authority that derives from it to successfully defy his rival, William, a poor peasant whose social standing comes to correspond to the 'lower', 'vulgar' and 'boorish' linguistic space within which Touchstone's intralingual translation positions him. 'Abandon' from the French *abandoun*, 'female' from the French *femelle* and Latin *femella* , and 'perishes' from the French *periss* and Latin *perire*: these bi- and trisyllabic words signify not only the meaning they express but also the higher social and cultural standing they embody compared to the shorter and more common Anglo-Saxon 'leave', 'woman' and 'die', by virtue, precisely, of their 'foreign' origin. So successful is Touchstone's class-based, French-flavoured linguistic intimidation that the poor 'rustic' responds to the final injunction and threat, 'Therefore, depart and tremble' – again, from the French '*departir*' and '*trembler*' – by leaving without uttering a word (5.1.43–52).

Nor, moving on to my final epigraph, is a chance to utter a word afforded to Portia's English suitor in *The Merchant of Venice*. According to Portia,

---

[40]   Ibid., p. 185.

communication is impeded by his lack of Latin, French or Italian, as well as by her poor English. It is clear, however, that as far as she is concerned the problem lies in the unsuitability of her monolingual suitor, not in her own linguistic limitations. After all, as Warren Boutcher has noted, during the Renaissance 'virtually nobody outside the British Isles ever dreamt of needing to learn English.'[41] By contrast, the publication of John Florio's bilingual dictionary and dialogues, as well as the English translations of Italian conduct manuals and courtesy books, from Baldassare Castiglione's *The Book of the Courtier* (1561) to Stefano Guazzo's *The Civil Conversation* (1574), illustrate that for the Elizabethan ruling class Italian language and cultural modes and models were very much part of a shared cultural horizon and cosmopolitan aspirations: 'Well to know Italian is a grace of all graces, without exception,' writes Florio in the dedication of the second edition of his dictionary.[42] The same goes for Shakespeare and his fellow dramatists, who copiously borrowed from both Italian theatre and literature, appropriating liberally from contemporary Italian comedies and novellas, and who also set a large chunk of their dramatic creations in Italian locations.

This is another perspective, then, from which Shakespeare comes to us 'already translated', for in the case of *The Merchant of Venice*, we have a play written in English, set in Italy and based on a plot from a collection of stories, Sir Giovanni's *Il Pecorone*, originally published in Italy in 1558 and subsequently translated into English but, as far as we know, never in a version as close to the original as Shakespeare's theatrical adaptation.[43] This series of cultural and linguistic permutations is partly mirrored by Portia's speech: an Italian character who speaks in English while pretending, according to theatrical conventions, to be speaking Italian and who, as a result, says that she is incapable of communicating with her English wooer, even though she manages to communicate with her other foreign suitors, the princes of Morocco and Aragon, perfectly well.[44] Perhaps they speak Italian. But whether they do or not, they remind us, in a play that is haunted by the cultural differences most powerfully evoked by the tragic figure of Shylock – a Venetian Jew, both native and alien, who, in yet another instance of linguistic creolisation, turns out to have a name of English provenance[45]– how a reading of the text inflected by a focus on translation as an act of simultaneous

---

[41] Quoted in Oakley-Brown, *Shakespeare and the Translation of Identity in Early Modern England*, p. 4.

[42] Quoted in Keir Elam, '"At the Cubiculo": Shakespeare's Problems with Italian Language and Culture', in Michele Marrapodi (ed.), *Italian Culture in the Drama of Shakespeare and His Contemporaries* (Aldershot: Ashgate, 2007), p. 109.

[43] John Russell Brown, introduction to *The Merchant of Venice* (London: Methuen, 1955), pp. xxx–xxxi.

[44] Some of the words Portia uses – such as 'converse' and 'picture' – have the same Latin roots as the related words in the language, Italian, that she declares foreign to English: *conversare* and *pittura*.

[45] John Drakakis, 'Shakespeare and Venice', in Michele Marrapodi (ed.), *Italian Culture in the Drama of Shakespeare and His Contemporaries*, p. 178.

bordering and border-crossing subverts the linguistic and cultural differences that are supposed to seal the borders between Venice and its linguistic and cultural others, including early modern England.[46]

In his overview of the presence of 'tropes of translation' in Shakespeare's plays, Michael Neill writes that translation is an apt metaphor for 'the experience of crossing over into the space of the Other', which in Shakespeare 'is figured in play after play', in that its broad range of meanings 'has as much to do with changing places as with shifting speech, with the crossing of seas as with linguistic frontiers, and with the bridging of cultural divisions as with the interpretation of unfamiliar tongues'. With my examples I have tried to suggest that even in what Neill describes as its 'narrowly linguistic application', a reconfigured notion of translation already encompasses the broader set of meanings that Neill evokes, and brings the confluence of the translational and the transnational into view.[47] Not only that, but it does so before a single word from Shakespeare has actually been translated.

---

[46]   The Venetian society represented in Shakespeare's and Ben Jonson's plays, writes Leo Salingar, was a 'refracted projection of London' ('Venice in Shakespeare and Ben Jonson', in Michele Marrapodi et al. (eds), *Shakespeare's Italy: Functions of Italian Locations in Renaissance Drama* (Manchester: Manchester University Press, 1997), p. 182). 'To the English, and particularly to Londoners', specifies Walter Cohen, Venetian mercantilism represented 'a more advanced stage of the commercial development they themselves were experiencing' (*Drama of a Nation: Public Theater in Renaissance England and Spain* (Ithaca, NY, and London: Cornell University Press, 1985), p. 200).

[47]   Neill, *Putting History to the Question*, pp. 401–2.

PART 2
Shakespeare, Mediated

Chapter 4
Foxe and the Fat Man, Shakespeare and the Jesuit: Oldcastle Revisited

Victor Houliston

In 1599 some English Catholic schoolboys, sent across the Channel to St Omer for a Jesuit education, mounted a short Latin play on the subject of St Thomas Becket. Presumably written by one of the Jesuit schoolmasters, it was designed to inspire young Englishmen to offer themselves to save their grieving country, oppressed by the Protestant heresy. The script of this little drama was scooped up by one of the rival English intelligence networks and eventually ended up amongst the Cecil Papers at Hatfield House in Hertfordshire. There it was read by South African scholar Guy Butler on one of his Shakespearean research expeditions. He was fascinated, and collected a large amount of information on the significance of St Thomas of Canterbury for the Elizabethan recusants and Catholic exiles, hoping there might be a connection with Shakespeare and his contemporary playwrights. In the event, the playscript led to nothing more than the publication of two obscure articles that launched the present writer's academic career.[1] But the whirligig of time has indeed brought in a Shakespearean connection. The founder of the Jesuit seminary at St Omer, now Stonyhurst College in Lancashire, was Robert Persons: unlike his fellow-Jesuit, John Donne's uncle Jasper Heywood, who was the first to translate Senecan tragedy into English verse,[2] he does not seem to have had much interest in drama, but a comment in one of his polemical works raises an intriguing question about Shakespeare's *King Henry IV, Part 1*.

[1]   Victor Houliston, '*Breuis Dialogismus* [text, with translation, commentary, and textual notes]', *ELR* 23 (1993): pp. 382–427, and 'St Thomas Becket in the Propaganda of the English Counter-Reformation', *Renaissance Studies* 7 (1993): pp. 43–70. Grateful thanks to the late Professor Guy Butler for permitting me to use his copy of the manuscript (Hatfield House MS Cecil Papers 139/116) and his extensive notes.

[2]   Hubert Chadwick, *St Omers to Stonyhurst: A History of Two Centuries* (London: Burns & Oates, 1962); Jasper Heywood's translations of Seneca's *Troas*, *Thyestes* and *Hercules furens* were published in 1559–61, while he was a Fellow at All Souls College, Oxford. See Dennis Flynn, 'Jasper Heywood' (*Oxford Dictionary of National Biography* [*ODNB*]).

Persons was eager to repudiate John Foxe's numbering of Sir John Oldcastle among the saints and martyrs.[3] In 1604 he wrote, '*Syr Iohn Oldcastle* a Ruffian-knight as all England knoweth, & commonly brought in by comediants on their stages ... was put to death for robberyes and rebellion under the foresaid *K. Henry* the fifth.'[4] Wittingly or unwittingly, Shakespeare thus provided the Jesuit with evidence for Oldcastle's unholy reputation among the common people. If we examine the immediate context of the composition of *1 Henry IV* in 1596, it raises some intriguing possibilities regarding Shakespeare's relation to contemporary religious conflict.

Two significant developments took place when the patron of the Lord Chamberlain's Men, Henry Carey, first Baron Hunsdon, Lord Chamberlain, died on 8 August 1596. Shakespeare's company was renamed 'The Lord Hunsdon's Men', after their new patron, George Carey, the second Baron Hunsdon; and Sir William Brooke, seventh Lord Cobham, became Lord Chamberlain and thus master of the Master of Revels. Cobham objected to the unflattering presentation of his ancestor Oldcastle (also called Lord Cobham after his marriage), and Shakespeare had little choice but to change the name of his primary comic character – to Falstaff. It has been suggested that the figure of Oldcastle in the play was designed to poke fun at the Puritan propensities of the Elizabethan Cobhams: Sir John Oldcastle was linked to the Lollards and treated as a proto-Protestant martyr by John Bale and John Foxe. There may have been further comic stage business at the Cobhams' expense when Shakespeare wrote *The Merry Wives of Windsor* for the installation of Sir George Carey as a Knight of the Garter in April 1597. In this play, Brook – the Cobham surname – is a false name assumed by the foolish citizen Francis Ford, whom Falstaff is intent on cuckolding. Much of this byplay can be attributed to Shakespeare's allegiance to George Carey's

---

[3]   A 'Kalender' of Protestant saints, not necessarily prepared or intended by Foxe, was prefixed to the 1563 and subsequent editions of the *Actes and monuments*; see Elizabeth Evenden and Thomas S. Freeman, *Religion and the Book in Early Modern England: The Making of John Foxe's 'Book of Martyrs'* (Cambridge: Cambridge University Press, 2011), p. 126, and Damian Nussbaum, 'Reviling the Saints or Reforming the Calendar? John Foxe and His "Kalender" of Martyrs', in *Belief and Practice in Reformation England: A Tribute to Patrick Collinson from his Students*, ed. Susan Wabuda and Caroline Litzenberger (Aldershot: Ashgate, 1998), pp. 113–36.

[4]   N.D., pseud. [Robert Persons], *A Treatise of Three Conversions of England from Paganisme to Christian Religion*, 3 vols (Antwerp: Arnout Conincx, 1603–1604), vol. 3, p. 31. For a survey of historical and polemical writings about Oldcastle, see Gary Taylor, 'The Fortunes of Oldcastle', *Shakespeare Survey* 38 (1985): pp. 85–100. He quotes Persons on p. 97, inaccurately identifying the pseudonym as 'Nicholas Dolman'. 'R. Doleman' was a pseudonym used (probably by Persons) for the author of the notorious *Conference about the Next Succession to the Crowne of Ingland* (Antwerp: Arnout Conincx, 1594/95). Persons used the pseudonym 'N.D.' for two polemical works directed against Sir Francis Hastings in the 'Watchword' controversy (1598–1603), prompting Matthew Sutcliffe, in reply, to dub him 'Noddie'. See note 29 below.

father, succeeded by Cobham. As it turned out, the second Baron Hunsdon in turn succeeded Cobham as Lord Chamberlain after the latter's death in May 1597 and the company resumed their old name. Falstaff, however, remained Falstaff.[5]

Two other events in the spring and summer of 1596 combined to add a wider significance to the composition, performance and censorship of *1 Henry IV*. This was a period of great anxiety over Queen Elizabeth's successor. In early 1595 a Catholic treatise, *A Conference about the Next Succession to the Crowne of Ingland*, had made its unwelcome appearance (to the embarrassment of the Earl of Essex, to whom it was dedicated). In May 1596 the probable authors of that work, Robert Persons, Joseph Creswell and the aged courtier Sir Francis Englefield, drew up a memorandum addressed to Philip II for an invasion plan that would clinch a Spanish succession. The new Armada was ready by October.[6] On the other side, those concerned to establish England's Protestant identity brought out a new edition of Foxe's *Actes and Monuments* in June 1596. Here the 20-folio defence of Oldcastle's reputation as a martyr, first included in the 1570 edition and reprinted in 1583, was once more put before the public.[7] Then on 22 July the London theatres were closed because of the plague.[8] The English people could read Foxe and wait for the Spanish fleet, while Falstaff toured the provinces.

These developments may well have amplified the resonance of the history plays with the political and religious turmoil of the 1590s. The *Conference about the Next Succession* had clearly come down on the side of Bolingbroke against Richard II, explicitly repudiating the newly minted doctrine of the absolute divine right of kings.[9] Shakespeare's *Richard II* seemed much more ambiguous, though it was apparently resurrected in 1601 to legitimise Essex's inglorious coup. In the

---

[5]   For the purposes of this article, see *Henry IV, Part 1*, ed. David Bevington, *The Oxford Shakespeare* (Oxford: Oxford University Press, 1987), and *Henry IV, Part 2*, ed. René Weis, *The Oxford Shakespeare* (Oxford: Oxford University Press, 1997). Both editors review the Oldcastle/Falstaff debate: Bevington, pp. 1–10, and Weis, pp. 7–16. See also T.W. Craik, introduction, *The Merry Wives of Windsor*, in *The Oxford Shakespeare* (Oxford: Oxford University Press, 1990), pp. 9–11, and Gary Taylor, 'William Shakespeare, Richard James, and the House of Cobham', *RES* 38 (1987): pp. 334–54.

[6]   Francis Edwards, *Robert Persons: The Biography of an Elizabethan Jesuit* (St Louis: Institute of Jesuit Sources, 1995), pp. 191–2. See also Albert J. Loomie, 'The Armadas and the Catholics of England', *Catholic Historical Review* 59 (1973): pp. 385–403.

[7]   John Foxe, *Actes and Monuments of matters most speciall and memorable, happening in the Church, with an universall history of the same* (London: Peter Short, 1596), pp. 523–40; see also the 1570 edition, pp. 676–99, and the 1583 edition, pp. 568–88.

[8]   René Weiss, introduction, *Henry IV, Part 2*, p. 9.

[9]   *A Conference about the Next Succession*, part 2, pp. 95–6; the work frequently opposes Pierre de Belloy, *Apologia catholica ad famosos et seditiosos libellos Coniuratorum* (Paris, 1584), translated as *A Catholicke Apologie against the Libels, Declarations, Advices and Consultations made, written and published by those of the League, perturbers of the quiet estate of the Realme of France* (London, 1590). De Belloy's absolutist stance was directed against the Catholic League in France, which resisted royal attempts at rapprochement with

context of 1595–96, civil war was anything but a remote historical phenomenon. Shakespeare's audience would have been divided, in what proportions who can know, but there was hardly a noble house in England that did not have a strong Catholic connection. Thomas Sackville, Lord Buckhurst, the author of *Gorboduc* and notable contributor to the *Mirror for Magistrates*, was a case in point. He was to succeed William Cecil as Lord Treasurer in 1599, but in 1574 he had helped Robert Persons when the latter, turning to Catholicism, was expelled from Balliol College, Oxford, and was about to go into exile. Sackville's son Thomas also became a zealous Catholic exile, and the old man himself, now the Earl of Dorset, was rumoured to have been received into the Church in 1608.[10] Such cases could be many times multiplied. The Catholics had not risen to support the Armada in 1588, but they remained an unpredictable community, hard to quantify. Many of those watching the history plays might have wondered what to make of Oldcastle, who, as Shakespeare put it in the epilogue to *King Henry IV, Part 2*, 'died martyr, and this is not the man'.

There is no way of knowing whether Shakespeare read Foxe's defence of Oldcastle the martyr, but it would be strange if he were not aware of the reprinting of the *Actes and Monuments*. Foxe was almost as familiar a staple of English religious discourse as the English Bible itself; indeed, copies of the great work were supposed to be on display in cathedrals and collegiate churches.[11] Given the chronology, it behoves us to read Foxe carefully to see what light his arguments may throw on Shakespeare's treatment of Oldcastle. The relevant section, 'A defence of the Lord Cobham, against Nicholas Harpsfield, set out under the name of Alanus Copus', shows the martyrologist fiercely on the defensive. Harpsfield, Archdeacon of Canterbury under Cardinal Archbishop Pole in the reign of Mary, had attacked Foxe in his *Dialogi sex* (1566),[12] using Cobham as one of his prime instances. Foxe, in turn, inserted his 'Defence' into the 1570 edition of the *Actes and Monuments*, but only in 1583 was he able to identify his opponent (who wrote under the pseudonym Alanus Copus) as Harpsfield. Thomas Freeman's authoritative headnote to this section, in the online edition provided by the

---

the Huguenots by King Henri III (d. 1589). Persons was closely associated with the League. Thus the Bolingbroke deposition was a politically sensitive topic.

[10]   See 'Four Papers Relative to the Visit of Thomas Sackville, afterwards Earl of Dorset, to Rome in 1563–64', ed. H.D. Grisell and J.H. Pollen, *Catholic Record Society Miscellanea II*, CRS 2 (London: Catholic Record Society, 1906), pp. 1–11, especially the headnote, and Rivkah Zim, 'Thomas Sackville' (*ODNB*). Dorset's will was explicitly Protestant, however.

[11]   See Elizabeth Evenden and Thomas S. Freeman, 'Print, Profit and Propaganda: The Elizabethan Privy Council and the 1570 Edition of Foxe's "Book of Martyrs"', *English Historical Review* 119 (2004): pp. 1288–307, who demonstrate that the book was not as widely displayed as was once assumed.

[12]   Nicholas Harpsfield, *Dialogi Sex contra Summi Pontificatus, monasticae vitae, sanctorum, sacrarum imaginum oppugnatores, et pseudomartyres* (Antwerp, Christopher Plantin, 1566).

John Foxe Project, comments that Foxe 'responded ... with a mixture of special pleading and incisive research', concluding that 'this section shows Foxe at both his best and his worst as an historian: on the one hand, his finding of documentary evidence to support his claims, and, on the other hand, his willingness to twist their contents and contexts to support his claims.'[13] The intensity of Foxe's animus against Harpsfield can be gathered from his opening broadside:

> with a foule mouth, and a stincking breath, [Cope] rageth and fareth agaynst deade mens ashes, taking now the spoyle of theyr good name, after theyr bodyes lie slayne in the field. His gall and choler being so bitter agaynst them, that he cannot abide any memory after them to remayne upon the earth. In so much that for the hatred of them, he spurneth also agaynst me, and fleeth in my face, for that in my Actes and Monumentes, describing the history of the Churche, I would say any thing in the fauour of them, whome the Romish Catholickes haue so vnmercifully put to death.[14]

Throughout the section he reverts to abuse of Harpsfield, sometimes witty and sardonic, always vitriolic, making this one of the most entertaining and hard-hitting passages of arms in the entire work.

The crux of the matter was whether Oldcastle was a traitor and a rebel, or a religious dissident who remained constant to death. Harpsfield's work took the form of a dialogue between Critobulus (the sceptic) and Irenaeus (seeking peace and unity), with Chapter 16 devoted to a scrutiny of Foxe's 'Pseudomartyrs'.[15] Critobulus protests that Cobham and his companion Sir Roger Acton should be absolved of any charge of sedition. In his view Foxe has exposed the falsehood of Polydore Vergil and shown the two knights to have proved their nobility by fighting bravely for the kingdom of Christ.[16] Whereas Irenaeus has (to the reader's supposed satisfaction) discredited several other pseudomartyrs, Critobulus insists that what Foxe has written about Cobham is more trustworthy. On the contrary, retorts Irenaeus, these lies are so prodigious that he can't think of anything that could outweigh Foxe in mendacity.[17] He brings the chroniclers Hall and Fabyan in as witnesses to support Polydore Vergil in establishing that Cobham was arraigned

---

[13]   Available online at: johnfoxe.org/index.php?realm=text&gototype=modern&editi on=1583&pageid=592#C148.1. The section is to be found in book 5 ('Thematic Division' 37). The 1596 edition, pp. 523–40, is used for all quotations and references.

[14]   Foxe, *Actes and Monuments*, p. 523.

[15]   Harpsfield, pp. 817–51.

[16]   'Iam quid nobilius Actono & Cobhamo? qui ad tantam generis, maiorem tamen generosi animi, pro Christi regno amplificando fortiter concertantes, nobilitatem adiecere' (*Dialogi sex*, p. 827).

[17]   'CRIT. Atqui sinceriora credo sunt, quae de Cobhamo atque Actono tradit. IREN. Sinceriora dicis? Certe tam prodigiose & hic mentitur, vt nesciam, quod cui mendacium praeponderet' (*Dialogi sex*, p. 832).

for treason; even though he was not actually present in St Giles' Field, when King Henry V was faced by 20,000 rebels, he was present in spirit and consent.[18]

These were the charges that Foxe was to return to again and again. The strength of his case rested on his claim to go beyond the chroniclers' narratives and interrogate the documentary evidence. Harpsfield, he averred, was 'like a spidercatcher sucking out of euery one [of his authors], what is the worst, to make vp [his] leystall ... a dunghill of dirtie Dialogues', whereas Foxe himself aspired to historiographical thoroughness and impartiality: 'diligence is required, and great searching out of bookes and authors.'[19] It was not enough to consult the chronicles: 'the records must be sought, the Registers must be turned ouer, letters also and ancient instruments ought to be perused, and authors ... wyth iudgement to be waied, with diligence to be labored, and wyth simplicitie pure from all addiction and partialitie to be vttered.'[20] As Foxe's own contemporaries, and modern commentators such as Thomas Freeman, have pointed out, it was only fitfully that he conformed to this ideal, so eloquently stated here.[21] In these pages, he shows an unmistakable bias against the Bolingbroke rebellion, even while protesting Oldcastle's loyalty to Bolingbroke's son, Henry V; it might be more accurate to say that he opposes rebellion tout court, citing as examples of the treasonable propensities of papism both the Archbishop of Canterbury, Thomas Arundel (who went into exile under Richard II and allied himself with Bolingbroke), and the Archbishop of York, Richard Scrope (who supported the rebels against Bolingbroke as Henry IV).

Shakespeare, dealing with these same events in *Richard II* and *Henry IV, Parts 1 and 2*, and relying for the most part on the chroniclers, was much more even-handed than either Foxe or Persons. His preferred source, Holinshed, we may say, was in a different class from Hall, Fabyan and Polydore Vergil. More than this, Shakespeare may have seen in the complex moral and political issues of the Bolingbroke era an opportunity to comment obliquely on the choices facing English Catholics as the Protestant state became simultaneously more entrenched and more nervous in the 1590s. In his interpretation of history, the chroniclers had a great deal more to offer than Foxe allowed, who commended them only for narrating 'vulgare and popular affairs' (battles and feasts and coronations and the like), where it did not matter much whether they were true or false.

---

[18] 'Non interfuit corporis, sed animi, consiliique praesentia. Post fugam eius, socij ipsius seditiose coierunt. At & Cobhamum quoque ex fuga postea reductum, vtriusque, id est laesae maiestatis atque haereseos fuisse conuictum, & vtriusque paenas dedisse, Fabianus & alij testantur' (*Dialogi sex*, p. 833). The chroniclers are Polydore Vergil, *Anglica historia* (Basle, 1546, etc.); Edward Hall, *The Union of the Two Noble and Illustre Famelies of Lancastre & Yorke* (London, 1548, etc.); and Robert Fabyan's *Chronicles* (London, 1516, etc.).

[19] Foxe, *Actes and Monuments*, pp. 530–31.

[20] Ibid., p. 532.

[21] '"Great searching out of bookes and authors": John Foxe as an Ecclesiastical Historian' is the title of Thomas S. Freeman's Ph.D. thesis, Rutgers University, 1995.

Shakespeare had an eye for what would make good theatre: nor was this merely an opportunistic approach to history. Drama entailed the fullness of realised human circumstance, rather than polemical hacking of evidence. In the case of Oldcastle, Shakespeare did not show much interest in the religious controversy, centred on pseudo-martyrdom. His histories of Henry IV and Henry V ignored the Oldcastle rebellion, but if he turned to Foxe he would have found there a line of argument that he could incorporate richly into his subplot and his celebrated conception: the Puritanical hedonist Oldcastle.[22]

Foxe's defence of Oldcastle against the charge of treason has the appearance of scrupulously reverting to primary sources but it depends largely on associations and analogies that may appear specious, as well as arguments from probability and negative evidence. Oldcastle faces accusations: so too did Susanna in the Bible,[23] and Foxe like Daniel has to weigh the truth of them. Is it likely, he asks, that a Christian (one who was ready to die for his version of the faith) and a gentleman-knight would seek to overthrow the commonwealth?[24] What faith might he have wanted to substitute for the Christian faith in England – the Turk's, the Jew's, the pope's? If he had no alternative to offer, then he would have been out of his wits to try to subvert the established order. Such speculations lack historically grounded pertinence to Oldcastle's case. Again, Foxe puts a charitable construction on the events in St Giles' Field: if men gathered in a field, why, perhaps they wanted to worship and listen to the word of God, just as persecuted Christians have done throughout the ages. After all, we have no records of the military organisation of the rebels in St Giles' Field. If there were 20,000 of them, why do we know the names of only three? In the light of such arguments, it may seem to the disinterested reader that Foxe can make no more substantial case for Oldcastle from the documents than Harpsfield can from the chroniclers, and the Lollard knight's reputation for treason has at least the support of tradition. Still, some of Foxe's arguments are suggestive, even if they have no more than rhetorical value in the interpretation of history.

Oldcastle's rebellion, Foxe suggests, may be a mere 'Chimera'.[25] The statute dealing with his case has a poem about rumours, congregations and insurrections, which Foxe pooh-poohs on the grounds that no one planning an insurrection would spread rumours about it and thus lose the element of surprise. The whole thing is a fabrication: 'And to make mountains of molhilles, first of rumours maketh

---

[22]   The Puritanical streak in Oldcastle/Falstaff is found in his mimicry of such phrases as 'saint' and 'labour in [my] vocation' (*1 Henry IV*, I, ii, 85–100).

[23]   The well-known story of Susanna and the Elders, a common subject for Renaissance painting, is to be found in Daniel 13 in the Vulgate, although it is not in the Hebrew Bible and was thus excluded from some Protestant translations. It was included in the 1560 Geneva Bible which appears to have been used by Shakespeare.

[24]   Foxe, *Actes and Monuments*, pp. 526–7.

[25]   This refers to the statute under scrutiny (p. 528), but by extension it refers to the subject of the statute, the Lollard threat.

congregations, & from congregations riseth vp to insurrections: where as in all these rumours, congregations, & insurrections, yet neuer a blow was geuen, neuer a stroke was stroken, no bloud spilt.' This is an uprising of the mind, the kind of exploit a man might boast about in a tavern. 'And peraduenture, if truth were well sought, it would be found at length, that in stead of armies and weapon, they were comming onely with theyr bookes, and with Beuerlay their preacher, into those thickets', no threat to any travellers passing by. It takes a great deal to mount a rebellion, 'the attempt so dangerous, the chances so vncertaine, the furniture of so manie things required', that we can hardly think that Sir John Oldcastle, 'beyng but a poore Knight by his degree, hauing none of the peeres and nobles in all the world to ioyne with him', would be able 'so sodenly, in such an hoat season of the yeare [this was January, supposedly], starte vp an army of xx. thousand fightyng men to inuade the kyng, to kill two Dukes his brethren, to adnulle Christian fayth, to destroy Gods law, and to subuert holy Church'. We might as well add that he would 'set also all London on fire, and ... turne all England into a fishepoole'. Only a Shakespearean Oldcastle could dream of such success, multiplying men in buckram until he came, perchance, even to the magic number of 20,000.

We cannot know. Yet when we put Shakespeare's play alongside Foxe's impassioned apologia for John Oldcastle, we are invited to ask whether Shakespeare did not see, in the twists and turns of the martyrologist's torturing of the evidence, a form of wild rhetorical inventiveness, the outrageous but infinitely energetic ability to be, as Edward Dowden put it in 1892, 'ever-detected yet never-defeated'?[26]

There we could let the matter rest, with Shakespeare the magpie. But we might also see him drawing the sting of religious controversy. The heat of accusation and counter-accusation, which would come to a head in the slanging match of the 'Watchword' controversy, could be given a comic turn. Out of the republication of Foxe came the antics of the 'Foxe-cub', as Persons was to call him, Sir Francis Hastings, warning against the Catholic threat. Any true-hearted Englishman, Hastings averred, would do well not to trust any Catholic,[27] and he supported his case by reference to those passages in Foxe which presented papally inspired churchmen as subversive to Christian kingdoms. The Oldcastle defence contained some of the most incisive of these accusations.[28] Over the next few years Persons, Hastings and Matthew Sutcliffe, a more deft but scarcely more objective controversialist than the clumsy layman to whose defence he came hastening, alternated broadsides on the 'watchword', with titles, increasingly convoluted,

---

[26]   Quoted by Michael Lablanc (ed.), *Shakespearean Criticism: Excerpts from the Criticism of William Shakespeare's Plays and Poetry from the First Published Appraisals to Current Evaluations* (Detroit: Gale Research, 2002), vol. 77, p. 119.

[27]   Sir Francis Hastings, *A Watchword to all religious, and true hearted English-men* (London: Felix Kingston, for Ralph Jackson, 1598).

[28]   See Foxe, *Actes and Monuments*, pp. 533–4.

making the most of warn-words, ward-words and waste-words.[29] At length Persons abandoned his ambitious attempt to produce an alternative ecclesiastical history, *Certamen ecclesiae Anglicanae*,[30] and decided to confront Foxe head-on in his *Treatise of Three Conversions*, two thirds of which was devoted to a rejection of all Foxe's Protestant and proto-Protestant martyrs.

When it came to Oldcastle, Persons's purpose was to emphasise how, in espousing the cause of the Lollard knight, Foxe excluded himself from the mainstream of English historiography. Where Harpsfield relied on Polydore Vergil, Fabyan and Hall, Persons refers us to John Stow, who enjoyed a reputation equal to Holinshed in Shakespeare's day.[31] He uses Foxe's own evidence to show that Oldcastle's beliefs with regard to transubstantiation and purgatory were far from anything Foxe and his fellow Protestants would allow, even though the *Actes and Monuments* prominently advertises the 'Christian beliefs of Sir John Oldcastle'. Other positions and actions of Oldcastle, such as his prophesying that he would be resurrected on the third day, approximate to the lunatic fringe. If this is the sort of witness Foxe summons to testify to the truth of the pure Protestant faith, Persons suggests, then he might as well associate himself with William Hacket, the notorious prophet put to death by Elizabeth's regime in 1591 – and Hacket's beliefs, Persons claimed, were closer to Foxe's than Oldcastle's.[32] All this goes to show, not only how devious and shifty Foxe's stratagems are, but what a dunghill his monument turns out to be. Persons rejects these new-made martyrs 'and as spotted and blemished ragges [we] do cast them out to the dunghill. Whome poore Fox gathereth vp againe with great diligence, putting them into his calendar, for Saints and cheife pillars of his new Church, & so consequently maketh his Church of our shue-clouts.'[33]

---

[29]   Robert Persons, *A Temperate Ward-word, to the turbulent and seditious Wach-word of Sir Francis Hastinges knight* (Antwerp: Arnout Conincx, 1599); Sir Francis Hastings, *An Apologie or Defence of the Watch-word* (London: Felix Kingston, for Ralph Jackson, 1600); Matthew Sutcliffe, *A Briefe Replie to a certaine odious and slanderous libel lately published by a seditious Jesuite, calling himself N. D. … entitled a temperate ward-word* (London: Arnold Hatfield, 1600); Robert Persons, *The Warn-word, to Sir Francis Hastinges Wast-word* (Antwerp: Arnout Conincx, 1602); Matthew Sutcliffe, *A Full and Round Answer to N. D. alias Robert Parsons the Noddie his foolish and rude Warne-word* (London: G. Bishop, 1604). See Peter Milward, *Religious Controversies of the Elizabethan Age: A Survey of Printed Sources* (London: Scolar Press, 1978), pp. 138–45.

[30]   Clitheroe, Lancashire, Stonyhurst Archives, MS A.II.12–15, 4 volumes. See Jos Simons (ed.), *Robert Persons, S.J.: Certamen Ecclesiae Anglicanae, A Study of an Unpublished Manuscript* (Assen: Van Gorcum, 1965).

[31]   John Stow, *The Annales of England, faithfully collected out of the most autenticall Authors* (London: R. Newbury, 1600), first published in 1580 and revised in 1592 and 1600.

[32]   Persons, *Treatise of Three Conversions*, vol. 2, pp. 250–51; see Alexandra Walsham, 'William Hacket' (*ODNB*).

[33]   Persons, *Treatise of Three Conversions*, vol. 1, p. 490.

It is probably no accident that the term 'dunghill' echoes Foxe's characterisation of Harpsfield's 'dunghill dialogues'. The dunghill is to be found outside the city, and Persons's polemical thrust is to marginalise Foxe and the radical Protestants. Such claiming of the centrist position is not only a common political strategy: it is an earnest of all Persons's polemic. The English schism, as Sander had argued and Persons and Allen had reiterated,[34] cut England off from Christendom's centre; Catholics were no true threat to political stability, because they believed in order, solid foundations and the universal Christian commonwealth, whereas Protestants were innovators, calumniators and voluntarists. The Calendar of Saints was a good index of this distinction, from Persons's point of view: the Catholic calendar contained only those saints who had been recognised by due process and made venerable by long tradition. The 'Kalender' attached to the *Actes and Monuments*, whether it was Foxe's doing or not, had no greater authority than the arbitrary will of the compilers.

Now it is notable that this manoeuvre, common enough in Catholic controversial writing, is performed partly by reference to Shakespeare, as the most easily identifiable of the 'comediants' who brought Oldcastle onto the stage as a 'ruffian-knight'. There seems to be an assumption here that Shakespeare, and probably the other Elizabethan dramatists, occupied the middle ground. If this was a widely shared perception – and the strategy implies that it was – it may be attributable to censorship, and the dramatists' careful avoidance of extreme political positions, especially after the notorious *Isle of Dogs* episode in 1597.[35] The impression that Shakespeare pitched his tent on the plain, in no-man's land, is no certain proof, therefore, that he was not a Catholic sympathiser. But what emerges from the Oldcastle episode is that he transposed the knight's reputation into a comic key, neither endorsing his status as a martyr nor dismissing him as a traitor. Instead, Shakespeare associates him with moral rebellion, but a delinquency that is entertainingly and even seriously defensible. One might even detect an analogy between Hal's truancy in Eastcheap and Shakespeare's guying of the Foxe position, aligning himself with the uncommitted and ludic chroniclers rather than the more intense martyrologist. And there is another, more significant element at play. If Shakespeare's Oldcastle was a token in the rivalry between the Cobhams and the Hunsdons, a badge, that is, of allegiance to Baron Hunsdon as his patron, we are invited to judge that the choices Shakespeare made in his presentation of Oldcastle were governed more by personal politics than by national religious questions. The Careys, father and son, were both involved in state action against the Catholic threat: Baron Hunsdon was sent north in 1578–79 to guard against possible uprisings in support of Mary Queen of Scots and especially the

---

[34]   Nicholas Sander, *De origine ac progressu schismatis Anglicani*, ed. E. Rishton (Rheims: J. Foigny, 1585); ed. R. Persons and W. Allen (Rome: Bartholomew Bonfadini, 1586).

[35]   D. Bevington, introduction, *Henry IV, Part 1*, pp. 9–10.

overthrow of the Protestant Morton regency in Scotland.[36] His son Sir George Carey sanctioned fierce harassment of Catholic recusants during the critical year 1584, when a Franco-Scottish invasion was feared.[37] There have been suggestions that Shakespeare was himself much captivated by Campion, the charismatic Jesuit missionary and martyr;[38] if so, this did not prevent him from enthusiastically welcoming Carey as his patron.

To interpret *1 Henry IV* as a plea for religious toleration, putting local obligations before ideology, is not to depoliticize Shakespeare. It is to restore to the term 'political' its primary meaning: consideration of life in community. Catholics faced with conflicting loyalties to the papacy and the monarchy often made choices, with regard to recusancy and conformity, that blurred the sharpness of division.[39] They were supported, as often as not, by their Protestant neighbours, for whom good neighbourliness was more important than the anxieties of Walsingham and Burghley at the court. By 1604 Persons himself, recognising that he had lost the contest for the succession, was rethinking how English Catholics could retain their integrity within a Protestant state.[40] The more we know about the actual circumstances of early modern English people, the less confident we should be about the drawing of party lines. Oldcastle or Falstaff, old lad of the castle or phallic catastrophe – the elusiveness is all.

---

[36]   See Wallace T. MacCaffrey, 'Henry Carey' (*ODNB*).

[37]   Robert Persons to Alfonso Agazzari, Paris, 11 June 1584, in *Letters and Memorials of Father Robert Persons, S.J.: Vol. I (to 1588)*, ed. L. Hicks, CRS 39 (London: Catholic Record Society, 1942), p. 210.

[38]   Most famously by Stephen Greenblatt in *Will in the World: How Shakespeare Became Shakespeare* (London: Jonathan Cape, 2004).

[39]   See Alexandra Walsham, *Church Papists: Catholicism, Conformity and Confessional Polemic in Early Modern England* (Woodbridge, Suffolk: Boydell and Brewer, 1993), and Michael C. Questier, *Catholicism and Community in Early Modern England: Politics, Aristocratic Patronage, and Religion, c. 1550–1640* (Cambridge: Cambridge University Press, 2006).

[40]   Victor Houliston, *Catholic Resistance in Elizabethan England: Robert Persons's Jesuit Polemic, 1580–1610* (Aldershot: Ashgate, 2007), pp. 135–60.

Chapter 5
'I, that am not shaped for sportive tricks': Playing with *Richard III*

Chris Thurman

Some of the ideas in this essay were first presented under the same title at a symposium on 'Sports, Games and Diversions in the Middle Ages and Renaissance'. As a Shakespearean – and one who easily loses his way in the field of medieval and Renaissance studies when he strays too far from Shakespeare – my response to the topic should perhaps have been a paper in which I discussed a sporting or gaming allusion in one of Shakespeare's plays. There are, after all, many instances in the plays in which Elizabethan and Jacobean leisure pursuits are invoked to metaphorical or narrative effect, from falconry (Pope noted more than 50 examples) and wrestling to bear-baiting and gambling. This would, however, have been treading ground already well-trod. The quotation in my title was, moreover, somewhat misleading. In his famous opening soliloquy, Richard Crookback (Shakespeare's villain, that is, as opposed to the historical king Richard III) complains that the apparent end of the conflict between the houses of Lancaster and York has resulted in men turning from conquests on the battlefield to conquests in the bedroom – 'But I, that am not shaped for sportive tricks ... cannot prove a lover' (1.1.14–28).[1] Here, then, sport is sex; hardly the form of sport, game or diversion suggested by the symposium's theme.

If 'sport' can refer to sex in Shakespeare's plays, it is also used to describe warfare. Alternatively, there is the duplicitous 'game of politics', which in *Richard III* is constantly on display; members of the court manoeuvre themselves and others like so many pieces on a chessboard. I chose, however, to 'divert' (if not digress) and discuss a comparatively new form of 'diversion': the movies. More specifically, I examined Al Pacino's 1996 film *Looking for Richard*, ostensibly a documentary – in fact a 'mockumentary' – recounting the actor's attempts to research, produce and perform *Richard III*. In this essay, I will re-engage with Pacino's film, noting various sporting connections along the way as I discuss certain 'national' anxieties pertaining to Shakespeare studies and performance. The first of my sporting instances has little to do with literature and drama, medieval or modern, but it will offer a useful framework for the discussion that follows.

---

[1] William Shakespeare, *King Richard III*, New Cambridge Shakespeare, ed. Janis Lull (Cambridge: Cambridge University Press, 1999). Subsequent references are to this edition.

The scoreline: England 1, United States of America 1. The fixture: the opening game of Group C at the FIFA 2010 World Cup, Royal Bafokeng Stadium, Rustenberg, South Africa. It was a match that the English were disappointed to draw, not least because the American goal came from a blunder by goalkeeper Robert Green (not to be confused with Robert Greene, author of the notorious 1592 pamphlet in which Shakespeare was derided as an 'upstart Crow'). The 1–1 result was widely described as an 'upset'. Sober consideration suggests, however, that England is not the world footballing power it is widely held to be: it has, after all, failed in every major international tournament since 1966. Reciprocally, the United States is no longer one of soccer's 'minnows'; since hosting the World Cup in 1994, it has steadily improved as a footballing nation and its record in recent FIFA tournaments is more or less equivalent to that of England. The point I'm making is that these two teams are on a par – when they play each other, a draw is the most likely result – and, just as there is no need for Americans to feel insecure when they play the English, so there is little cause for the English to assume superiority over the Americans. This affirmation, I want to suggest, provides a paradigm for understanding the anxiety that seems to attend a composite Anglo-American Shakespeare. It is, to put it bluntly, similar to the conclusion that Pacino reaches in *Looking for Richard*.

***

The early years of the twenty-first century have seen some controversial displays of solidarity, in response to geopolitical events, between the governments of Great Britain and the United States. British foreign policy has, of course, been heavily criticised within the United Kingdom, just as there have been corresponding voices of dissent across America. Attitudes of disdain (from the British) and distrust (from the Americans) have continued to characterise aspects of the 'special relationship' between these two countries. It has become customary to assess this changing relationship through a post-9/11 lens and, accordingly, *Looking for Richard* – predating that seminal event by five years – seems to inhabit a different world. Nearly two decades after its release, however, the film continues to speak to a knot of cultural anxiety: indeed, both its subject matter and its formal qualities encourage a 'long view', not only of current transatlantic (that is, North Atlantic) interaction but also of wider cultural context, literary authority and the media of stage and film.

It is tempting to suggest that the two most significant events in the almost 400-year history of Shakespeare studies took place in the decade after his death: the publication of the First Folio in 1623 and the voyage of the Mayflower three years earlier. The Folio claim is not controversial – the book's publication did, after all, initiate a process by which Shakespeare's name was removed from the grubby commercial world of Elizabethan and Jacobean theatre and turned into that of a revered Author. His work survived the closure of the theatres and Restoration adaptations, his reputation gained a boost from the likes of David Garrick and the nascent Shakespeare cottage industry in Stratford, the Romantics canonised their 'Genius' – and by the nineteenth century Shakespeare was well established as England's national poet. As a result, the *Collected Works* was exported, representative of British culture, to the furthest reaches of the empire; in Stephen Greenblatt's words, 'Shakespeare's theatre had become a book.'[2]

Could the departure for America, in 1620, of a hundred or so English separatists (Puritan dissenters of the same kind as were opposed to Shakespeare's licentious theatre) really be comparable? Well, not in and of itself; but, as a reading of any American high school history textbook bears out, the pilgrims are a potent symbol of freedom from 'the old country'. It took a couple of hundred years for a self-consciously national American literary tradition to develop, but by the mid-nineteenth century writers such as Hawthorne, Whitman and Melville were emphasising their desire to create an autonomous local literature – which meant jettisoning Shakespeare precisely because he represented an English canon whose influence was deemed unwelcome. Yet *Moby-Dick* is full of Shakespearean echoes; the same is true of any number of 'American classics'.

The early years of the twentieth century saw the rise of a new creative medium: (silent) film. Shakespeare offered the ideal source material for aspirant film-makers – both because many of his plays were so well known that plot and characterisation could easily be conveyed in a short time without using the spoken word, and because there were no copyright restrictions. Judith Buchanan, in her assessment of silent Shakespearean films from the 1916 tercentenary year, focuses on J.M. Barrie's satire *The Real Thing at Last: The 'Macbeth' Murder Mystery* – which 'specifically caricatured a set of perceived differences between British and American approaches to Shakespeare'.[3] In the same year, however, a more ardent filmic rendering of *Macbeth*, directed by John Emerson and starring Sir Herbert Beerbohm Tree, anticipated a later pattern in Anglo-American Shakespearean film collaborations. Barrie's spoof notwithstanding, the Tree *Macbeth* demonstrated a growing 'film industry confidence in its own suitability and efficacy as a medium for interpreting Shakespeare' and was not unsympathetic towards the 'po-faced, reverential approach to Shakespeare of most official tercentenary events ... in a year in which the conservative weight of the Shakespearean establishment was at its most conspicuous'.[4] A 'talkie' version of *The Taming of the Shrew* in 1929 ushered in a new era of Shakespeare-in-performance; over the next 80 years, for many people Shakespeare would be not a book or a play but a movie.

It is worth noting the parallel development, on the one hand, of Anglo-American tensions over the 'right' to adapt Shakespeare to film and, on the other, of the 'special relationship' as a strategic political and ideological alliance. World War II was decisive in both regards. America added morale and military might to

---

[2]   Greenblatt, *Shakespearean Negotiations: The Circulation of Social Energy in Renaissance England* (Berkeley: University of California Press, 1988), p. 163.

[3]   Judith Buchanan, *Shakespeare on Silent Film: An Excellent Dumb Discourse* (Cambridge: Cambridge University Press, 2009), p. 191.

[4]   Ibid., pp. 191–2.

the Allied war effort when it joined belatedly in 1941. In the field of Shakespeare-on-screen, however, Britain and America remained competitors. Laurence Olivier's 1944 *Henry V* was very clearly a rallying call to his compatriots; it was not completed in time to contribute to wartime propaganda (if that is not too strong a term), but its success in boosting post-war British patriotism entrenched Olivier's position as the national Shakespearean torch-bearer and made possible his subsequent film versions of *Hamlet* (1948) and *Richard III* (1955). Not to be outdone, American actor/director Orson Welles matched this trio with one of his own: *Macbeth* (1948), *Othello* (1952) and, some time later, the Falstaffian composite film *Chimes at Midnight* (1965 – the same year as Olivier's stage-to-screen National Theatre *Othello*). Yet by the 1960s Anglo-American national rivalries over Shakespeare had begun to give way to a collusion more appropriate to the 'special relationship': Britain provided the cultural capital (Shakespeare's plays and, often, a glut of actors to perform them), while Hollywood saw to the production, financing, marketing and distribution.

It is tempting to see, in Italian director Franco Zeffirelli's *The Taming of the Shrew* (1967) and *Romeo and Juliet* (1968), films representing the 'internationalisation' of Shakespeare – one could also point to Akira Kurosawa's Japanese appropriations of *Macbeth* (*Throne of Blood*, 1957) and *King Lear* (*Ran*, 1985), or Grigori Kozintsev's Russian *Hamlet* (*Gamlet*, 1964) and *King Lear* (*Korol Lir*, 1971). Zeffirelli's *Shrew* was, however, precisely the kind of collaboration described above: Hollywood stars Richard Burton and Elizabeth Taylor – as if direct from the set of *Who's Afraid of Virginia Woolf?* – brought their off-screen controversy to their on-screen roles, a confluence that no doubt pleased the folk at Columbia Pictures. If Burton (an 'Americanised' Welshman) and Taylor (born in England to American parents) were exemplars of transatlantic Shakespearean film production in the 1960s, three decades later the Shakespeare film industry capitalised more explicitly on this model. A list of films and actors should suffice to prove the point: Zeffirelli's *Hamlet* (1990) starred Mel Gibson, Glenn Close, Helena Bonham Carter and Paul Scofield; Kenneth Branagh's *Much Ado about Nothing* (1993) had Emma Thompson, Keanu Reeves, Denzel Washington, Michael Keaton and Branagh himself (he would also co-star with Lawrence Fishburne in Oliver Parker's 1995 *Othello*, and his 1996 *Hamlet* included Derek Jacobi, Kate Winslet and Billy Crystal); Richard Loncraine's *Richard III* (1995) boasted Ian McKellan, Annette Bening and Robert Downey Jr.

Shakespeare on film as a specifically Anglo-American phenomenon arguably reached its apex in the 1998 blockbuster *Shakespeare in Love*. Here we had an English director (John Madden), an American screenwriter (Marc Norman) working with a renowned British playwright (Tom Stoppard) and a host of 'British' stars with 'American' CVs: Gwyneth Paltrow, Joseph Fiennes, Judi Dench, Rupert Everett, Colin Firth and others. A year later, an Anglo-American cast filled the roles in Michael Hoffman's *A Midsummer Night's Dream*: Kevin Kline, Michelle Pfeiffer, Stanley Tucci, Everett again, Anna Friel, Calista Flockhart, Dominic West and Christian Bale. Other notable Hollywood Shakespearean appropriations in this decade included teen idols Leonardo DiCaprio and Clare Danes in Baz Luhrmann's *Romeo + Juliet* (1996) and Michael Almereyda's *Hamlet* (2000) starring Ethan Hawke, Bill Murray and Julia Stiles – who, to complete the circle, also appeared (with Heath Ledger) in *Ten Things I Hate about You*, the 1999 adaptation of *The Taming of the Shrew*.

Why, then, despite these apparent affirmations of a special Anglo-American Shakespearean 'filmic' relationship in the 1990s, does Pacino's film go to such great lengths to explore American anxieties about performing (and understanding) Shakespeare?

***

At the start of *Looking for Richard*, the camera pans from the black-and-white silhouette of a barren tree to a grand old cathedral as a familiar, soft-spoken English voice (it belongs to Jeremy Irons, who does not appear elsewhere in the film) presents a prologue in measured tones. It seems an odd choice – Prospero's meditation on evanescence:

> Our revels now are ended. These our actors,
> As I foretold you, were all spirits and
> Are melted into air, into thin air:
> And, like the baseless fabric of this vision,
> The cloud-capp'd towers, the gorgeous palaces,
> The solemn temples, the great globe itself,
> Yea, all which it inherit, shall dissolve
> And, like this insubstantial pageant faded,
> Leave not a rack behind. We are such stuff
> As dreams are made on, and our little life
> Is rounded with a sleep.
>
> (*The Tempest*, 4.1.148–58)[5]

As the voice continues, the 'cloud-capp'd towers' of the stone cathedral 'dissolve' – or rather, cut – to high-rise buildings dominating an inner-city basketball court. This sporting allusion is a potent symbol: basketball is, along with the other American 'big three' sports of baseball and gridiron football, a marker of national cultural identity. Pacino, moving in slow motion around the court with an unidentified opponent, is here clearly allied with 'American' qualities: youth, urban energy, the modern 'edge'. Our attention is returned, for a short time, to 'Shakespeare's England': the cold, 'solemn temple' and, briefly, the pages of an open book. Once spoken, the famous lines that adorn Shakespeare's cenotaph in Westminster Abbey, redolent of English cultural capital, are challenged by Pacino's iconoclastic New York accent, asking: 'Who's going to say action?' Moments later, his baseball

---

5   William Shakespeare, *The Tempest*, Arden Shakespeare, 6th edn, ed. Frank Kermode (Walton-on-Thames: Thomas Nelson, 1998).

cap turned backwards on his head, he walks nervously onto an unconvincingly reconstructed 'Elizabethan' thrust stage and confronts the taciturn person of 'Shakespeare' himself, alone and unmoved in the empty auditorium.

This opening sequence firmly establishes the dynamic examined in *Looking for Richard*: a conflict between the perceptions of tradition, of ownership and of literary/dramatic authority that shape our understanding of Shakespeare. For the film's writing-acting-directing-producing team, these concerns foreground a fundamental problem experienced by Americans engaging with Shakespearean drama – the problem of 'Englishness'. Does a lack of familiarity with medieval English history obstruct the appreciation of *Richard III*? Is it necessary to recreate period costume and setting in order to be 'authentic'? Do difficulties with the vocabulary of early modern English justify a departure from the Shakespearean text? Pacino declares himself an unashamed bardolater at the start of the film, and we are reminded throughout of the sense of inferiority that burdens American actors wishing to perform Shakespeare. Richard's opening soliloquy is delivered in an English accent, an ostensibly unself-conscious demonstration of what Homi Bhabha might call colonial mimicry. Likewise, the search for Richard – it is explicitly described as a 'quest' – seems to be inexorably linked to the film-makers' pilgrimage to England.

By the end of the film, it would appear that Pacino and his journeymen have not escaped this predicament. The closing sequence mirrors the first: 'Shakespeare' gives a disparaging shake of the head; the basketball court is again contrasted to the visuals of the old cathedral; the voice-over that had been out of place as a prologue is repeated as an appropriate epilogue, dismissing the 'insubstantial pageant'; and, finally, the production team are seen dwarfed against the imposing towers of the Palace of Westminster. Despite wishing to present a Shakespeare that is accessible to their fellow Americans, it appears that they have remained bound to an incongruously Anglocentric or Anglophilic vision of the play. Certainly, we are given the impression that would-be American Shakespeareans are radically different to their English counterparts, and that their status is diminished by the comparison. The Americans formally interviewed in the film (James Earl Jones, Kevin Kline) offer only personal anecdotes about their formative experiences of Shakespeare – both positive and negative – while it is left to venerable English scholars (Emrys Jones, Barbara Everett) and veterans of English theatre (Peter Brook, John Gielgud, Vanessa Redgrave) to offer 'informed', albeit somewhat detached, critical comment. In the film's construction, apparently, there are no equally distinguished American Shakespeare academics or acclaimed American Shakespeare actors.

All of this is patently inaccurate. Furthermore, as much as the Wars of the Roses are portrayed as entirely alien to Americans, in the cosmopolitan social environment of Britain today knowledge of medieval history is neither expected nor considered by many to be inherently valuable or relevant. As for the issue of language, which is represented as the greatest deterrent to American schoolchildren enjoying Shakespeare: any teacher in a British school would readily echo Pacino's description of faces that 'didn't know what I meant' in response to the opening lines of *Richard III*. Co-star and co-producer Frederic Kimball is exasperated because 'Nobody knows the play ... nobody!' – nobody, that is, in America – but John Gielgud's suggestion that the reason Americans are not acquainted with Shakespeare's world is 'they don't go to picture galleries and read books as much as we [English] do' constitutes a frankly inane generalisation.

The challenge of making Shakespearean language and historiography accessible could more persuasively be described, in the above terms, with reference to countries where illiteracy, lack of education, limited arts funding and, of course, English language difficulties produce substantial obstacles. Even then, as the popularity of Shakespeare in the developing world – the 'east' and the 'south' – has shown, these are not insurmountable barriers. (I will turn to the question of Shakespeare in South Africa at the end of this essay.) Either way, they do not provide an appropriate scale of comparison if distinctions between America and Britain are to be formulated. Both are rich, media-dense and primarily English-speaking; both provide a comprehensive infrastructure for dramatic and literary endeavours. Assessing and comparing the reception of Shakespeare in America and Britain/ England (I note that it is problematic to use these descriptors interchangeably) requires a subtler approach than Gielgud's statement offers.

***

The film's apparent attempts to locate itself within an orthodoxy or tradition of Shakespearean play- and film-making seem, to the viewer who is familiar with *Richard III*, fairly naive and crude. On the one hand, Shakespeare's words are not allowed to stand on their own: historical and political context is explained, we are subjected to a lengthy explanation of Gloucester's opening monologue (including the basic pun on 'sun/son of York') and the cast are constantly shown paraphrasing the text as they discuss plot, characterisation and psychological motivation. These interpolations are deemed necessary for the (American) 'people on the street' who have been casually interviewed and who are shown in the early parts of the film expressing either indifference or ignorance regarding Shakespeare's plays.[6] On the other hand, not even the (American) actors seem to have a solid grasp on the subject of their film; Pacino himself frequently professes confusion over historical details or concepts such as iambic pentameter. Moreover, the period costumes and settings, like the intermittent and inconsistently feigned English accents – insofar as they form part of a project to produce Shakespeare 'accurately' or 'faithfully' – are uninspired if they are earnest. Creative cinematic renditions of Shakespeare's plays moved away from this style long ago.

---

[6]   The one American 'man on the street' – an eccentric indigent – who expresses enthusiasm for Shakespeare is something of a comical figure; his British equivalent, a homeless man with a broad Scottish accent, strikes the keynote for the film by asking the American crew, 'What the fuck do *you* know about Shakespeare?'

It would be a mistake, however, to assume that Pacino's treatment is as ingenuous as these aspects of the film would suggest. *Looking for Richard*, as we shall see, searches for Richard of Gloucester through a process that makes manifest that character's ability to manipulate the relationship between 'seeming' and 'being'. Kim Fedderson and J.M. Richardson, in a skeptical response to the film, recognise this 'dissonance' but argue that it betrays a sinister motivation on the part of the film-makers.[7] I would like, instead, to emphasise the playfulness that underscores the irony and equivocation of Pacino et al. – a playfulness that nonetheless makes a serious case.

According to Fedderson and Richardson, the mythical 'quest romance' that the film purports to offer presents the divide between English and American experiences of Shakespeare as a potential tragedy given a comic resolution. Their reading of Pacino's search as a 'modern hero' realigns the characters of *Richard III*. The sick King Edward is likened to British dramatic and academic institutions, seen to be dying a slow death; or, worse, the dead King Edward is the suffocated spirit of Shakespeare. Pacino, on the other hand, is a prince in the Tower – a rightful inheritor, with youthful vigour and hope – who escapes to accede to the throne, enacting his prerogative to wield the thrilling power of Shakespeare. Fedderson and Richardson argue, however, that this is merely a mask for the covert intentions of a smiling murderer: the chief protagonist of both *Richard III* and *Looking for Richard*. They identify a 'repressed narrative' in which the driving force behind the film (Pacino) and the malignant schemer in the play (Richard) are uncomfortably affiliated; in the play's terms, 'both are false' in their 'heart' as well as in their 'tongue' (*Richard III*, 1.2.197–9). Thus Pacino-Richard, the aggrieved American individualist, usurps Shakespeare's crown from the legitimate English heirs. English voices in the film are treated with restrained mockery; the 'powerful young prince' of British-filmed Shakespeare, Kenneth Branagh, is killed off after a brief appearance early on; and other rival film-makers are pushed aside (one notable omission is Ian McKellen, who starred in Richard Loncraine's *Richard III*, which was released towards the end of 1995). Indeed, the 'impudent' Pacino is accused by Fedderson and Richardson of wooing English audiences for financial gain by performing Shakespeare 'for a while' before returning to mainstream Hollywood productions – comparable to Gloucester wooing Lady Anne and proclaiming, 'I'll have her; but I will not keep her long' (1.2.233).

Unfortunately – perhaps inevitably for a somewhat contrived allegation – Fedderson and Richardson do not clarify whether or not they believe Pacino is aware of the 'repressed narrative' within his film. Rather, their most substantial indictment of Pacino is that his supposed quest is based on a misreading of Anglo-American Shakespearean relations. They react strongly to the idea

---

[7]   Kim Fedderson and J.M. Richardson, 'Looking for Richard in *Looking for Richard*: Al Pacino Appropriates the Bard and Flogs Him Back to the Brits', *Postmodern Culture* 8.2 (1998).

that America is 'missing out on Shakespeare', as inferred from Pacino's street interviews and unsuccessful school workshops: 'the implicit premise in this film – that Shakespeare's work is in need of resuscitation – is, of course, completely wrong: never before have Shakespeare's works been made so accessible to the American public.' This assertion, although made in direct opposition to those who wrongly assume that the American cultural climate is not suitable for cultivating Shakespeare enthusiasts, is nevertheless contestable.

Gary Taylor is one of many critics who question the 'reputation' of Shakespeare in America, not persuaded by statistics that 'his works are studied by twenty million American schoolchildren every year' or the recollection that 'Baz Luhrmann's *Romeo + Juliet* was the number one grossing film in America the weekend it opened'.[8] The popular Shakespeare, Taylor argues, is a modern fallacy; he was best appreciated and understood (in both England and America) in the nineteenth century, and he has been steadily disappearing from the public imagination since then. As Pacino mischievously points out, there is 'a tendency to confuse the plays'. Shakespeare may be widely read in schools and acclaimed as universal, but

> a text can only belong to everybody if everybody is forced to adopt it. Universality, never the product of free choice, can only be imposed by totalitarian means. And the very imposition of a text itself creates resistance to it. As a result, even when Shakespeare is taught, he doesn't stick. People don't internalise him the way they used to.[9]

Luhrmann's *Romeo + Juliet* was successful because it managed to turn the most commonly used Shakespearean set text into a product for 'pop-culture-addict adolescents' – and it sold, not by association with the name of Shakespeare, but because of the names Leonardo DiCaprio and Claire Danes. Indeed, insofar as 'Shakespeare' is a commercially successful commodity, that designation is increasingly distant from the author and the plays to which it once referred: his name may roll easily off the public tongue, but according to Taylor, his works are superficially apprehended in the public imagination.

This is not simply a post-structural affectation, acknowledging a death of the author through which the signifier 'Shakespeare' is largely detached from the disparate signifieds of historical figure, performed play or souvenir edition. Peter Smith describes a 'Shakemyth ... the complex of cultural ideas surrounding the plays, the social institutions through which they are represented and the mythologised persona of Shakespeare' that has been developing for more than three centuries.[10] The myth is perpetuated by a Shakespeare industry that has grown

---

[8]　　Gary Taylor, 'Afterword: The Incredible Shrinking Bard', in Christy Desmet and Robert Sawyer (eds), *Shakespeare and Appropriation* (London and New York: Routledge, 1999), p. 197.

[9]　　Ibid., p. 202.

[10]　　Peter Smith, 'Shakemyth: The Fabrication of Shakespearean Culture', in *Social Shakespeare* (Basingstoke: Macmillan, 1995), p. 219.

in the pursuit of financial gain rather than through dramatic or literary conviction.[11] The pervasive 'artistic' appropriation of Shakespeare is typically seen as a result of his enduring influence, but as Richard Finkelstein points out (echoing Taylor's sentiments on trivial or gratuitous allusions to Shakespeare), 'resemblances to Shakespeare can seem generic or coincidental.'[12] Moreover, the nature of this appropriation is dictated by a commoditised market in which 'corporations and the Shakespeare Industry authorize one another.'[13]

Shakespeare's forced complicity with a capitalist ethos is analogous to his establishment as an icon of British imperialism. Taylor describes a Shakespeare who was at his height in the Victorian age, which unfortunately has also made him (to some) synonymous with the injustices of the colonial process. As an Englishman interviewed in New York notes wryly towards the beginning of *Looking for Richard*, Shakespeare is 'a great export'. Virginia may have been one of the first colonies of what would become the British Empire but, four centuries later, America and England are often seen as allies in 'a renewed form of cultural imperialism, an attempt by Anglo-America to (re)impose' itself on the world.[14] (The place of Shakespeare in this process is perhaps most emphatically, and problematically, demonstrated by the addition of *Henry V* to the Pentagon's proposed reading list for US troops – collapsing the distinction between ideological and actual warfare. Many American soldiers fighting the war in Iraq, following the example of their World War II precursors, had read and could quote from the play.)

Other commentators maintain a more sanguine attitude: Curtis Breight celebrates 'popular audiences ... having Shakespearian greatness thrust upon 'em in lively films, clever adaptations and subtle allusions' precisely because Shakespeare is available for appropriation internationally.[15] It is therefore not fitting to talk about 'a renewed form of cultural imperialism' because this neglects 'the multi-national quality of the resurgence'. After all, 'even Hollywood displays multiple attitudes to Shakespearian raw materials', which remain 'a touchstone for struggle within tumultuous societies such as the USA'.[16] These exciting contests notwithstanding, Taylor is right to encourage wariness. It is clear that the film industry would survive without Shakespeare. The converse is more intriguing: how much does 'Shakespeare' depend on the film industry?

---

[11] See Graham Holderness, 'Bardolatry: or, The Cultural Materialist's Guide to Stratford-upon-Avon', in *The Shakespeare Myth* (Manchester: Manchester University Press, 1988), pp. 2–15; and Graham Holderness, *Cultural Shakespeare: Essays in the Shakespeare Myth* (Hatfield: University of Hertfordshire Press, 2001).

[12] Richard Finkelstein, 'Disney Cites Shakespeare: The Limits of Appropriation', in *Shakespeare and Appropriation*, p. 194.

[13] Ibid., p. 195.

[14] Curtis Breight, 'Elizabethan World Pictures', in John Joughin (ed.), *Shakespeare and National Culture* (Manchester: Manchester University Press, 1997), p. 297.

[15] Ibid., p. 296.

[16] Ibid., p. 297.

It seems we are left at an impasse. Despite Fedderson and Richardson's confidence, it cannot be denied that even the populations of English-speaking Western nations such as England and America need Shakespeare to be 'dismantled' if the plays themselves are to be valued and made 'relevant'. In Pacino's view, this necessitates a rudimentary explanation of the play texts. We can accept his stated aim as sincere: 'It has always been a dream of mine to communicate how I feel about Shakespeare to other people ... a Shakespeare that is about how we feel and how we think *today*.' On this level, as an exercise in secular evangelism, the film is guaranteed to win converts to Shakespeare out of the masses of bored agnostics. The famous names that accompany Pacino on the cast list – including Alec Baldwin, Kevin Spacey, Winona Ryder and Aidan Quinn – ensure a broad potential audience for the film. The tone is frequently light, and as a piece of entertainment the production is eager to distance itself from the sober reserve of high culture that might be associated (however erroneously) with Shakespearean drama. Furthermore, as Kenneth Rothwell has written, although his intention is to teach, Pacino 'never [talks] down to the audience', adopting 'a Socratic pose of ignorance to win it over'.[17]

The greater challenge (and again a proselytising metaphor is apposite) is that of preaching to the converted – both those who blindly follow the 'Shakemyth' and those who would consider themselves enlightened believers. If the only impetus behind the evolution of *Richard III* into *Looking for Richard* were the latter's efficacy as a rough educational tool, the film would be limited in its artistic and intellectual scope: it would reduce Shakespeare to a sum of parts, and the thorough mitigation of the text might estrange viewers with a more sophisticated understanding of the playwright and the play. Fortunately, this is not the case; the 'Socratic pose' is an act by a consummate actor and stems from the same distinguishing attribute of the film that Fedderson and Richardson misconstrue as 'subtle, false, and treacherous' (*Richard III*, 1.1.37). Pacino *is* consciously feigning the role of the naive quest hero, but he does so neither to condescend to the inexperienced viewer, nor to pander to the bardolater, nor to deceive the learned Shakespearean. Rather, the simple, documented search for the essential elements of *Richard III* – a search that makes Shakespeare accessible – becomes a dramatic rendition of the cultural baggage that is inextricable from Shakespeare; as a result, *Richard III* is made more and not less complex.

***

Neil Sinyard, reflecting on the postmodern 'fragmentation' of *Looking for Richard*, highlights the film's 'eclectic, elusive style' and an 'incompleteness' that

---

[17] Kenneth Rothwell, *A History of Shakespeare on Screen: A Century of Film and Television* (Cambridge: Cambridge University Press, 1999), p. 227.

hints at the predominant consideration of genre.[18] This is foregrounded by a heated discussion between the members of the production team:

> 'We're never going to finish this movie.'
> 'It's organic, it's got to be what it is.'
> 'How much more are we going to shoot? It's becoming a movie about a play. We're making a documentary.'

Is *Looking for Richard* a film version of a play or a movie about a play? Is it a film about putting on a play or a movie about the process of turning a play into a film? It is all these things simultaneously, and this multiplicity offers a useful insight into the awkward relationship between any Shakespeare film and the stage performances that have preceded it. Many of the scenes from *Richard III* that are 'officially' performed in the film seem to be more theatrical than cinematic, and the mise en scene often contains an actual stage. Towards the end of the film, Pacino and Kimball take to the stage of a medieval banquet hall, hoping to summon the spirits of past thespians as they rehearse the ghost scene (5.3). Following this, Pacino delivers King Richard's pre-battle oration; the speech is shot from a low angle, as if the camera were part of a theatre audience. These elements suggest that filmed Shakespeare is inevitably indebted to, cannot escape from and, importantly, is complemented by the tradition of staged Shakespeare. Nevertheless, *Looking for Richard* fully exploits the advantages that cinema holds over theatre, in particular the technique of juxtaposition, which is appropriate to the film's postmodern inclinations as described by Sinyard: a 'montage that leaps about in time and place with a mobility that only cinema can manage'.[19] He gives the example of 'that subliminal memory flash of Queen Margaret's dire prophecy that occurs to Buckingham after his rejection by Richard – a striking moment since ... Margaret essentially stands for memory in the play.' Montage is also used in the ghost scene.

The blurring of performance media and genres is integral to the progressive excoriation of an Anglocentric Shakespearean tradition. As both documentary and drama, the film continually crosses the boundary between fiction and non-fiction, confusing the (re)created world of fifteenth-century England with the scenes that detail 'the making of' that world. Fedderson and Richardson claim that only four scenes from the play are performed; in fact, many more scenes are performed or at least presented, if only in part. As the story of *Richard III* goes on, however, the paraphernalia associated with the 'faithful' reproduction of period and location (such as costume, accent or music) are cleverly manipulated. For example, the scene in which Gloucester consults the men hired to murder Clarence (1.3.340–55) is performed in contemporary, casual dress. It seems that we are watching a plainclothes rehearsal – the murderers wear jeans, Pacino has

---

[18]   Neil Sinyard, 'Shakespeare Meets *The Godfather*: The Postmodern Populism of Al Pacino's *Looking for Richard*', in Mark Thornton Burnett and Ramona Wray (eds), *Shakespeare, Film, Fin de Siecle* (Basingstoke: Macmillan, 2000), p. 59 and pp. 70–71.

[19]   Ibid., p. 70.

his overcoat and glasses on – but this *is* the performance. Later, Kevin Spacey sports a jacket and tie to speak his part as Buckingham. King Richard's fiery, climactic exhortation to his soldiers is filmed with Pacino wearing his distinctive outfit of black trousers and jacket, baseball cap characteristically turned backwards on the head; by the end of the film, we associate the modern costume with King Richard as readily as we associate it with Al Pacino.

The protagonists' accents are similarly adjusted. When Pacino mouths the opening monologue in the affected tones of Received Pronunciation, the effect is incongruous but we accept it as a 'behind-the-scenes' view of an actor experimenting with intonation. After the first scene is played in costume, it becomes clear that Pacino intends to speak Richard's part with a 'high English' inflection throughout – an accent that jars with the American brogues of Baldwin, Spacey, Ryder and most of the other cast members, although the accents of Margaret and Hastings could also loosely be described as 'Anglo-American'. Through the medium of the docudrama, however, the sound-images of Pacino 'performing' in an English accent are spliced with footage of him 'rehearsing' in his native New York drawl. The latter is both more convincing and more emotive than the former, and permeates the 'performance' of King Richard. By the time the battle of Bosworth has been fought and won, it does not strike us as peculiar that the victorious Richmond (Quinn) should close the action of the film – and the play – wearing chain mail armour but speaking in a broad American accent: the clash is deliberate. (On the matter of accents, of course, it is worth noting that certain American English pronunciations are probably closer to those of sixteenth-century England than words spoken today in 'the Queen's English'.)

The music that accompanies the title sequence and echoes throughout the film, a medieval refrain clearly intended to evoke a period atmosphere, is also deconstructed. Midway through the action of the movie (after 2.1 in the play), this music is playing as the camera zooms in through the window of an apartment in which the cast are having a party. Our gaze then passes over a group of young musicians playing a harpsichord, a lute and a recorder as the source of the tune is revealed: what had been non-diegetic music becomes anachronistically diegetic and consequently loses its 'medieval' quality. This is followed by a bizarre sequence in which the (royally clothed) King Edward's death seems to take the (casually dressed) production team by surprise: having viewed footage of his death on a video monitor, they are next seen as if standing over his corpse, horrified expressions on their faces.

Immediately afterwards, Pacino and Kimball are glimpsed traipsing through a wood, trying to bury the (fictional) king. A voice asks, 'Is that in the play?' and the action cuts to a wake for the same (fictional) king, held by the grieving cast members; the gathering then becomes a lively rehearsal as the cast continue to read through the play. This defamiliarising development fuses the American actors with their historical-dramatic English characters, as historical drama becomes recreated docudrama. The film demonstrates a keen awareness that not even its documentary components can claim to represent reality – many of the 'authentic' documentary scenes appear staged and acted (such as that in which Pacino knights a kneeling Kimball, 'Ph.D.'). This has a thematic resonance: as Barbara Everett points out in one of the interviews, *Richard III* is one of the earliest plays in which Shakespeare depicts 'human beings as actors'.

Pacino awards Kimball his doctorate for a melodramatic defence of actors as 'the proud inheritors of the understanding of Shakespeare', possessors of a dramatic tradition more vital and valuable than that of any literary critic. As we have seen, in *Looking for Richard* academics are readily (mis)understood as analogues for the stifling Englishness that alienates Shakespeare from 'the people', whereas actors (mis)represent a liberating American crusade to promote Shakespeare in popular culture. We have also seen that this is an erroneous distinction: after all, Kimball refers to scholars at American institutions like 'Columbia or Harvard', and he derides Pacino's allegedly obsequious 'quest'. Moreover, by collapsing such false dichotomies, the film anticipates (perhaps even warns against) the political rhetoric that would subsequently emanate from the corridors of power in the United States under the Bush administration – the unabashed use of 'crusade' terminology, the hollow emphasis on 'liberation' – precisely because *Looking for Richard* explodes the myths surrounding Anglo-American Shakespeare, and so reminds the perceptive viewer of many other entrenched myths and histories that separate us from the person and works of Shakespeare. As the film-makers' parodied visit to the holy land of Stratford and their uninspiring footage of a half-built new Globe theatre on Bankside prove, Shakespeare (like Richard Crookback, and *Richard III*) is not easily found.

***

British-American tensions over the 'right' to perform, teach and research Shakespeare's work re-emerged in the wake of Roland Emmerich's film *Anonymous* (2011), which gave new impetus to the Shakespearean authorship controversy (and which, with an American-authored screenplay, had a cast of British stars including Derek Jacobi, Vanessa Redgrave, Rhys Ifans and Joely Richardson). The California-based Shakespeare Authorship Coalition (SAC), an organisation dedicated to fostering 'reasonable doubt about the identity of William Shakespeare',[20] used the launch of the film as a platform from which to attack the Stratford-based Shakespeare Birthplace Trust (SBT) – in particular, Stanley Wells (Honorary President) and Paul Edmondson (Head of Learning and Research) – for its condescending rejection of enquiries into the authorship issue. Michael York, another English actor who enjoys transatlantic popularity (and who, as it happens, made his screen debut in Zeffirelli's *Taming of the Shrew*), added his voice to those of the authorship 'doubters', many of whom are also English.[21] Nonetheless, the

---

[20] The Shakespeare Authorship Coalition, 'Declaration'. Available online at: doubtaboutwill.org/declaration.

[21] John Shahan, emailed press release (21 November 2011).

antagonism between the SAC and the SBT is very clearly inflected by discourses of national 'culture' and 'heritage'.

Looking for Richard speaks directly to such ongoing anxieties around Anglo-American Shakespeare/s – anxieties that find further, unexpected filmic expression. Consider another film released in 2011, *My Week with Marilyn*, featuring the 'powerful young prince' of British Shakespeare-on-screen, Kenneth Branagh, whose crown (if Fedderson and Richardson are to be believed) Pacino sought to steal. Here Branagh, not so young any more, completes his imitation of Laurence Olivier – comparisons between the two have been standard critical fare since Branagh's *Henry V* in 1989 – by actually portraying his famous cinematic forebear. *My Week with Marilyn* is the story of a fleeting relationship between Colin Clark, a young man trying to find work in the film industry (played by Eddie Redmayne), and Marilyn Monroe (Michelle Williams), which developed when the American actress travelled to England in 1956 to act with Olivier under his direction in *The Prince and the Showgirl*. It was an undertaking that was doomed to bring both of them 'agony' because, as Colin tells Marilyn, '[Olivier]'s a great actor who wants to be a film star, and you're a film star who wants to be a great actress. This film won't help either of you.'

Olivier finds working with Monroe infuriating: she is always late, she is paralysed by insecurity, she is in the thrall of Method acting even though she often seems utterly unsuited to her vocation ('Trying to teach Marilyn how to act is like trying to teach Urdu to a badger,' he complains). Yet all this translates, magically, into an accomplished performance on screen; watching a projection of her from the editing booth once filming is over, Olivier declares to Colin, 'She's quite wonderful. No training, no craft, no guile, just pure instinct. Astonishing.' In this final scene, still watching the footage of Monroe, Olivier speaks as Prospero to Colin's Ferdinand: 'You do look, my son, in a moved sort, as if you were dismayed. Be cheerful, sir. We are such stuff as dreams are made on, and our little life is rounded with a sleep.' He may be reflecting on the various simulacra created by the film industry; his lines may be a proleptic expression of the pathos of Monroe's death at the age of 36. But the quotation from *The Tempest* is also a kind of valediction. Olivier seems to be marking a transition that demands a farewell on his part. Somehow, the centre has shifted – from Olivier to Monroe, from stage to screen, from England to America.

Olivier would, however, go on to make many more film and stage appearances after *The Prince and the Showgirl* (1957). His speech at the end of *My Week with Marilyn* is affecting but it is also an exaggeration. That his somewhat-misplaced epilogue is a contracted version of the same lines Pacino chooses to frame *Looking for Richard* (from *The Tempest*, 4.1) is an instructive coincidence. If the history of Shakespeare-on-screen in the second half of the twentieth century can be understood in terms of transatlantic cooperation or 'equilibrium', rather than a wrestling for power between America and England, then the ironic and playful use of Prospero-Shakespeare's prologue-epilogue in *Looking for Richard* is arguably more appropriate than its elegiac application in *My Week with Marilyn*.

***

Let us return, then, to our scoreline from the 2010 England-USA World Cup footballing encounter.

As host nation, South Africa surprised most international observers – and, to be fair, many of its own citizens – by producing a successful tournament. Yet what can be made of the on-field performance of its team, nicknamed 'Bafana Bafana'?[22] After their opening fixture, both England and the United States went on to qualify for the second round before being eliminated by Germany and Ghana respectively; Bafana Bafana, despite achieving a draw against Mexico and beating an under-strength French side, could not progress beyond the group stages. Can we apply the footballing metaphor to Shakespeare in/and South Africa?

Certainly, over the last few years Bafana Bafana should have achieved better results than they have. There is no shortage of talent; indeed, the country's top players have become the darlings of major football clubs in England and across Europe. The national team's underperformance is largely attributable to poor administration and management – which, one could argue, is a legacy bequeathed to the game by apartheid (it was dismissed by white Nationalist ideologues as a 'black' sport). Football is extremely popular, Shakespeare is largely neglected – and yet some intriguing comparisons can be made. As with football, so with Shakespeare. There is no shortage of talent; indeed, expatriate South African actors and directors are feted in London and Stratford, while overseas-based South African scholars have produced important work in the field. Equally, Shakespeare in/and South Africa is problematic precisely because of apartheid educational and cultural practices and the centuries of colonial exploitation that preceded them.

If football in South Africa is not quite on a par with football in England or America – probably best represented by Bafana Bafana's 1-0 loss to Team USA in a friendly match a few months after the 2010 World Cup – there is no doubt that the same could be said of Shakespeare: while a small cohort of plays remain entrenched in South African high school and university syllabi, Shakespeare studies are a marginal concern to most literary scholars, professional stage productions are few and far between, and films are non-existent (apart from a handful of 'educational' adaptations to the small screen like the *Shakespeare in Mzansi* series and para-Shakespearean enterprises like *Otelo Burning*). Shakespeare is more of a going concern in both England and America. Yet, insofar as there is in South Africa 'a tendency to confuse the plays'; insofar as 'nobody knows' the history of Richard III or the play *Richard III*; insofar as students are baffled, bewildered and bored by Shakespeare as a compulsory presence on school syllabi, to the point that not even the most charismatic attempt to rejuvenate his plays in their minds will succeed ... well, here we are not that far, after all, from the American context

---

[22]   A phrase from the Nguni language group that can be loosely translated as 'The Boys'.

sketched by Pacino in *Looking for Richard*, nor from the context of a generation of young Britons to whom Shakespeare is as remote as Illyria was to sixteenth-century Londoners.

South Africans are wont to adopt a kind of exceptionalism when reflecting on the country's status: it has the most ethnically diverse population, it achieved the least violent transition to democracy, it is currently beset by the worst criminal practices and the most widespread state corruption in the world. None of these declarations is statistically accurate, and even though South Africa is a country of extremes, neither its best features nor its greatest problems are entirely unique. It is no less immersed in the effects of globalisation than any other country. If Shakespeare is 'universal' – whatever we take that to mean – he is present in South Africa as both a South African and a global phenomenon. Perhaps, then, while there is still important work to be done in freeing Shakespeare from the stigma of colonial/imperial expansion (and the ways in which this expansion has always shaped our country's history, and continues to shape its present), we cannot be too earnest in our attempts to make Shakespeare 'local'. Like Pacino, we need to be play-ful in our approach to Shakespeare. This means, on a basic level, emphasising again and again the importance of the *player* – making sure that adolescents and adults alike encounter Shakespeare on the stage or screen as much as the page. It also means giving creative artists more *play* – that is, room to adapt Shakespeare more freely, to manipulate language and genre and setting in invigorating ways. Finally, it means treating our understandable anxiety about Shakespeare ironically; this, after all, is what makes *Looking for Richard* such an enjoyable appropriation.

Chapter 6
Traditions of English Criticism: Shakespeare's Late Plays in the Early Twentieth Century

Brian Pearce

Introduction

This essay focuses on Shakespeare's late plays. It addresses a critical period in the interpretation of the plays from the late 1890s to the 1930s, when the late plays underwent a dramatic change in fortune – from being viewed as idyllic works written in Shakespeare's retirement to being central Shakespearean texts. The essay forms part of a greater body of work attempting to uncover how and why this change in critical reception occurred. I have long been convinced that such major new traditions of literary interpretation were directly the result of emerging traditions of stage performance of the late plays, and that the English literary critics during this period were reading Shakespeare according to the conventions of production with which they were most familiar. In other words, major changes in styles of performance directly resulted in new styles of literary interpretation which allowed the late plays to become comprehensible and valued texts. In my work on this period, I have concentrated on Sir Henry Irving's production of *Cymbeline* (1896), William Poel and his production of *The Tempest* (1897), Beerbohm Tree's productions of *The Tempest* (1904) and *The Winter's Tale* (1906), Edward Gordon Craig and Harley Granville-Barker's production of *The Winter's Tale* (1912) and other productions of the late plays in London and Stratford-upon-Avon.[1] What follows is a focused discussion of criticism of the late plays during the period.

At the end of the nineteenth century, the predominant critical view of the late plays was that they were serene works written during the playwright's retirement, the 'doctrine' against which Lytton Strachey rebelled in 1904. Strachey's criticism might be seen as an attempt to demystify the plays, to indicate their remoteness

---

[1]   See Pearce, 'Beerbohm Tree's Production of *The Tempest*, 1904', *New Theatre Quarterly* 11.44 (1995): pp. 299–308; 'Granville Barker's Production of *The Winter's Tale*, 1912', *Comparative Drama* 30.3 (1996): pp. 395–411; 'The Reception of Shakespeare's Late Plays in the Early Twentieth Century', *Shakespeare in Southern Africa* 9 (1996): pp. 41–8; 'Sir Henry Irving's Interpretation of Iachimo: The Actor as Literary Critic', *Speech & Drama* 45.2 (1996): pp. 12–17; 'William Poel and the Elizabethan Drama', *Shakespeare in Southern Africa* 10 (1997): pp. 44–8.

from reality, the plays being seen as essentially escapist. This view was influenced by the new realistic criticism that was already evident in the theatre criticism of William Archer and George Bernard Shaw at the time of Irving's production of *Cymbeline*.[2]

Criticism from 1896–1938 of the late plays can be divided into five main categories. First, there is the biographical criticism against which Strachey in part rebelled. Then there is the 'realistic' criticism of the period which attempts either to defend or attack the plays according to realistic criteria. The other traditions might be seen as having developed in direct response to this kind of criticism. Formalist criticism would focus on 'the text itself', following the belief that the plays are autonomous works of art rather than representations of life. Such critics focus on understanding the conventions of the late plays and they tend to be particularly concerned with questions of style, artifice and workmanship, Shakespeare being seen as a highly conscious artist, a craftsman. Symbolic criticism, in contrast, analyses the plays as 'myths of the unconscious', exploring the symbolic substructure of the plays, recognising that the late plays are works of the imagination rather than failed attempts at representing the real world. Finally, the historicist tradition might be defined as those scholars and critics who attempted to analyse the plays in relation to the Elizabethan and Jacobean world, and includes the kind of criticism which focuses on the plays in light of Beaumont and Fletcher, the revenge drama, the romance tradition, the court masque and Elizabethan/Jacobean historical and political events. Again, such criticism might be seen to address the concerns of the realists, showing how the plays related to the social and historical context in which they were written.

Biographical Criticism

Lytton Strachey's essay, 'Shakespeare's Final Period' (1904), is the pivotal work of criticism during this early period. Strachey exposed one of the myths of the late nineteenth-century critical tradition, the widely held view that the late plays are serene expressions of the playwright's old age, that 'at last, in his Stratford home again, peace came to him, Miranda and Perdita in their lovely freshness and charm greeted him, and he was laid by his quiet Avon side.'[3] Strachey associates this doctrine with the major critics of the time – Furnivall, Dowden, Brink, Gollancz, Brandes and Lee – and he refutes it by drawing attention to Shakespeare's frequent 'violence of expression' and to those aspects of the late plays which do not fit into the 'scheme of roses and maidens'.[4] Reading through the critical literature

---

[2]   See Archer, '*Cymbeline*', in *The Theatrical World of 1896* (London: Walter Scott, 1897), pp. 260–76 and Shaw, 'Blaming the Bard', in *Our Theatres in the Nineties – Vol II* (London: Constable & Co, 1906), pp. 195–202.

[3]   Strachey, 'Shakespeare's Final Period', in *Books & Characters* (London: Chatto & Windus, 1922), p. 48.

[4]   Ibid., p. 53.

on the late plays at the turn of the century, one is struck by the soundness of his judgement in grouping together the various critical opinions and seeing them as representing the single doctrine of Shakespeare's 'serene' late period. Rarely can such consensus of opinion have existed in relation to a group of Shakespeare's plays, and Strachey's criticisms were undoubtedly revolutionary. However, Strachey's conclusion that Shakespeare was bored – 'bored with people, bored with real life, bored with drama, bored, in fact, with everything except poetry and poetical dreams' – has provoked controversy.[5] Pafford writes that 'Strachey himself overstated his case and gave an uncritically biased picture'; Nosworthy, another Arden editor, argues that 'Strachey merely drives the Victorian heresy to an opposite extreme.'[6]

Strachey's idea that Shakespeare was bored is a development of the notion that the late plays exhibit the serene and mellow tranquillity of Shakespeare in retirement – the view which he had himself just refuted. One can certainly find earlier critics hinting at the conclusion that if Shakespeare was not bored he was weary. F.S. Boas, in *Shakespeare and His Predecessors* (1896) writes,

> The general impression left upon us by the work of the final period is that the dramatist, exhausted by the gigantic creative effort of the preceding years, was writing in leisurely fashion, not swept along, as before, by the irresistible might of his own imagination, but content to glide by gentle stages down the slow-moving stream of romance.[7]

One of the best examples of the biographical approach to the romances was that of Morton Luce in the original Arden edition of *The Tempest*, first published in 1902. Luce closely identifies Prospero with Shakespeare. He makes an interesting comparison between the style of *A Midsummer Night's Dream* and *The Tempest*, which may have influenced Max Beerbohm's comments on the two plays in his review of J.H. Leigh's production of *The Tempest* in the following year.[8] In the late plays, Luce claims, Shakespeare writes 'if not carelessly, at least with less of concentrated artistic determination and purpose; the evolution of a drama has

---

[5]   Ibid., pp. 59–60.

[6]   Pafford, introduction to the Arden edition of *The Works of William Shakespeare: The Winter's Tale* (London: Methuen, 1981), pp. xxxvii–xliv; Nosworthy, introduction to the Arden edition of *The Works of William Shakespeare: Cymbeline* (London: Methuen, 1955), pp. xl–xlvii.

[7]   Boas, *Shakespeare and His Predecessors* (London: Oxford University Press, 1896), p. 506. Brandes, one of the critics whom Strachey most closely identified with the doctrine, also mentioned Shakespeare's 'weary tolerance' while writing the late plays, in *William Shakespeare* (1898). In 1913, a New Variorum edition of *Cymbeline* was published. The editor, H.H. Furness, follows the pre-Strachey view of Shakespeare's late period (pp. v–xx). The biographical view of Shakespeare's late period survived well into the new century.

[8]   Beerbohm, 'The Tempest', in *Around Theatres* (London: Rupert Hart-Davis, 1953), pp. 293–7.

become more of a recreation, less of a matter of business; his attitude is often that of an onlooker both as regards the body and the spirit of his work.'[9] As Edwards notes, Luce's starting point is that 'Style is a revelation of soul', that by studying the changes of style in Shakespeare's writing, one can best understand the personal feelings of the author.[10] Luce's viewpoint seems at once orthodox and original, the most important new element being the emphasis he places on style.

E.K. Chambers, in *Shakespeare: A Survey*, a collection of essays originally published between 1904 and 1908, returned to the biographical view, directly linking Shakespeare's writing of the late plays with a state of mental relaxation.[11] However, Chambers also anticipates later criticism when he writes that *The Winter's Tale* 'sets the unities at nought in a way which would be difficult not to regard as deliberate'. He compares the play to *The Tempest*, in which a story of similar character 'is presented in a form of perfect classical regularity' and argues that if Shakespeare 'wanted art', it is clear 'that the lack arose from no incomplete mastery, but from an effort ... after an unlimited freedom of technique'.[12] Here Shakespeare is seen as deliberately flaunting convention rather than passively ignoring the rules during his flights of poetic fantasy. This view anticipates Harley Granville-Barker's perception of the artifice of the late plays.

Walter Raleigh, in 'The Last Phase', in his *Shakespeare* (1907), apparently oblivious of Strachey, also follows the doctrine of the serene late period. Raleigh counts the tragedies as Shakespeare's finest achievement; the fact that the playwright 'turned at last to happier scenes, and wrote the Romances, is evidence, it may be said, that his grip on the hard facts of life was loosened by fatigue, and that he sought refreshment in irresponsible play' (211). Once again, the late plays are regarded as fanciful and escapist, as not completely 'serious' works of art.

Henry James's response to the fairy-tale quality of Irving's *Cymbeline* seems to prefigure his fine essay on *The Tempest*, which first appeared in 1907. He begins his essay by remarking on the questions presented by the play – questions that 'hover before us in their most tormenting form'.[13] To confess to such bafflement, he writes, is 'no unworthy tribute to the work'. It is not 'the tribute most frequently paid, for the large body of comment and criticism of which this play alone has been the theme abounds much rather in affirmed conclusions, complacencies

---

[9] Luce, introduction to *The Arden Shakespeare: The Tempest* (London: Methuen, 1926), pp. ix–lxx.

[10] Edwards, 'Shakespeare's Romances: 1900–1957', *Shakespeare Survey* 11 (1958): p. 2.

[11] Chambers, *Shakespeare: A Survey* (London: Sidgwick & Jackson, 1925), pp. 292–3.

[12] Ibid., pp. 298–9.

[13] Henry James, *Selected Literary Criticism* (London: Heinemann, 1963), p. 297. See his review of Irving's *Cymbeline*, 'Mr. Henry Irving's Production of *Cymbeline*', in *The Scenic Art: Notes on Acting and the Drama 1872–1901* (London: Rupert Hart-Davis, 1949), pp. 282–5.

of conviction, full apprehensions of the meaning and triumphant pointings of the moral'. This perception of the problematic nature of the work, more than any other, heralds the way to modern criticism, which has found *The Tempest* to be a particularly contradictory, ambiguous work, open to a wide variety of interpretations and meanings. James argues against the biographical view of late Shakespeare while partly succumbing to it: 'The man himself, in the Plays, we directly touch, to my consciousness, positively no-where: we are dealing too perpetually with the artist.'[14] He writes that 'the man everywhere, in Shakespeare's work, is so effectually locked up and imprisoned in the artist that we but hover at the base of thick walls for a sense of him.' In James's terms the plays are an autobiography not of the man, but of the artist. James pictures Shakespeare in *The Tempest* as 'a divine musician who, alone in his room, preludes or improvises at close of day', a musician 'who plays for his own ear, his own hand, his own innermost sense, and for the bliss and capacity of his instrument.'[15]

James testified to the play's greatness more explicitly than any previous critic had done. This led him to ask a fundamental question: why did Shakespeare, at such a moment of artistic mastery, choose like Prospero to relinquish his powers? Here he assumes the importance of discovering Shakespeare the man, while simultaneously exposing the impossibility of that task: 'The figured tapestry, the long arras that hides him, is always there, with its immensity of surface and its proportionate underside.'[16] James's essay represents one of the most thoughtful and probing of biographical approaches to *The Tempest*, affirming the unique importance of the play as a self-reflective plunge into the author's own art – which would lead directly to later perceptions about the artifice of the late plays.

Realistic Criticism

Samuel Johnson anticipated the realistic criticism of the late nineteenth century when he wrote that *Cymbeline*

> has many just sentiments, some natural dialogues, and some pleasing scenes, but they are obtained at the expense of much incongruity. To remark the folly of the fiction, the absurdity of the conduct, the confusion of the names, and manners of different times, and the impossibility of the events in any system of life, were to waste criticism upon unresisting imbecility, upon faults too evident for detection, and too gross for aggravation.[17]

---

[14]   Ibid., p. 300.
[15]   Ibid., p. 302.
[16]   Ibid., p. 310.
[17]   Johnson, *Johnson on Shakespeare: The Yale Edition of the Works of Samuel Johnson*, vol. 8, ed. A. Sherbo (London: Yale University Press, 1968), p. 908.

Hazlitt challenged Johnson's view of the play, but during the nineteenth century *Cymbeline* lost favour among producers and audiences, while earning the admiration of at least two influential poets. Tennyson, on his death bed, called for his copy of Shakespeare and turned to this, his favourite play, which was then buried with him; Swinburne, in his book on Shakespeare, turned to Imogen for his final comments on the playwright.[18] At the time of Irving's production in 1896, this contradictory view of the play was echoed in the criticism of Shaw and Archer. Like Johnson, they condemned the absurdities and illogicality of the play, while following the Imogen cult of the Victorians. It was a play which, to Archer and Shaw, seemed deliberately to be constructed in defiance of common sense. Paradoxically, such negative realistic criticism came closer to an understanding of the play's style than the more romantic appreciations of Tennyson or Swinburne, who ignored the incongruities, while concentrating only on the play's poetic qualities.

Indeed, one can see the realistic criticism of the late nineteenth century as effectively liberating the late plays. These works appeared to be so defiantly at odds with realistic conventions; hence, they were all the more highly valued by the emerging avant-garde in their reaction to the hegemony of the naturalist movement. Surveying the criticism of this period, it is interesting to note how often the late plays are either criticised or appreciated by recourse to realistic criteria.[19] The mixture between realism and fantasy annoyed Shaw, but in spite of his prejudices, he found substance enough in the play to engage him in lengthy correspondence. In 1897, he turned his attention to a tragedy, *Othello*, which was running at the Lyric theatre. Having already castigated late Shakespeare in his review of *Cymbeline*, he now found *Othello* less realistically convincing than *The Winter's Tale*. He wrote that Othello's jealousy 'is purely melodramatic jealousy. The real article is to be found later on in *A Winter's Tale*, where Leontes is an unmistakable study of a jealous man from life' – and so we find the unusual situation of a romance being commended for its realism when compared to a tragedy.[20]

In the same year, Arthur Symons commended *The Winter's Tale* for its *lack* of realism, for the fact it is 'constructed in defiance of all probabilities, which it rides over happily'.[21] Like Henry James, who responded to the fantasy of Irving's

---

[18]   See Tennyson, *Alfred Lord Tennyson: A Memoir by His Son*, vol. 2 (London: MacMillan, 1897), pp. 428–9, and Swinburne, *A Study of Shakespeare* (London: Chatto & Windus, 1880), p. 227.

[19]   In 1898, Rudyard Kipling made a foray into Shakespearian criticism, writing an essay on *The Tempest*. Kipling uses realistic criteria to attempt to explain the fantastic elements in the play; the 'absurdities' of the play are accounted for by reference to a 'real life' situation ('The Vision of the Enchanted Island', in *A Book of Homage to Shakespeare*, ed. Israel Gollancz, pp. 200–203).

[20]   Shaw, *Shaw on Shakespeare*, ed. E. Wilson (Harmondsworth: Penguin, 1961), p. 171. Shaw returned to this idea in his sketch, 'A Dressing Room Secret' (1910), in which he again made the comparison between Othello and Leontes (p. 252).

[21]   Symons, *Studies in Two Literatures* (London: Leonard Smithers, 1897), pp. 42–3.

production of *Cymbeline*, Symons writes of the play's fairy-tale charm while also noting its seriousness and its tragic mood. He is particularly responsive to the play's defiance of realistic convention. Here we have the argument – which, ironically, Shaw used that year in support of Poel's staging of *The Tempest* – that too much realism can actually destroy the effect of illusion. Symons's view is essentially a reaction to the realistic perspective and is similar to Tree's justification for the play's anachronisms in his programme notes for a production in 1906.

Robert Bridges, writing about *The Winter's Tale* in 1907, used realistic criteria to stress the play's psychological implausibility. Where Shaw had argued for the credibility of Leontes's jealousy, Bridges complained of its senselessness and absurdity and noted the lack of adequate motivation. He was, however, most critical of the division between the two halves of the play and the 'impossibility' of the ending.[22]

If we move ahead in this survey, to 1912, we find F.W. Moorman, editor of the Arden edition of *The Winter's Tale*, attempting to supply the reader with the kind of realistic detail which might make the last scene more comprehensible. Moorman followed Bradley in assuming that Shakespeare's characters have a 'real' life offstage, which it is the business of the critic to consider. Hence, Moorman attempted to explain why Hermione's withdrawal of herself from her husband's society is not simply the result of 'unforgiving chastity' or the 'resentful nursing of an injury' – 'in reality', he writes, Hermione's withdrawal 'is an act of heroic submission' to the will of the gods.[23] Here we have an absurdly novelistic attempt to supply the reader with the kind of background information which might make the play seem plausible.

Such realistic criticism was to resurface throughout the period, but another interesting example is that of D.G. James in 'The Failure of the Ballad Makers' in *Scepticism and Poetry* (1937). He does not consider the plays an artistic success: 'We hover between apprehension of momentous significances, of a luxurious imagination, and of absurdities.'[24] James gives little sense of having considered the plays in performance, and one can suppose only that he was unresponsive to the contemporary productions which were proving to critics like Wilson Knight and Tillyard that the plays *were* artistic successes. His aesthetic bias is towards the realism which had dogged earlier critics, from Shaw to Bridges; however, even when compared to Shaw, James's criticisms are severe:

> It is absurd ... that Imogen should have mistaken the dead body of Cloten for that of Posthumus, even though his head was off and he was wearing the clothes of Posthumus ... what Shakespeare was anxious to convey he attempted to convey

---

[22] Bridges, *Collected Essays: The Influence of the Audience on Shakespeare's Drama* (London: Oxford University Press, 1927), pp. 21–2.

[23] Moorman, introduction to *The Arden Shakespeare: The Winter's Tale* (London: Methuen, 1912).

[24] James, *Scepticism and Poetry: An Essay of the Poetic Imagination* (London: George Alien & Unwin Ltd, 1937), p. 210.

at the expense of his art, about which he seems in these plays to have cared so little ... the coming to life of the 'dead' obsessed his imagination to the point of making his work silly to a degree it never had before been.[25]

Later critics noted the limitations of James's essay. For Edwards, 'the "silliness" of the plays is not so apparent to readers more at home in fairy-tale than James appears to be.'[26] There seems to be a conflict in James's essay between his recognition of the plays' mythical dimensions and his censure of their lack of realism. Like Strachey before him, D.G. James's bias towards realism allowed him a clear perception of the plays' qualities yet prevented him from evaluating them positively.

Formalism

Both Morton Luce and Henry James stressed the importance of style in relation to *The Tempest*, and James had argued for the independence and autonomy of the work of art. The formalist tradition would focus attention on Shakespeare the craftsman rather than Shakespeare the man. Behind the formalist tradition we find the influence not only of the aestheticist movement but also of William Poel, who focused attention on the dramaturgical structure of Shakespeare's plays. A.H. Gilbert's article, '*The Tempest:* Parallelism in Characters and Situations', which appeared in 1915, is valuable; here we have an example of a new trend towards structural criticism, examining the interrelationship between the various characters – a trend that seems to be directly influenced by Poel's staging techniques, which concentrated on dramatic action rather than on poetry.

An earlier example of structural criticism is R.G. Moulton's *Shakespeare as a Dramatic Thinker* (first published in 1903). Moulton believed in the primacy of the plot in understanding Shakespeare and argued against approaches based on individual characterisation or on poetry: 'The position here taken is that it is the construction of the plot, not the dialogue of the scenes, that contains a dramatist's philosophy.'[27] For Moulton, 'plot is dramatic perspective: the harmony of all details in a unity of design.' He believed that 'Shakespeare's plots are the key to Shakespeare's thought ... in story construction philosophy is dramatically presented.' The book devotes one chapter to *The Winter's Tale* and *Cymbeline*, focusing on the theme of 'Wrong and Restoration'. Although one might describe Moulton's approach as formalist in that he focuses attention on the construction of the plays, his interpretations move into the realm of moral criticism, a tradition of criticism that has not been of great importance in the critical re-evaluation of the romances.

---

[25] Ibid., pp. 232–3.

[26] Edwards, 'Shakespeare's Romances', p. 10.

[27] Moulton, *Shakespeare as a Dramatic Thinker: A Popular Illustration of Fiction as the Experimental Side of Philosophy* (New York: Macmillan Company, 1912), p. 5.

Sir Arthur Quiller-Couch's *Shakespeare's Workmanship* was first published in England in 1918. The title of this work is worth noting. Here we have moved well away from the biographical approach towards an analysis of Shakespeare's 'workmanship', which is itself a reaction to the Romantic and Victorian view of Shakespeare as the inspired and inspirational artist, concerned less with technique than with the children of his fertile imagination. This interest in Shakespeare's workmanship would be developed by later writers, for example by F.S. Boas in his *Introduction to the Reading of Shakespeare* (1927). Granville-Barker, too, both anticipated and developed the idea, while Muriel Bradbrook, in *Shakespeare the Craftsman* (1969), could be seen to follow in this tradition. Nosworthy writes that 'the most valuable element in [Quiller-Couch's] study of *Cymbeline* and its fellow Romances lies in its recognition of their experimental nature, especially in relation to the new opportunities for spectacular staging which the Jacobean theatres provided.'[28] Edwards, too, testifies to the significance of Quiller-Couch's book, noting its influence on later criticism, particularly Nosworthy's own emphasis on the experimental quality of *Cymbeline* and the other late plays.[29] Pafford also writes that 'the keynote of modern criticism is that the plays are experiments' and believes that this view may first have been expressed by T.R. Price in 1890.[30] However, it would seem that Quiller-Couch was the writer who was most responsible for popularising notions about the plays' experimental qualities, which would become if not a critical commonplace, at least an essential starting point for later criticism.

In his discussion of *Pericles*, Quiller-Couch agrees with Sidney Lee and Israel Gollancz, among others, that Acts I and II are 'un-Shakespearean, or at least not Shakespeare of this period'.[31] However, he supports the view of Raleigh that Shakespeare was acquainted with the 'darker side of town' and that the brothel scenes in Act IV were written by him. For 'the very greatest artists are not afraid of ugliness; since only by understanding, by plumbing the mire of our nature, can the beauty that springs from it be shown in highest triumph.' Likewise, in his chapter on *The Winter's Tale*, Quiller-Couch writes that

> no one can begin to understand Shakespeare's later plays who does not perceive that they have one common and constant aim – to repair the passionate errors of men and women in the happiness their children discover, and so to renew the hopes of the world; to reconcile the tragedy of one generation with the fresh hope of another in a third form of drama.[32]

---

28   Nosworthy, introduction to *Cymbeline*, p. xlviii.

29   Edwards, 'Shakespeare's Romances', p. 16.

30   Price's 'The Construction of *The Winter's Tale*', *Shakespeariana*, October 1890, is quoted by Pafford, introduction, p. xliv.

31   Quiller-Couch, *Shakespeare's Workmanship* (London: T. Fisher Unwin Ltd, 1918), p. 250.

32   Ibid., p. 286.

Nonetheless, he does not consider *The Winter's Tale* to be an artistic success, for the play 'abounds in careless workmanship'.[33] He maintains that Shakespeare, in his presentation of Leontes, 'bungled it', and failed to make the character's jealousy credible. He agrees with Coleridge's remark about the playwright's apparent indolence not to have provided in the oracle 'some ground for Hermione's seeming death and sixteen years' voluntary concealment', writing that 'the resurrection of Hermione thus becomes more startling, but at a loss of dramatic irony.'[34] He criticizes Florizel's sudden change of costume in 4.4, and views the bear as a 'naughty superfluity', a true offence 'against economy of workmanship'. Antigonus too is regarded by Quiller-Couch as superfluous to the plot. The greatest fault of all, however, is the recognition scene, which he believes has been 'scamped'.[35] Quiller-Couch does not object to the anachronisms of *The Winter's Tale*, which he believes are justified in terms of the play's fairy-tale nature. His criticisms are to do only with 'those laxities of construction, of workmanship'; he writes that the play 'never lodges in our minds as a whole, is never compact', that 'it leaves no single impression.'[36] (One might contrast this view of the play with that of Harley Granville-Barker, as expressed in his preface to the Heinemann edition of 1912, which stresses the workmanship of the play, most particularly in the recognition scene.)

Quiller-Couch believed *The Tempest* to be Shakespeare's supreme achievement. While he admired that play's artistry, however, he had not quite escaped from the sentimental view of the late nineteenth century. In *Shakespeare's Workmanship*, in a spirit of patronising colonialism, he writes that Caliban 'is not a bad monster' and that if he were 'to come fawning into the room, our impulse would be to pat him on the head – "Good old doggie! Good monster!" – that would be the feeling'.[37] Of *The Tempest*, Quiller-Couch writes that 'every artist of the first class tires of repeating his successes, but never of repeating his experiments.'[38] In his opinion, Shakespeare had come to realise that forgiveness is nobler than revenge and, accordingly, in the last plays, Shakespeare sought to reach something finer than tragedy: his aims 'brought him at last "up against" the limitations of his art'.[39]

Granville-Barker is the writer who best exemplifies the formalist school of criticism. He was first to suggest the idea of 'artifice' in relation to a late play, an idea which was explored in the visual design of his production of *The Winter's Tale*. His preface to *Cymbeline* first appeared in 1923 in an edition of the play published by Victor Gollancz (it was then considerably reworked before reappearing in 1929 in its more familiar form as part of his series of *Prefaces*). The earlier version is

---

[33] Ibid., p. 290.
[34] Ibid., pp. 291–2.
[35] Ibid., p. 294.
[36] Ibid., p. 297.
[37] Ibid., p. 353.
[38] Ibid., p. 331.
[39] Ibid., p. 233.

in many ways the more revealing, particularly in terms of how Granville-Barker himself may have conceived of the play in production terms. The illustrations for the edition were by Albert Rutherston, who had designed the settings for his *Winter's Tale*, and again one senses a close collaboration between the two, as if they had seriously considered a stage production. Granville-Barker writes of the problem of finding a setting for the play, with its 'make-believe' story. He stresses the link between *Cymbeline* and the court masque. The play's whole action smacks 'of the close oncoming of the scenic idea, of pageantry, of the spirit of the masque'.[40] He writes that 'the elaborate battle is meant to be more like pageantry than real fighting.' One is reminded of Henry James's comment about the battle scene in Irving's production, implying that the battle seemed extremely masque-like in its visual effect (again, one can sense the influence of Irving's production on Granville-Barker).

Of the cave of Belarius, Granville-Barker writes that this

> pretty piece of make-believe which was still a novelty upon the public stages, definitely influences the dramatic conduct of the scenes that take place before it ... the bringing on of Cloten's head and the whole episode of the headless body will be intolerable if its acting is not at one with the artificiality of the painted canvas that is meant to form its background.

In this scene, with its double trick of the potion, and its constant moralising, 'all is make-believe and in the spirit of the masque.' The play's masque-like quality affects the way in which a designer can approach his task. According to Granville-Barker, the vision of Jupiter 'lifts us clear of all responsibility to this century or that, lodges us in a world of fancy where anachronisms are no offence'. If the designer 'rejects the hint that the masque's influence affords him, his task must still be to find, if he can, a decorative equivalent to the romantic and slightly bizarre mood with which Shakespeare has informed the play'.

Insofar as the keyword in Granville-Barker's analysis is 'artifice', this becomes explicit in the later version of the preface. In the earlier version, he writes about Shakespeare's 'deliberate craftsmanship', for example, his use of convention to prepare the audience for the play's overall style:

> To begin with – and at the very beginning – we are not to question the likelihood of one gentleman telling another such an admirably concise tale of all *we* need to know of the scandal at Cymbeline's Court. We accept the convention and we also note – and request the actors to note – that it is a pattern scene in matter and manner both, that it sets the tune and pace of what is to come. It gives us the temper of the play.

This recognition of the play's use of convention is probably the most revolutionary aspect of Granville-Barker's criticism; in other respects, he relies heavily on older

---

[40] Granville-Barker, *Prefaces to Shakespeare: The Winter's Tale – Cymbeline* (London: B.T. Batsford Ltd, 1984), p. 94.

opinions, for example the well-received notions that '*Cymbeline* is held to be a product of the time of Shakespeare's retirement to Stratford' and that 'one can indeed divine in it the work of a man somewhat weary, yet doing what he does at his ease.' However, he continues, if Shakespeare was weary when he wrote *Cymbeline*, 'it would seem that he knew how to turn even this disability to some account.' Granville-Barker's reliance on earlier perspectives is always hedged with a certain ambivalence.

Nosworthy, while recognising the importance of Granville-Barker's preface, especially for 'its masterly analysis of various kinds of artifice that went to the making of the play', writes of certain obvious defects:

> The disintegration theories which were in the air when it was written left him perplexed and over-credulous, and his discussion of the characters of the play shows that he was still responsive to the methods of A.C. Bradley, so that his Imogen, his Posthumus, his Cloten are invested with a reality that can scarcely be reconciled with Shakespeare's presumed intentions.[41]

J.L. Styan, noting Granville-Barker's 'lame observations', is altogether less sympathetic.[42] Yet Styan simply ignores the important new insights that the preface contains, while concentrating only on its more conventional aspects. Granville-Barker's emphasis on the play's style and its use of artifice led discussion well away from the Shaw-Archer school of realistic criticism.

Another critic who, like Granville-Barker, is associated with the perception of the artifice of Shakespeare's plays is E.E. Stoll. Much of his work is devoted to the tragedies, but he also wrote a provocative essay on *The Tempest*, first published in 1932. In *Shakespeare Studies* (1927), he had attempted to destroy 'the autobiographical illusion' of the Victorians and Edwardians: 'From the plays, at all events, the dark period in his life cannot justifiably be inferred. If to these critics the plays seem gloomy and misanthropic, still the man at that moment may not have been. The imaginative mood runs often contrary – is a relief, a counterpoise.'[43] In Stoll's book one can note the strong influence of Wilde:

> Literature is, of course, not life, neither history nor material for history, but a scroll whereon are traced and charactered the unfettered thoughts of writer and reader – a life within a life, fancy somewhat at odds with fact. But by critics and historians this is often forgotten – 'to pass from the art of a time to the time itself,' says Wilde, 'is the great mistake that all historians commit.'[44]

---

[41]   Nosworthy, introduction to *Cymbeline*, p. xlv.

[42]   Styan, *The Shakespeare Revolution: Criticism and Performance in the Twentieth Century* (Cambridge: Cambridge University Press, 1977), pp. 119–20.

[43]   Stoll, *Shakespeare Studies* (New York: Macmillan, 1927), p. 81.

[44]   Ibid., pp. 39–40.

In his essay on *The Tempest*, Stoll set out to attack allegorical interpretations, claiming that there is not any allegory, symbolism, or 'veiled biography' in that play. In *Art and Artifice* (1933), Stoll discusses the various conventions of Shakespeare's plays – among which he numbers the stories of disguise, mistaken identity, deception, eavesdropping, apparent deaths and revivals, oracles, or the fateful finding of rings, letters and handkerchiefs. These devices, he writes, are often seen as being artificial, outworn and taboo, 'but alike they are only the traditional means of attaining the contrast or conflict, the compression and condensation, which drama of necessity seeks. In themselves they are devices of accumulation and simplification.'[45] Stoll seems to be suggesting that the plots of Shakespearian drama are themselves 'devices', conventions proclaiming their artificiality, their purpose being not to reflect life, but to provide the basis for each play's poetic and dramatic structure. Stoll's view of Shakespeare's art could hardly be more opposed to G. Wilson Knight's highly symbolic view of the plays. While the two writers share a rejection of earlier realistic critical assumptions, Stoll singles out Wilson Knight for criticism, claiming that he does not observe the primary duty 'of regarding the author's meaning, of reading the text'.

Symbolic Interpretations

Symbolic interpretations of the late plays fall into three broad categories: allegorical interpretations, mythical approaches and the study of image patterns. These categories are not mutually exclusive and the major critics in this tradition – like Wilson Knight – do not fit into a single category. F.C. Tinkler examined mythical symbolism in *The Winter's Tale*, while Caroline Spurgeon clearly focused on a study of image patterns. Although Wilson Knight is clearly important in the realm of myth criticism, it would only be in the post-war period, following the influence of Northrop Frye, that this tradition would disentangle its own concerns from those of the allegorists.

At the turn of the century, there were a number of allegorical readings of the late plays, particularly of *The Tempest*. Biographical criticism might even be seen as an early example of this trend. In such interpretations Prospero was identified with Shakespeare and Milan with Stratford. Edward Dowden believed that Prospero's advice to Ferdinand could be taken to represent Shakespeare's own advice to his young colleague, John Fletcher. Such crude allegorical interpretations would be replaced by more complex ones. In 1908, Churton Collins published an essay on *The Tempest* (in the *Contemporary Review*) that is remarkable for being one of the first to focus on the symbolism of Prospero's island, and as such is a forerunner of a great deal of later criticism. Collins tentatively suggested an allegorical reading of *The Tempest*, asking, 'Is the island the world, the *dramatis personae* mankind, the government and central purpose of Prospero symbolic of life and life's control by

---

[45] Stoll, *Art and Artifice in Shakespeare* (Cambridge: Cambridge University Press, 1933), p. 3.

Heaven?'[46] For Collins the allegory of *The Tempest* is essentially a Christian one; the idea that the play is a religious allegory would be developed by later critics, like Colin Still, although along less orthodox lines. (The notion that the island represents the world also constituted a remarkable new interpretation, anticipating Jan Kott.) In 1921, Still's *Shakespeare's Mystery Play* appeared – a study of *The Tempest* that was to be lavishly praised by Wilson Knight, whose comments about it in *The Crown of Life* (1947) are pertinent. *The Tempest* could now be seen as 'a dramatic representation of the Mystery of Redemption, conceived as a psychological experience and expressed in mythological form ... a myth of creation woven from his total work by the most universal of poets'.[47]

John Dover Wilson's *The Essential Shakespeare* (1932) included a chapter entitled 'The Enchanted Island'. Dover Wilson, as a critic, had closer links with the formalist tradition of Quiller-Couch – he echoed Quiller-Couch's view that the late plays are experiments – than with the symbolism of Wilson Knight, yet in his interpretation of *The Tempest* he moved into the world of symbolic criticism. For example, he writes that Prospero 'has learnt that Desire may prove a savage beast, and has chained it up in a rock beneath his cell'. Here we have an example of how stagings of the play may have unlocked its potential symbolism, for Dover Wilson's interpretation depends on a visual, theatrical image. He was one of the first critics to suggest that Caliban is an aspect of Prospero's own identity, an idea which would be explored by later critics like Kott. For Dover Wilson, Prospero 'is more than Shakespeare, he is Dramatic Poetry; just as the island is more than Life, it is Life seen through the mirror of ripe dramatic art'. This interest in the symbolism of Prospero's island would also be explored by John Middleton Murry in his *Shakespeare* (1936): 'the Island is a realm where by Art or Nurture Prospero transforms man's Nature to true Human Nature.'[48] This notion that the island is 'a realm', a symbolic world, can be seen to be a direct result of the new traditions of staging, inspired by Poel, which freed the island from the literalistic confines of the nineteenth-century stage.

In *Shakespeare's Imagery* (1935), Caroline Spurgeon offers various insights into the imagery of the late plays and makes the claim that '*Pericles* alone of the romances has no sign of any running "motive" or continuity of picture or thought in the imagery, a fact sufficient in itself to throw grave doubt on its authorship.'[49] However, as Spurgeon discerns a similar absence of continuity in the imagery of both *The Tempest* and *The Winter's Tale*, her conclusion is not convincing. She notes two chief strains in the imagery of *Cymbeline*: on the one hand the predominance of country images of trees, flowers and birds, the play being 'alive

---

46   Collins, 'Poetry and Symbolism: A Study of *The Tempest*', in *Contemporary Review* 97 (January 1908): p. 78.

47   Wilson Knight, *The Crown of Life* (London: Methuen, 1985), p. 226.

48   Murry, *Shakespeare* (London: Jonathan Cape, 1936), p. 396.

49   Spurgeon, *Shakespeare's Imagery* (Cambridge: Cambridge University Press, 1935), p. 291.

with the movement and sound of birds'; on the other, the theme 'of buying and selling, value and exchange, every kind of payment, debts, bills and wages'.[50] In *The Winter's Tale* Spurgeon does not see 'any one symbol occurring clearly and repeatedly' but is conscious rather 'of something more indirect and subtle, not a picture, but an *idea*, dominant in the poet's mind'.[51] This dominant idea seems 'to be the common flow of life through all things, in nature and man alike'; above all, it is 'the oneness of rhythm, of law of movement, in the human body and human emotions with the great fundamental rhythmic movements of nature herself'. The dominant image in *The Tempest*, by contrast, is

> something more subtle than we have yet encountered, in that it is not expressed through any one single group of images which fall easily under one heading, but rather through the action itself and the background, reinforced by a number of images taken from many groups, all illustrating or emphasising one single sensation ... It is the sense of *sound* which is thus emphasised, for the play itself is an absolute symphony of sound, and it is through sound that its contrasts and movement are expressed, from the clashing discords of the opening to the serene harmony of the close.[52]

Spurgeon's approach is similar to that of Wilson Knight, except that Wilson Knight went further than simply observing the various image clusters. He was much more concerned with linking poetic images with the ideas and themes of the plays.

F.C. Tinkler, in an essay on *The Winter's Tale* published in *Scrutiny* in 1937, begins with the positive statement that the play 'is an assured artistic success'. Tinkler's essay is valuable for stressing the links between the play and fertility rituals, examining the play in the context of 'the folk drama of England'. His interpretation may well have been inspired as much by Eliot's poem, *The Waste Land*, as by its primary source, Jessie Weston's *From Ritual to Romance*, which appeared in 1920. The following year, in another *Scrutiny* essay on *Cymbeline*, Tinkler argued that the play 'should be considered, not as a fashionable romance, but as a play which continues the achievement of the great tragedies in another form' – again, we have the view that a late romance needs to be taken as seriously as any of the tragedies. Of course, here Tinkler was following in the wake of Wilson Knight's argument that the late plays represent a development from the tragedies.

Wilson Knight's most influential and revolutionary essay on the late plays was *Myth and Miracle*, first published as a booklet in 1929. Thirty years later, in 'New Dimensions in Shakespearian Interpretation', Wilson Knight would explain in detail the process which led to his recognition of the significance of the late plays. In the 1920s he had grown dissatisfied with the usual division of Shakespeare's art into 'characters' and 'poetry', believing that 'the dramatic people were themselves

---

50   Ibid., p. 296.
51   Ibid., p. 305.
52   Ibid., p. 300.

poetic.'[53] He also found himself unsympathetic towards the dominant strain of criticism of the time, 'realistic' criticism, concerned primarily with sources and the kind of study 'which appeared to believe ... that a proper understanding of the Elizabethan stage and Elizabethan prompt books and printing would serve if driven far enough to render up the Shakespearian secret'. In 'New Dimensions', reviewing the attitudes towards the late plays that were current in the 1920s – the idea that Shakespeare was imitating Fletcher, the Victorian view of the serene mood of the plays, Strachey's reaction to the sentimental readings – Wilson Knight describes his own sudden comprehension of the plays' significance:

> We were to see a mystical or miraculous statement pushing through the form and structure of a conventional play. Everything at once fell into place: questions of authorship settled themselves. We had no reason to suppose that the greater part of *Pericles* or the Vision of Jupiter in *Cymbeline* was spurious; on the contrary, the new reading made it highly probable that these were purposive and coherent.[54]

With *Myth and Miracle*, Wilson Knight set out to show that 'those improbabilities of plot texture and curiosities of the supernatural descending on the purely human interest' are not 'the freaks of a wearied imagination', nor the work of the 'incompetent coadjutor', 'but rather the inevitable development of the questioning, the pain, the profundity and grandeur of the plays they succeed'.[55] His method was

> to regard the plays as they stand in the order to which modern scholarship has assigned them; to refuse to regard 'sources' as exerting any limit to the significance of the completed work of art; to avoid the side issues of Elizabethan and Jacobean manners, politics, patronage, audiences, revolutions and explorations; to fix attention solely on the poetic quality and human interest of the plays concerned.

This brings Wilson Knight's critical intentions surprisingly close to those of A.C. Bradley (indeed, 'New Dimensions' acknowledges a debt to Bradley). Although reacting to his emphasis on 'character', Wilson Knight regarded Bradley's discussion of the poetic 'atmospheres' of *Macbeth* and *King Lear* as anticipating his own approach, realising 'that what Bradley had done for a few plays might be done in greater detail and on a wider scale'.[56] In regarding 'Elizabethan and Jacobean manners, politics, patronage, audiences, revolutions and explorations' as

---

[53]   Wilson Knight, 'New Dimensions in Shakespearian Interpretation', in *Shakespeare and Religion* (London: Routledge & Kegan Paul, 1967), p. 197.

[54]   Ibid., pp. 198–9.

[55]   Wilson Knight, 'Myth and Miracle', in *The Crown of Life* (London: Methuen, 1985), p. 9.

[56]   Ibid., pp. 200–201. Other influences which Wilson Knight acknowledges are John Masefield's 1924 Romanes Lecture *Shakespeare and Spiritual Life* and Colin Still's *Shakespeare's Mystery Play* (1921).

side issues, Wilson Knight's critical approach is far removed from the historicist tradition of Tillyard.

Myth and Miracle also dispenses with problems relating to Shakespeare's intentions by deciding to 'leave any discussion of consciousness and unconsciousness, intention and inspiration, as unnecessary to a purely philosophic discussion of the text'. Here Wilson Knight might be seen to anticipate structuralist criticism. He believes that to the critic of the poetry, 'the word "Shakespeare" stands alone for the dynamic life that persists in the plays, and any other "Shakespeare" is pure abstraction.'[57] Effectively, Wilson Knight returns to the biographical view – with one significant difference: 'Shakespeare' has, for the purposes of criticism, no independent existence beyond the work of art itself. This approach must surely be seen as a development of the idea implicit in Henry James's essay of 1907, that there are in fact two Shakespeares – the man and the artist – and that if the plays constitute an autobiography then it is of Shakespeare the artist. Later in the essay, Wilson Knight writes of *The Tempest* in a way that echoes James:

> In this work Shakespeare looks inward and, projecting perfectly his own spiritual experience into symbols of objectivity, traces in a compact play the past progress of his own soul. He is now the object of his own search, and no other theme but that of his visionary self is now of power to call forth the riches of his imagination.[58]

Earlier in the essay, Wilson Knight compares *Pericles* and *The Winter's Tale*, observing that the two stories are remarkably alike. He also notes the atmosphere of mysticism which permeates the plays and the 'pseudo-Hellenistic' theology, from the Delphic Oracle to the temple of Diana: 'A reader sensitive to poetic atmosphere must necessarily feel the awakening light of some religious or metaphysical truth symbolized in the plot and attendant machinery of these two plays.'[59] He regards the scene of the reviving of Thaisa as 'one of the pinnacles of Shakespeare's art' and states that this scene, and those of the restoration to Pericles of Marina and Thaisa, are alone sufficient to establish his thesis 'that the author is moved by vision, not fancy; is creating not merely entertainment, but myth in the Platonic sense'.[60] Thus, he affirms, 'the blindness of past Shakespearian criticism is at no point more completely in evidence than in the comments on this play. To the discerning mind it will be evident that we are here confronted with the furthest reach of Shakespeare's poetic and visionary power.'

He continues his comparison between *Pericles* and *The Winter's Tale* by drawing attention to the central significance of the storm imagery:

---

[57] Ibid., p. 9.
[58] Ibid., p. 23.
[59] Ibid., p. 14.
[60] Ibid., pp. 15–16.

In both these plays we have the theme of a child bereft of its mother and threatened by storm and thunder. The emphasis on tempests is insistent, and the suggestion is clearly that of the pitifulness and helplessness of humanity born into a world of tragic conflict. That the tempest is percurrent in Shakespeare as a symbol of tragedy need not be demonstrated here at length. Its symbolic significance is patent from the earliest to the latest plays – in metaphor, in simile, in long or short descriptions, in stage directions. The individual soul is the 'bark' putting out to sea in a 'tempest': the image occurs again and again.[61]

This idea – a revolutionary one in Shakespeare criticism, seeing an underlying thematic structure which gives unity and coherence to the entire body of Shakespeare's work – was subsequently to be expounded upon in detail in *The Shakespearian Tempest* (1932).[62]

Wilson Knight's discussion of *Cymbeline* centres around the vision of Jupiter, which he regards as 'Shakespeare's clearest statement', in terms of 'anthropomorphic theology', of the significant themes in the final plays. This scene, which had so often in the past been attributed to the 'incompetent coadjutor', Wilson Knight considers, for the purposes of his study, to be 'by far the most important scene in the play'.[63] *Myth and Miracle* is a seminal piece of criticism, not only for first expressing the idea of the tempest-music antithesis in Shakespeare's works but also for the re-evaluation it offered of both *Pericles* and *Cymbeline*. Further, by seeing the late plays as 'myths of immortality', Wilson Knight profoundly influenced the course of later criticism. Indeed, one can discern his influence on various subsequent interpretations of *The Tempest*. For example, in *Myth and Miracle* he writes, '*The Tempest* is at the same time a record of Shakespeare's spiritual progress and a statement of the vision to which that progress has brought him. It is apparent as a dynamic and living act of the soul, containing within itself the record of its birth: it is continually re-writing itself before our eyes.'[64] One might trace a direct line of descent from this idea, through Tillyard's analysis of re-enactment in the play, to Jan Kott's notion that *The Tempest* is a re-playing of Shakespeare's 'history of the world', to Peter Brook's 1968 production, which explored Kott's ideas, or to Peter Greenaway's 1991 film, *Prospero's Books*, with its subtle exploration of the theme of 're-writing' and its visual interpretation of the play's symbolism.

---

[61]   Ibid., pp. 17–18.

[62]   In *The Shakespearian Tempest* (London: Methuen, 1960), Wilson Knight begins, 'In any intellectual study we expect first some principle of unity; but it is exactly this that has been lacking to our understanding of Shakespeare. If no unity be apprehended, the result will be an intellectual chaos such as has surely emerged throughout recent investigation. My purpose here is to replace that chaos by drawing attention to the true Shakespearian unity: the opposition, throughout the plays, of "tempests" and "music"' (p. 1).

[63]   Ibid., p. 19.

[64]   Ibid., p. 27.

Furthermore, Wilson Knight's essay 'Tolstoy's Attack on Shakespeare' (1934) is notable for its response to the realistic criticism which had directed itself at Shakespeare's art at the turn of the century. Just as Strachey had exposed the preconceptions behind the biographical view of the 'serene late period', Wilson Knight here attempted to expose the preconceptions behind the realistic method. He writes that there are some elements in Shakespeare's work which, by their nature, cannot be 'the fine pieces of realistic exactitude to which his idolators have raised them'.[65] He believes that it is precisely because of the romantic overemphasis on the virtues of Shakespeare's characterisation that his art becomes most subject to criticism. He argues that if by 'characterisation' is implied 'verisimilitude' then it will be found that this is 'not only not the Shakespearian essence, but actually the most penetrable spot to adverse criticism that may be discovered in his technique'. Wilson Knight focuses on the critical perspectives of two writers, Tolstoy and Bridges, who had both addressed themselves to the question of Shakespeare's artistic worth. He argues that their attacks on Shakespeare are 'based on a fundamental misunderstanding of his art'; Bridges 'complains of Shakespeare's carelessness, disregard of improbabilities in plot-texture, faults of "characterisation", and want of taste', while Tolstoy 'continually complains of Shakespeare's vulgarity'.[66] Yet 'Tolstoy's violent attack on Shakespeare is primarily aroused, not by Shakespeare, but by the Shakespearian commentators. ... Applying the hackneyed opinions to Shakespeare, they found that these qualities refused to fit: Tolstoy therefore rejects Shakespeare wholesale; Bridges [rejects only] those elements which repel him.'[67]

Although Tolstoy was misguided, he was, according to Wilson Knight, 'nevertheless correct in his feeling that the Shakespearian commentary he knew was often quite out of touch with the facts'. Tolstoy's attack on Shakespeare 'is thus at root a healthy attempt to break free from the "hypnotism" ... of romantic criticism'. Bridges's complaints, like Tolstoy's, 'are a step towards understanding'.[68] However, as no defence against their criticism was forthcoming, 'realistic' criticism 'was loosed on the twentieth century'. Here Wilson Knight clearly identifies the historicist tradition as 'realistic' – that is, based in an attempt to read the plays in the light of the 'real', historical circumstances of the age in which they were written. Shakespeare, now regarded as a writer pandering to vulgar tastes, therefore had to be explained by reference to his historical circumstances: 'Failing to find any inherent unity in the art-form, the critic has to overstep the limit of aesthetic commentary and try to account for the artistic essence in terms of its "causes", its "circumstances", its supposed inartistic "purposes". Thus

---

[65] Wilson Knight, 'Tolstoy's Attack on Shakespeare', in *The Wheel of Fire: Interpretations of Shakespearian Tragedy with Three New Essays* (London: Methuen, 1983), p. 270.

[66] Ibid., p. 273.

[67] Ibid., pp. 274–5.

[68] Ibid., p. 279.

our modern "realistic" criticism of Shakespeare came into being: aptly, it soon developed into disintegration.'[69] It would surely be wrong to attribute the entire 'realistic' (historicist) critical tradition to the impact of the criticism of Tolstoy and Bridges. The realistic critical perspective was itself a phenomenon of the age when naturalism was the dominant intellectual and aesthetic ideology. We have noted a similar realistic emphasis in the criticism of Shaw, Archer and Strachey. Bridges and Tolstoy simply took the realistic criticism of Shakespeare to a naive extreme. It may be fair, however, to claim – as Wilson Knight did – that realistic criticism 'is plainly a reaction from the extravagant praise and rhetorical appreciation that so long and so loud sounded throughout the nineteenth century'.

To understand Shakespeare, Wilson Knight argues,

> one must make this original acceptance: to believe, first, in people who speak poetry; thence in human actions which subserve a poetic purpose; and, finally, in strange effects in nature which harmonize with the persons and their acts; the whole building a massive statement which, if accepted in its entirety, induces a profound experience in the reader or spectator.[70]

His description of the Shakespearean world is one which seems to echo the Freudian idea of the unconscious:

> The Shakespearian world is not the world we habitually see. Yet it is the world we experience: the poignant world of primal feeling, violent subterranean life, and wayward passionate thought, controlled, denied, hidden often, then up-gushing to surprise ourselves; the inner world we experience, the world we live and fear, but not the world we normally see, nor the world we think we understand.

'Tolstoy's Attack on Shakespeare' is not just an answer to the criticism of Bridges and Tolstoy but also to the criticism of Archer and Shaw in their reviews of Irving's *Cymbeline*, and indeed to a great deal of the commentary that had attempted either to defend or dismiss the late plays according to realistic criteria. However, Wilson Knight's tendency to see the historicist critical tradition as 'realistic' is misleading, for the historicists, through a study of the literary and theatrical conventions of the period, were themselves discovering the non-illusionist, symbolic nature of Shakespeare's art.

Historicism

This tradition places the late plays in relation to other works during the period, to romance literature, Jacobean drama, the court masque, or to the ideas of the age. Ashley Thorndike, in *The Influence of Beaumont and Fletcher on Shakespere* (1901), attempted to locate the late plays in the 'factual' historical realm by

---

[69]   Ibid., p. 293.
[70]   Ibid., p. 284.

examining the relationship between these works and Jacobean court drama. His study is valuable for drawing attention to the similarities between *Philaster* and *Cymbeline*. As Edwards notes, Thorndike's main thesis is 'that Shakespeare imitated Beaumont and Fletcher', an idea which would be later refuted by both Wilson Knight and Tillyard.[71] However, one might see Thorndike's study as the beginning of the historicist tradition, which attempted to study the late plays within the context of the literature and theatre of the period. This interest in Beaumont and Fletcher's plays and their relationship to Shakespeare can be directly related to the work of Poel and the Elizabethan Stage Society, who in 1898 staged *The Coxcomb*.[72]

In 1920, in an interesting essay entitled 'The Wager in *Cymbeline*', W.W. Lawrence argued that 'Posthumus and Imogen and Iachimo are too often treated as if they were persons of the nineteenth century, and their acts interpreted like those of characters in a modern realistic novel, instead of a tale the outlines and spirit of which had been determined by centuries of literary and social tradition.'[73] Again, this is an attempt to understand the play within its own historical context. Lawrence relates the wager plot to various sources and earlier examples of the story. He asks how the Elizabethans may have understood it as they saw it on the stage and what they would have thought of Posthumus. Through this analysis, Lawrence attempts 'a substantial vindication' of Posthumus 'as blameless and even praiseworthy in accepting the wager', as a character 'acting in accord with the ethics of his day and the conventions of romantic drama'.[74] He argues that 'much in the play which seems absurd and improbable today becomes, in the light of Elizabethan ethics and social conventions, natural and reasonable.'[75] This hints at the realistic perspective and the need to account for the play's incongruities. However, Lawrence recognises that the play as a whole remains elusively implausible, that it can be taken seriously only until the end of the second act, after which 'it goes to pieces, as far as naturalness is concerned, and becomes a kind of – dare we say it? – variety-show, in its multitude of dramatic situations, many of them wildly improbable, mingled with a procession of ghosts, the stage trick of Jupiter, the eagle, the thunderbolt, political prophecy, and so forth.' Yet he avoids a negative judgement, or indeed any judgement: 'How far we can afford to chide Shakespeare when he pours out the whole cornucopia of stage-tricks before us, in this reckless and prodigal fashion, and accuse him of "unresisting imbecility," is a question which shall be left to others to decide.' For all the insights of his essay, Lawrence concludes on a somewhat conservative note.

---

[71] Edwards, 'Shakespeare's Romances', p. 4.

[72] See Speaight, *William Poel and the Elizabethan Revival* (London: Heinemann Ltd, 1954), p. 281.

[73] Lawrence, 'The Wager in *Cymbeline*', *Publications of the Modern Language Association of America* 35.4 (1920): p. 395.

[74] Ibid.: p. 396.

[75] Ibid.: p. 431.

Another influential writer to examine the relationship between the late plays and the drama of the period was Enid Welsford, whose *The Court Masque: A Study in the Relationship between Poetry and the Revels* (1927) focuses particular attention on *The Tempest*, comparing the play to Jonson's masques. She writes that 'if Shakespeare is following Ben Jonson, he is following not his theories as a classicist, but his practice as a writer of masques.'[76] Unlike the classical drama which is concerned with the final phase of a conflict, the masque, she notes, deals 'with a moment of transformation; it expresses not uncertainty, ended by final success or failure, but expectancy, crowned by sudden revelation; and even when the opposition of good and evil is symbolised by masque and antimasque, this opposition is shown as contrast rather than as a conflict.'[77] She argues that in this respect '*The Tempest* is more masque-like than dramatic, for Prospero addresses Miranda in the tone of a masque presenter and, throughout the play, he manipulates the human characters as surely as he manipulates the spirit masquers.' Far from being founded upon a conflict, 'the play does not even contain a debate.' She acknowledges that behind *The Tempest* 'lie that conflict between two opposing parties and that conflict within the soul of the hero which was always the subject of Shakespearian tragedy'; however, 'Shakespeare is now hymning the victory instead of describing the battle, the lyrical element has almost usurped the place of drama, time has almost disappeared into eternity.' Here then is an interpretation based on the play's relationship to the conventions of the court masque, which supports through historical evidence the broad outline of Wilson Knight's interpretation.

Una Ellis-Fermor's study, *The Jacobean Drama: An Interpretation* (1936), contains an insight into the late plays that Tillyard would later quote in *Shakespeare's Last Plays*. She writes of the influence of Beaumont and Fletcher on Shakespeare and of how he had transcended their influence: 'The fairy-tale with him becomes charged with those implications which the more immediate types of story could not present, becomes the vehicle of imaginative experience and interprets the real world more truly than do the records of actuality.'[78] This again might be seen as an answer to Lytton Strachey and as a positive affirmation of the artistic seriousness of the late plays.

In 1938, R. Warwick Bond, one of the most interesting critics of Irving's 1896 production, returned to the subject of *Cymbeline* in a short essay, 'The Puzzle in *Cymbeline*' (published in his *Studia Otiosa*). Bond attempts to answer the question of why Shakespeare combined a tale of early Britain 'with a heroine of some twelve centuries later, to whose comfort and convenience he boldly sacrifices all

---

[76] Welsford, *The Court Masque: A Study in the Relationship between Poetry and the Revels* (Cambridge: Cambridge University Press, 1927), p. 338.

[77] Ibid., pp. 339–40.

[78] Ellis-Fermor, *The Jacobean Drama: An Interpretation* (London: Methuen, 1936), p. 268.

we should naturally expect of a picture of Britain at this early date?'[79] He writes that 'at once we feel the anomaly far greater than the occasional anachronism in other plays' – here the anomaly 'is pervading, inherent, not a mere incidental detail to make his audience feel more at home'. Bond's answer is that it must have occurred to Shakespeare 'that this period of the first contacts of Rome and Britain is a golden opportunity for linking together his two great series by a play that may serve as it were as coping-stone to his whole historical edifice'. He concludes, 'Had this motive of linking the two series Roman and English, occurred to Johnson he might have dealt less harshly with what most of us feel as among the poet's richest, tenderest and most fascinating works.'

Like Wilson Knight's *Myth and Miracle*, Tillyard's *Shakespeare's Last Plays* (1938) is a seminal work of criticism. Its chief importance lies in its reassessment of previous criticism and in its argument that the late plays supplement the tragedies. Tillyard also stresses the links between the late plays and romance literature and argues for the close interrelationship between the individual plays, seeing them as a closely knit group. Unlike Wilson Knight, Tillyard tends to underplay the importance of *Pericles*, and his study is directed mainly at *Cymbeline*, *The Winter's Tale* and *The Tempest*. He begins by directing his attention at earlier criticism, noting, on the one hand, the view that the plays are experiments, while, on the other, quoting Strachey's opinion that Shakespeare was bored. He thinks that Granville-Barker may have echoed this view when he noted the artifice of *Cymbeline*: 'This art that displays art is a thing very likely to be to the taste of the mature and rather wearied artist.'[80] However, he writes, 'this acute and temperate comment on a single play is remote from Strachey's imputation of weariness to the whole group.' Tillyard argues that Strachey's essay is at complete odds with his own opinion: 'There is no lack of vitality, Shakespeare is not bored with things; and my conviction of this springs from the rhythms, the imagery, in fact from those most intimate poetical qualities about which it is futile to argue.' He quotes Middleton Murry's view that even in *Cymbeline*, 'the verse is sinewy from first to last: manifestly the work of a poet in whom the faculty was at height.'

Tillyard then turns to the question of the influence of the court theatres and particularly to the influence of Beaumont and Fletcher. He argues that if Shakespeare followed Fletcher, then this 'does not in the least mean that he resembled Fletcher in final poetic effect'.[81] Shakespeare 'transformed an alien suggestion into something entirely his own'. He suggests that it is wrong to ignore the influence of Beaumont and Fletcher, but that 'it is equally wrong to suppose that the things Shakespeare derived from them were exclusively their property' –

---

[79] Warwick Bond, 'The Puzzle of *Cymbeline*', in *Studia Otiosa: Some Attempts in Criticism* (London: Constable, 1938), pp. 69–74. See his review of Irving's production, '*Cymbeline* at the Lyceum', *Fortnightly Review*, November 1896, pp. 635–47.

[80] Tillyard, *Shakespeare's Last Plays* (London: Chatto & Windus, 1938), pp. 2–3.

[81] Ibid., pp. 9–10.

behind their work lies 'a stock of romantic incident, the common property of the Jacobean age' (in updated critical parlance, Tillyard might be seen to be advocating an intertextual reading). He goes on to note that much of this material appears in the romance literature of the period, particularly in the work of Philip Sidney: 'We shall not understand what Shakespeare's contemporaries expected from the romantic material and the types of feeling they thought it capable of treating, unless we remember what they thought of *Arcadia*.' Tillyard argues for the importance of understanding the seriousness with which romance literature was regarded during the period:

> Sidney in writing *Arcadia* not only gave the romantic material a new popularity but, by treating this material with such academic correctness, immensely raised the whole status of the romance in the eyes of the Elizabethans and Jacobeans. The notion, so wide spread today, that Elizabethan drama dealt with life while Elizabethan romance escaped from it, is as alien to Elizabethan opinion as it should prove itself false to any modern who troubles to read *Arcadia* with sympathetic attention.[82]

Shakespeare, in using such romantic material, instead of Holinshed or Plutarch, did not necessarily seek to 'escape' or to be less serious: 'The "feigned" history he chose to draw on was taken quite as seriously by his contemporaries as the true history he abandoned.' This argument is in some ways similar to Lawrence's defence of the wager in *Cymbeline*. Both writers stress the cultural and historical differences between the Renaissance and the twentieth century which result in misconceptions about the 'seriousness' of the plays. Tillyard takes issue with Wilson Knight and D.G. James over the question of *Pericles*, writing that in using this play as a base on which to erect their symbolic interpretations, they 'are taking the gravest risks'.[83] It may have been 'the merest accident' that Shakespeare handled the Pericles story: 'As a seminal play, rich in undeveloped possibilities, we may heed it, but not as something embodying any fully formed experience in Shakespeare's mind.'

Tillyard believes that *Cymbeline* is the least successful of the late plays, that Shakespeare, writing in a new idiom, 'is as yet uncertain how to manipulate; in what proportions to blend the preponderatingly human treatment of character he used in the tragedies with the more symbolic treatment found generally in romance'.[84] He writes that Imogen 'is at times a human being, at times a Griselda of the medieval imagination' – a view which seems to echo Shaw. Tillyard also agrees with Granville-Barker's remarks about the sophisticated artlessness of the play but argues that 'these qualities do not account for the strenuousness that went to create Imogen and to write certain great scenes.' In *The Winter's Tale*, by comparison, Shakespeare more successfully separates out the symbolic

---

[82]   Ibid., pp. 11–12.

[83]   Ibid., p. 24.

[84]   Ibid., pp. 31–2.

and realistic elements; hence Hermione is 'the real woman', while Perdita is the symbol. He then compares the mixture of realism and symbolism in the late plays with D.H. Lawrence's method in *Women in Love*. Lawrence, in moving from realism to symbolism, 'shows the same process and the same confusion during the period of transition'.[85] One might disagree with Tillyard's judgements about *Women in Love*, which in spite, or because of its 'confusion' of idioms, is regarded today as one of Lawrence's finest works. Similarly, it does not necessarily follow that *Cymbeline* is less successful – on these particular grounds – than *The Winter's Tale*.

Returning to Granville-Barker's criticism of *Cymbeline*, Tillyard suggests that Granville-Barker may be wrong in limiting the play to a piece of technical sophistication:

> He says, 'Shakespeare has an unlikely story to tell,' and proceeds to explain, relying especially on the theatrical conditions, with what artifice he did the job. But to say 'Shakespeare has an unlikely story to tell' is to beg the main critical question. And this is: why did Shakespeare choose so unlikely a story? Or, more fully, why did Shakespeare take the trouble to go to three quite different originals, thus letting himself in for a dramatic task of extreme difficulty, which he can perform only by forfeiting the kind of dramatic probability which he normally accepted?[86]

This comment highlights the kind of limitation, noted before, in Granville-Barker's work both as a director and as a critic. He ignores questions of 'meaning', while devoting his attention primarily to questions of 'style'. For this reason, Granville-Barker seems to me to be a less important *interpreter* of the late plays than has often been supposed.

Tillyard is also responsive to the metatheatrical elements in the late plays, writing in detail about the theme of 're-enactment' in *The Tempest*. He is also perceptive in dealing with the masque, remarking on similarities between *The Tempest* and the plays of Pirandello. Furthermore, he appears to answer the criticism of Bridges, repudiating the view that Shakespeare 'was merely pleasing the fugitive and accidental tastes of his audience or was trying to escape more serious thoughts'. For Tillyard, 'It may indeed well be that he had in mind the growing taste for masques and spectacle; but no more in his last than in his previous plays did the public appetite, to which he certainly paid heed, compromise his personal, artistic necessities.'[87] Tillyard also stresses the tragic character of *The Tempest* (finding support in Dover Wilson). He writes that 'Antonio is one of Shakespeare's major villains.' How far removed this is from the serene play imagined by the Victorians.

Tillyard's study is notable for stressing both the realistic and the symbolic elements at work in the late plays. His is probably the most balanced study of

---

[85] Ibid., p. 36.
[86] Ibid., p. 70.
[87] Ibid., p. 60.

the late plays to appear during the period, drawing as it does on the wide variety of scholarship then available. His study is effectively a summing up and a development of earlier perspectives, acknowledging the insights of both the realistic and the symbolic views. For all this, his criticism is less revolutionary than Wilson Knight's, which must be regarded as the most provocative approach to the plays to emerge during this period.

Conclusion: Stage Performance and the Critical Traditions

The three important traditions of criticism of the late plays during the period might each be seen to have been inspired by the new traditions of theatre production. The formalist tradition was influenced by the 'modernist' idiom of Granville-Barker. Indeed, Granville-Barker is the central figure in the tradition, his criticism of *The Winter's Tale* and *Cymbeline* arising out of his own production methods, which stressed the artifice of *The Winter's Tale*. His production, although inspired by Poel, did not attempt to return the play to an Elizabethan historical context; rather, it accepted the play's ability to communicate directly to a modern audience. The assumption behind this method was that the play did not need explaining or historicising, that it was a dramatic entity which could be understood on its own terms, that the acting of the full text in a contemporary setting would automatically allow the play to communicate its own set of meanings. Granville-Barker believed in the autonomy of the text, that the play, if clearly presented, contained the key to its own interpretation. His criticism follows a similar pattern. Although greatly interested in the conventions of the Jacobean theatre, he directed this knowledge towards the question of the play's structure, of how the various elements of characterisation, action, verse, tragic and comic conventions, and the masque combine to produce the play's form, and of how a suitable style might be found for the play in the modern theatre. In stressing the artifice of the play, he removes it from the realm of realist-based criticism, placing it in the theatre and emphasizing Shakespeare's workmanship and artistry. This is an approach primarily concerned with questions of style and form made possible by twentieth-century theatricalism. In literary criticism, there are similarities between this approach and the tradition of New Criticism, with its close focus on the individual text, without reference to the historical, social or ideological context. However, the New Critics were primarily concerned with questions of meaning, symbolism and imagery, whereas Granville-Barker was not at all interested in the plays' symbolic meanings. His criticism is directed mainly at their dramaturgical structure and style.

The symbolic tradition focuses primarily on the mythological element in the plays – a tradition which has close connections with an anthropological interest in fertility symbolism, religious interpretations and what was to become a Jungian concern with the relationship between the symbolism of the plays and the collective unconscious. Here, the two main influences are Tree and Craig, influences which Wilson Knight himself acknowledged. Wilson Knight also suggested the possible influence of Tree's production of *The Tempest* on Colin Still's allegorical reading of the play, which examined the text in the light of initiation ceremonies.

The historicist tradition, best represented by the work of Tillyard, was anticipated by the productions of William Poel and the Elizabethan Stage Society. It is significant that the director whose work Tillyard mentions in his study of the late plays is Nugent Monck, who in the 1930s best exemplified the Poel tradition. Tillyard, more than Wilson Knight or Granville-Barker, was concerned with understanding the plays in their historical context – understanding the conventions of the plays not just from the perspective of the theatre, but in relation to romance literature and in relation to the ideas current during the age. He was of course influenced by both Wilson Knight and Granville-Barker, but the tradition which he represents is broader than either of theirs, and he is more eclectic in his approach. Hence, he is able to relate the plays to other works of literature, to Sidney's *Arcadia*, to Pirandello's drama, to Lawrence's novels. His approach is essentially comparative. Tillyard is also the critic most responsive to the metatheatrical element in the late plays, to questions about illusion and reality, recognising this as an important thematic and structural component of the works.

The production from which the beginning of this critical re-evaluation may be dated is Sir Henry Irving's *Cymbeline* in 1896. After the play had been neglected for many years, Irving's production stimulated critical interest and became a popular success. Ellen Terry played Imogen and her costumes (designed by Lawrence Alma-Tadema) became fashion items, echoing Wilde's view that life imitates art. Irving anticipated Strachey in his own portrayal of Iachimo, finding the tragic and sinister aspects of the character. The fairy-tale aspect of the play and its masque-like effect, while criticised by Archer and Shaw, influenced Henry James's more positive assessment. It was out of the dialectical argument set up by this production, between realistic criticism on the one hand and defences of the play's artifice and symbolism on the other, that later criticism developed. Edward Gordon Craig, who pioneered a symbolic approach to the production of Shakespeare (and influenced Wilson Knight), acted in Irving's *Cymbeline*; Granville-Barker saw the production and was influenced by it in his perception of artifice in the late plays. The original reviewers, including Shaw, James and R. Warwick Bond, all played a significant role in subsequent criticism of the late plays. Irving's production began the process which eventually led not only to emerging traditions of staging the late plays but also to the critical re-evaluation of the late plays as a group.

PART 3
Butler's Shakespeare Reconsidered

Chapter 7
Shakespeare's Dramatic Vision[1]

Guy Butler

I am going to attempt to say a very great deal in a very short space. Much of it may be 'old hat', but it is necessary for my argument. First, I shall make a few comments on neglected elements in Shakespeare's dramatic vision – a vision of the universe and the destiny of man which derives directly from the medieval Christian civilisation of which he and Milton were perhaps the last great literary exponents. This vision is much closer to that of St Augustine, Dante and Chaucer than it is to that of Marx or Freud or Shaw or Samuel Beckett. Second, I shall emphasise certain aspects of the Elizabethan theatre and some of the opportunities and limitations it offered to a dramatist attempting to express this vision. Third, I shall suggest certain obvious and less obvious dimensions of reading and performing a Shakespeare text – dimensions that producers and actors should attempt to project.

Readers of Shakespeare have been helped in recent years by studies of Shakespeare's background such as E.M.W. Tillyard's *The Elizabethan World Picture* and Walter Clyde-Curry's *Shakespeare's Philosophical Patterns*; what follows is indebted to works of this kind. Yet the generation of Curry and Tillyard could still assume that most readers knew the elements of the Christian doctrine of man, so that no explication of this seemed necessary. Judging from some recent critical works, however, and from the muddled paganism of many of my students, this assumption can no longer be made. Enlightened post-Christians, who still believe that the great works of the European past are worth studying, all need to be reminded of this Christian scheme from time to time – particularly when writers like Jan Kott believe that they are doing Shakespeare some sort of a favour by calling him our contemporary – as if it were a great honour to be dragged from the pinnacle of the English Renaissance to paddle with us in the 'filthy modern tide'.[2]

I believe that it can be demonstrated that Shakespeare accepted, with improved Renaissance amplifications, the great medieval synthesis or myth. For all our achievements since, we have not managed to replace it. We live in a fragmenting cosmos.

'Had we but World enough and Time', cries Andrew Marvell to his coy mistress. There is never enough world and never enough time for man, because

---

[1]   'Shakespeare's Dramatic Vision' was delivered as a lecture c. 1978.

[2]   See Jan Kott, *Shakespeare Our Contemporary* (London: Methuen, 1967), and W.B. Yeats's poem 'The Statues'.

of his divine origins and his infinite appetites; 'the desire is boundless and the act a slave to limit' (*Troilus and Cressida*, 3.2.90). Let us remind ourselves of the Elizabethan sense of World and Time: if each individual life is subject to limits, so is the very world itself. One of the major efforts twentieth century man has to make is to recapture the 'feel' of medieval cosmology in regard to Space and Time.

First, Time. At some stage in the past, before time began, there was war in heaven – a war to which I will return. One of the results of this war was the creation of the world, that is, the natural world composed of the elements of earth, air, fire and water. This event, according to Archbishop Ussher, took place at 9 am in 4,004 BC. The 'great while ago [when] the world began' about which Feste sings in *Twelfth Night* (5.2.425) was, to the Elizabethans, some 5,600 years before; the world was moving towards its end, which could be expected at any time, and almost certainly within the next 4,000 years – at which point, as Prospero says,

> The cloud-capped towers, the gorgeous palaces,
> The solemn temples, the great globe itself,
> Yea, all which it inherit, shall dissolve,
> And like this insubstantial pageant faded
> Leave not a rack behind.
>
> (*The Tempest*, 5.1.148–52)

Of course, scientists now estimate the age of planet Earth at around 4,600 million years.

Next, Space (or World). For Shakespeare and his contemporaries, all things begin and end in God, in the realm of divine spirit. God is ultimately unknowable – although we can learn about him by studying two main books, the Book of Nature and Holy Writ. In Him all paradoxes are ultimately solved. Creation is of very short duration and in the Christian vision it has, like an Aristotelian drama, a beginning, a middle and an end. Christians live between the middle and the end. Creation or nature as God's handiwork is good, marvellous, glorious; indeed to read in the book of nature as Prospero does is to get closer to understanding His mind. But nature has been wrenched from its perfect function by the Fall of Adam and the entire human race into sin. Old-fashioned as the notion of sin has become, I am afraid we cannot avoid its importance in Shakespeare's thinking; in fact it is absolutely central, far more central to a proper understanding of his dramatic vision than 'order' or 'degree'. Here it will be valuable to glance at the first sins, which form the paradigm for all that is to follow.

The first sin takes place in heaven in the realm of the spirit. Lucifer commits the great sin of pride, of revolt against the Committee of Heaven. His sin is essentially one of self-love. This results in the cosmic disaster, war in heaven, the expulsion of the rebel angels and the establishment of hell in opposition to heaven. Hell is the home of pride, envy, hatred and malice, the home of Iago, by which he swears (*Othello*, 2.3.310). Only later are the fleshly sins of lust, gluttony and sloth added to these.

The second great paradigm is of equal importance. Man is fashioned of the dust of the earth, yet in the image of God himself. His double nature is everywhere apparent in Shakespeare: we can understand neither Hamlet's disillusionment nor Cassio's chivalrous devotion to Desdemona unless we recapture this sense of mankind's divine origins. Upon man God bestowed countless gifts; let us briefly consider two – love and freedom.

All Shakespeare's plays deal with love and its enemies. Love between man and woman, parent and child, brother and sister. One of the first steps in studying any Shakespearean play, in my view, is to examine the family relationships involved. In general, his comedies deal with the triumph of love, the establishment of new families, 'the more the merrier' – while his tragedies always involve the agonised destruction or disintergration of a family or families due to some failure or defeat of love. The family is man's greatest, most joyful and most difficult achievement. It is the chief garden in which nature and nurture collaborate, in which the flowers of grace may grow. Destroy it and you destroy man. Wherever there is a garden, however, there is a damned serpent (as we hear in *Hamlet*: ''Tis given out that, sleeping in my orchard / a serpent stung me', 1.5.35–6). It was the love between Adam and Eve, their mutual trust and fulfilment, that filled Lucifer with envy and shame. Love is an assault on Satan, an intolerable insult to self-lovers like Iago.

The other gift of God is freedom: freedom of choice, and for the right exercise of choice we are given reason and love. Freedom involves risk, a real choice between good and evil. It is through choice that we not merely reveal our characters but in some degree make them. Satan tempts Eve through an appeal to her vanity; Adam fails because he loves Eve more than he loves God. His reason is fogged by his passion. This opposition between reason and passion, judgement and blood, patience and rage, runs through play after play. The consequences of choice for the individual and his/her descendants are profound and far-reaching. Hence, moments of choice and decision are of prime importance in our lives and the lives of our families and nations. Man's soul becomes a battleground for the forces of good and evil; he lives with eternal consequences as well as temporal consequences suspended over his head.

What was Shakespeare's view of history *after* the Fall?

In the first great period of history man is a creature whose only God is nature and his imperfect understanding of an obedience to her laws. The next great period is ushered in by written law, the great law of Moses. It was believed that at about the same time all over the world societies received written laws, which in their essentials were similar to those of Moses. Written law was given to assist mankind: 'Human statute purged the gentle weal' (*Macbeth*, 3.4.77). These written laws did not outdate the laws of nature, however, but supplemented them. With the development of statutes, a vastly more complex type of life had emerged – what we call 'civilisation', what Shakespeare would call 'nurture'. Between the life of nature and of nurture there develops an increasing distance and tension. Adherents to either are subject to error and excess – many a Shakespeare play demonstrates man's need for both. The action starts in a court, is moved to a forest, or to a sheep shearing, or to an island full of noises, before returning back to Athens or Bohemia or Milan.

Yet neither the unwritten laws of nature nor the written laws of societies – the 'moral laws / Of nature and of nations' to which Hector refers in *Troilus and Cressida* (2.2.184–5) – prove adequate to the human situation. It becomes clear that strict justice, the application of the lex talionis (an eye for an eye and a tooth for a tooth), is too demanding. As Hamlet observes, 'Use every man after his desert, and who shall 'scape whipping?' (2.2.541). So God tempers justice with mercy, and the great transformation of primitive sacrifice into moral generosity and self-giving begins to emerge: forgiveness, that is, giving up or giving away what would seem to be yours by right, in the course of love, devotion or duty. The great debate between the old written law and the new law of mercy is central to an understanding of plays like *The Merchant of Venice* and *Measure for Measure*. There are countless scenes of forgiveness and reconciliation in Shakespeare, usually near the ends of plays: 'Exchange forgiveness with me, noble Hamlet,' as Laertes cries at his death (*Hamlet*, 5.2.340).

This spiritual evolution reaches its climax with the Incarnation, the central act, the climax, the hinge of all time and history, in which God, assuming human form, gives himself into the power of the world – to provide man not with a written law, but a living model of behaviour. This incursion of the Divine into time and into the world marks the arrival of grace: but there are many signs of grace before the Incarnation, forshadowings of its advent, as Shakespeare shows in those plays set in pre-Christian historical periods. Take *Antony and Cleopatra*, for instance:

> CLEO: If it be love indeed, tell me how much?
>
> ANT: There's beggary in the love that can be reckoned.
>
> CLEO: I'll set a bourne how far to be loved.
>
> ANT: Then must thou needst find out new heaven, new earth.
>
> (1.1.14–17)

Another fine example from the same play is Antony's action in sending his treasure after the deserter, Enobarbus. These 'Heavens of Grace' are everywhere in Shakespeare, nowhere more notably than in the darkest of tragedies, *King Lear*. Cordelia, Edgar and Kent are all people who – in spite of appalling wrongs done to them – continue to seek the good of those who have injured them. They are governed by something more then the principle of Justice. The effects of gracious behaviour are incalculable. Hamlet's open and generous apology to Horatio leads to Laertes's confession of the plot and to the exposure of Claudius in full court, which enables Hamlet not merely to assassinate the King as if in a blood feud, but to execute him as the criminal he is now proved to be.

There is another kind of grace in Shakespeare: the grace transforming power into beauty. Influenced in due course by that strong platonic strain of medieval and

Renaissance thought, Shakespeare saw in the superlatively beautiful a reminder that the Divine dimension is a powerful force, as much as in the superlatively moral.

I have remarked that this universe, this world and time, is limited. The end of it all was one of the great themes of medieval art and meditation: the day of Doom, the Last Judgement. The whole world of space and time was moving towards that event. All men would be judged according to the true record by a Judge to whom all desires are known and from whom no secrets are hid. Two of the most popular books of the late sixteenth and early seventeenth centuries were Jeremy Taylor's *Holy Living* and *Holy Dying*. It was not important merely to live well, but to make a good death. This accounts for the outrage felt by Hamlet senior at the manner of his death. It also sets strict limits to human justice. Earthly judges and executors must give people, found guilty according to human laws, a chance to make their peace with God before they die. So Othello, before he kills Desdemona, asks her 'Have you prayed tonight? ... I would not kill thy Soul' (*Othello*, 5.2.24–32) and, in *Measure for Measure*, we have the delightful comedy in the prison (4.3) when the reprobate and rogue Barnardine, who is due for execution, is let off the hook because he stoutly claims that he has a terrible hangover and is in no fit state to make his peace with God.

Nature and grace are full of reminders of renewal: the perpetuation of a race through the processes of mating, birth, ageing and death; the death and resurrection of the world itself. The former need little comment; we are fully aware of the miraculous recreations of life. We are less conscious of the mysterious workings of grace, which touch even Edmund in *Lear*. Grace usually becomes available only after insight, repentance and purpose of amendment. So, for all their severe pre-occupation with judgement, Elizabethans felt their lives to be full of chances of renewal and redemption (awe-inspiring as life under judgement might be, it is filled with hope). They were assured on two counts: the universe is just and makes moral sense; and the universe is full of mercy, of renewals, of fresh beginnings, of rescuing and redeeming operations. The amount of justice and the amount of mercy necessary would be determined by the behaviour of the people involved. I believe that we find the operations of justice and mercy in all of Shakespeare's plays.

For Shakespeare these three dispensations – of Nature, Law and Grace – operate in all societies. This does not mean to say that all societies are the same. Shakespeare was acutely conscious of how very different societies could be, and that in some, grace had very little chance of operating. The great indictment of the city of Rome in *Coriolanus* is that both nature and grace are inhibited by the distorted nurture of the city. Volumnia, Coriolanus's mother, is nature perverted. Coriolanus's wife, Virgilia – the one morally sensitive person in the play – has no scope in such a world. In his noble, if limited, manner Coriolanus recognises this when he calls her 'my gracious silence' (*Coriolanus*, 2.1.171). Shakespeare judges men and whole societies by their response to the three great bonds; he was at pains to depict their application in different societies, and did so with astonishing success.

These bonds are not for the mere creation, man, but are also the intimate concern of God (or the gods). What happens on this little 'O', the earth, is of vital concern to the heavens, to supernatural beings. It is essential, when studying Shakespeare, to try to recapture this sense of supernatural participation in human affairs. The degree and type of involvement varies enormously from play to play: Oberon and Titania and the fairies in *A Midsummer Night's Dream*; the wide range of ghosts, from the sequence in *Richard III* to the dead king in *Hamlet* to Banquo in *Macbeth*; witches, cosmic storms, earthquakes, omens, perplexities and terrible courses fulfilled; oracles of Apollo consulted and the god angered; the strange music of Caliban's island in *The Tempest* and the goddesses appearing at the wedding of Ferdinand and Miranda; the fickle goddess fortune turning her wheel; the planetory influence on mortals.

***

Now let us turn to Shakespeare's theatres, the instruments he inherited from the Middle Ages – first the medieval theatre in the round, with its central staging; second the circular London theatres, consisting of tiers or galleries enclosing a space into which the main stage thrust itself forward. This provided the dramatist with at least three acting levels: the main stage, the inner stage on the same level and one or more upper stages. There were trapdoors through the main stage and, in later theatres, flying devices suspended from what was known as 'the heavens'. So we have nether regions below the stage, from which the agents of hell can appear; the main stage itself to represent the world; and the upper stages for God or his deputies on earth, like kings, and the heavens appointed with the signs of the zodiac. We notice too that much of the audience looked down on the action like gods. The whole theatre is circular in shape, a wooden 'O', an unroofed building open to the skies – a fact of incalculable importance. A gesture under the open sky is likely to be very different from one made in a drawing room. Drama seems to lose a certain cosmic and elemental force once it takes place in a roofed building; too much nurture, no reminder of great nature, let alone the heavenly audience.

Let us consider briefly some of Shakespeare's reminders of the very old comparison between the world and the stage. The most famous is from *As You Like It*: 'All the world's a stage, / And all the men and women, merely players ...' (2.7.88ff). Here the stage simply *is* the world – but in the following quotation from *Macbeth*, what happens on the stage of the world clearly calls for a response from the cosmos: 'Thou seest, the heavens, as troubled with man's act / Threaten his bloody stage' (2.4.5–6). In *Pericles* we see a conscious appeal to the heavenly audience: 'Oh you powers / That give heaven countless eyes to view men's acts' (1.1.72–3). This heavenly audience is not emotionally detached from the spectacle on the stage of the world, as we learn in *Measure for Measure*: 'man, proud man! / Dressed in a little, brief authority ... Plays such fantastic tricks before high heaven / As makes the angels weep' (2.2.118–23). Over the topmost tier of the Globe theatregoers, we are to imagine tier upon tier of angelic spectators.

Shakespeare was, of course, aware of the limitations of his instrument, as the opening chorus to *Henry V* shows; but he was supremely fortunate to have inherited a stage and audience accustomed to seeing the war of the mighty kingdoms of hell and heaven contending for man's soul on 'unworthy scaffolds' (Prologue.10), an audience for whom drama was not merely a matter of life and death but a dimension of salvation. So the substitution of the houses of York and Lancaster, or of England and France, or of Rome and Egypt, was not an impossible demand on their credulity. He also knew that he could, at any moment, by the apt choice of an image, surround his historical action with the old ambience of eternal judgement and mercy. (The religious dimensions of *Henry V* have not been adequately explored; that play is, I believe, Shakespeare's reply to Marlowe's *Tamburlaine*.)

Let us now turn from the cosmos or the universe of the actor, to the actor himself. 'I think the King is but a man as I am. His ceremonies laid by, in his nakedness he appears but a man,' says Henry, disguised as a common soldier (4.1.101). Later he discourses upon ceremony, relating it to the symbolical clothing that a king wears:

'Tis not the balm, the scepter, and the ball,
The sword, the mace, the crown imperial,
The intertissued robe of gold and pearl,
The farced title running 'fore the King
The throne he sits on, nor nor the tide of pomp
That beats upon the high shore of this world.

(4.1.258–63)

I quote this to remind you that the actor has three main instruments with which to serve the dramatist: his body (in its nakedness or clothed), gestures, movements, postures; his costume, which is always more-or-less symbolic; and of course his voice. Shakespeare was a master at exploiting all three, and his plays abound in evidence of his professional understanding of these matters. Many of his greatest moments are non-verbal. He uses sounds besides those of the human voice, and a glance at the scene in *Macbeth* in which Duncan is murdered shows that he also knew the power of silence. There is electrifying stage direction in *Coriolanus*: '*holds her hand silent*' (5.3.183).

Any reader or viewer of *Antony and Cleopatra* or *King Lear* cannot fail to be impressed by the symbolic changes of costume, but we will fail to understand their significance unless we achieve (or are given) a proper understanding of the text. I propose to end, therefore, with some very simplified pieces of advice to producers and to actors as to how to 'read' a Shakespearean play.

First, accept Aristotle's definition of a play as an imitation of an *action* that has a beginning and a middle and an end. What is the *time* of the play? What is the world or *space* of the play? What action has to be concluded before its allotted time is spent? What kind of a judgement is there on the action at the end of the play? Try and define the 'right' and 'wrong' choices, the mistakes or the crimes, the retributions, the reconciliations that take place. Having mastered the story, mark the climaxes, the peaks of excitement, tension, horror, joy, relief and so on. The whole strategy of play-making is determined by the playwright's need to build towards these climactic moments, to exploit their results and to move to a conclusion. Second, study each scene to see how it advances the action; what decision is reached during its course; what choices are made? Debate, discussions and soliloquies are most revealing if looked at in this way. Third, pay particular attention to all verbal references to actions performed by the actor's body, and all references to props. For instance, the crown in *Richard II* is the great prop of the deposition scene, but long before we arrive at this scene the crown appears many times in the text. Cleopatra commits suicide with the aid of an asp, but long before she does this there are several references to serpents in the text; Antony commits suicide on his sword, but long before he does this his sword has come to symbolise his soldier's honour. And so we could go on. Much of the imagery in the poetry relates to the props, to parts of the actor's body (for example, hands in *Macbeth*) and to costume. If the action is the heart of the play, much of the imagery in the poetry prepares us for it and exploits it.

There is, however, another important source of imagery: the action in a Shakespeare play always takes place within a most carefully constructed universe of beliefs and values. The dramatist sets his action not only geographically and historically but also in a clearly defined world or metaphysical system. It is my belief that Shakespeare, by the time he wrote *Othello*, was acutely aware of the manner in which his heroes and heroines were either given scope or limited by the universes they chose or inherited. His greatness in character creation has been fully acknowledged; his ability to create distinct worlds for his characters to inhabit has not. It is from the tensions between characters and their worlds, quite as much as between the characters themselves, that his tragic dramas take their power. In *Macbeth* there are many images that place us clearly in the medieval Christian universe – not only the many religious references but also those deriving from the great chain of being. Perhaps the commonest sort of image springs into existence in the mouth of the actor in his attempts to relate his actions to his universe. To demonstrate briefly and crudely: in *Macbeth*, a king is killed at midnight; he is old and he is innocent. That is plot, a rare history that could nonetheless happen in a dozen societies or ages. But the moment he is called 'gracious', or 'the Lord's anointed temple' (2.3.68), the action has been placed in a specific religious and political universe. An attack on God's deputy on earth is not a mere political murder, but an assault on the divine order of the cosmos as well: the murder is 'most sacrilegious' (67), blasphemous evil. Shakespeare must somehow invest the bare circumstances of a plot with the appropriate resonances. How does he do this? Most striking, of course, is his transformation of Holinshed's Weird Sisters from 'goddesses of destine, or else some nymphs or faeiries' into Macbeth's witches, repulsive and malign agents of hell and confusion.[3] (The play opens with the ominous non-verbal image of thunder – the witches' signature tune.)

---

[3]   See 'The Chronicle of King Duncan' in Raphael Holinshed's *Chronicle of Scotland* (1587).

Let us take two other examples of a more restricted kind. One of the essential circumstances of the action is the time of the murder. With archetypal appropriateness, this simple temporal detail is converted into a symbol of the morally dark nature of the deed. Well before the night of the murder descends, Lady Macbeth invokes night (as the ancient ally of hell) to hide the projected deed from heaven – and, most significantly, from herself:

> Come, thick night,
> And pall thee in the dunnest smoke of Hell,
> That my keen knife see not the wound it makes,
> Nor heaven peep through the blanket of the dark,
> To cry 'Hold, Hold!'
>
> (1.5.46–50)

The place that is to be enveloped by the dunnest smoke of hell is, of course, Macbeth's castle. We first see it from the outside as sunlit, as having a pleasant seat, as providing resting places for temple-haunting martlets. But once the deed has been done, it is transformed into a lively image of hell itself by the drunken porter. Glynne Wickham has pointed out, conclusively I think, that the porter scene is a parody of one of the Corpus Christi plays, 'The Harrowing of Hell', in which Christ hammers on the infernal gates and throws the demons and the guilty into terror and panic.[4] Hell was presented on the medieval stage as a combination of a castle and a dragon. So both the time of the murder and the place of the murder have been located imaginatively in hell, or, shall we say, have become subject to hell as a result of the prayers and actions of the protagonists and the witches. Note, however, whose words have done this placing: those of Lady Macbeth and the totally uninvolved porter. There is an unconscious collusion of the characters, major and minor, to use words and images that keep placing the action firmly between hell and heaven.

In conclusion: Shakespeare's theatre, although it exploited spectacle for many purposes, was not dominated by the eye; the passion for visual realism had not yet triumphed and pushed the action behind the proscenium arch and a picture-frame stage. Shakespeare's theatre was still a symbolic instrument for projecting the interior struggles of the soul. The little worlds of men and the times of the actions of these plays are significant because, like the world itself, like the time itself, they contain histories that are also moral and spiritual pilgrimages towards the divine. Keats remarked that Shakespeare sought the world of soul-making. Our secular society needs to be reminded of the nimbus, the potential halo, the grace and the glory which quivers and sometimes shines with a supernatural authority in certain scenes. To project this, the actor needs to give the full range of his/her body, mind and soul to the task of interpreting and projecting the meaning of the words – to

---

[4]   See Glynne Wickham, *The Medieval Theatre* (Cambridge: Cambridge University Press, 1974).

be as fully articulate as possible. Yeats was enraged by the impoverishment of theatrical range, the dwarfing of the dimensions of man inflicted upon the theatre by naturalism and realism. I end, then, with the final stanza from his poem 'The Old Stone Cross':

> But actors lacking music
> Do most excite my spleen,
> They say it is more human
> To shuffle, grunt and groan,
> Not knowing what unearthly stuff
> Rounds a mighty scene ...

Chapter 8
Shakespeare, Daniel and Augustus Caesar: Kingdoms in *Antony and Cleopatra*[1]

Guy Butler

1.

> In those days the Emperor Augustus decreed that the whole world should be enrolled.
>
> —Luke 2:1

Any person wishing to write about *Antony and Cleopatra* encounters certain major difficulties of interpretation. It is not such a puzzle as, say, *Hamlet*, but more of a puzzle than *Macbeth* or *Coriolanus*. Before we say of the work of so great a master as Shakespeare, 'He was nodding, like Homer' – or, worse, 'The ambiguity and lack of clear focus is intentional' – before we resort to excuses, we should ask ourselves: is it possible that a shift in attitude between his age and ours is responsible? Was Shakespeare taking certain things for granted (such as traditional ways of looking at important historical events and figures), which have since slipped out of focus owing to a change in the lens of the beholder?

Antony and Cleopatra are overcome by Octavius. He is their antagonist. What sort of a man is he? What does he stand for? If we look at the play alone, we have precious little material to go on. He is on the stage for 14 of the total 42 scenes – in other words, for less than one third of the playing time is he before our eyes. Yet his presence is felt in almost every scene. Unlike Antony and Cleopatra, he is not much discussed. The references to his character are brief and, when they come from Antony and Cleopatra, unforgivable, or from Enobarbus, satirical. As a piece of characterisation, he is inconsistent, and not at all dynamic or attractive. He does not rank among Shakespeare's great character creations. This is remarkable, because in most other plays, the antagonists are very carefully and vividly drawn: Claudius in *Hamlet*, Iago in *Othello*, the villains in *Lear*, Banquo and Macduff in *Macbeth*, Aufidius in *Coriolanus*. Nor has he been fully characterised in his earlier appearance in *Julius Caesar*, as Henry V had been as Hal in the *Henry IV* plays. It therefore is worth asking: is he a partially allegorical figure, rather like the enigmatic Duke in *Measure for Measure*? A stock figure, whose main traits

---

[1]   This is a collated version of two lectures: 'Shakespeare and Augustus Caesar' and 'The Defeat of Antony, the Four Kingdoms of Daniel, and Astral Portents', delivered c. 1978.

were known and largely determined by his place within an ancient and popular tradition? In other words, was Shakespeare relying, to some extent at least, on an automatic response to his name alone? And, being the expert at theatrical economies and shortcuts that he was, he did not waste time – but only modified and departed from that stock figure when his theme demanded it?

There were several stock dramatic figures in existence in the popular Elizabethan mind that have since died, such as the various vices of the old morality plays and figures from the miracle plays – most notably Herod of Jewry, to whom Shakespeare refers eight times in his plays, five times in *Antony and Cleopatra*. This repeated reference to Herod may be significant. Herod, as we know, slaughtered the innocents: he was a bloody, raging tyrant, addicted to rant and tearing passions to tatters. He was one of the group of monarchs who formed a fateful historical constellation round the cradle at Bethlehem, as dramatised in the miracle plays. Octavius Caesar was another such. This, I think, is the important point. Antony and Cleopatra were not given extensive story treatment in the Middle Ages, nor were they put on stage until shortly before Shakespeare's time: they were a Renaissance 'find', as it were. Octavius, on the other hand, *was* an extremely popular medieval figure – indeed, it is likely that he was the best known Roman after Pilate – depicted in stained glass windows, murals, poems and on the popular medieval stage. He is a commonplace of later medieval Christian art.

This medieval Octavius stands behind Shakespeare's, his cosmic power and temporal function well known to Shakespeare and his audience. To understand Octavius we need to recall some medieval historiography, in particular the way it interpreted Roman history. A good starting point is provided by R.G. Collingwood in *The Idea of History*:

> Any history written on Christian principles will be of necessity universal, providential, apocalyptical and periodised.
>
> *Universal*: it will be universal history, or history of the world, going back to the origin of men. It will describe how the various races of men came into existence, and peopled the various habitable parts of the earth. Graeco-Roman ecumenical history is not universal in this sense, because it has a particular centre of gravity. Greece or Rome is the centre round which it revolves. Christian universal history has undergone a Copernican revolution, whereby the very idea of such a centre of gravity is destroyed.
>
> *Providential*: It will ascribe events not to their human agents, but the workings of Providence preordaining their course.
>
> ...
>
> *Apocalyptic*: It will set itself to detect an intelligible pattern in this general course of events, and in particular it will attach a central importance in this pattern to the historical life of Christ, which is clearly one of the preordained features of the pattern. It will make its narrative crystallise itself round that event, and treat earlier events as leading up to it or preparing for it, and subsequent events as developing its consequences. It will therefore divide history at the birth of Christ into two parts, each having a particular and unique character of its own: the first, a forward-looking character, consisting in blind preparation for an event not yet

revealed; the second a backward-looking character depending on the fact that the revelation has been made. A history thus divided into two periods, a period of darkness and a period of light, I shall call apocalyptic history.

Periodical: having divided the past in two, it will thus naturally tend to subdivide again; and thus to distinguish other events, not so important as the birth of Christ, but important in their way, which make everyone after them different in quality from what went before. Thus history is divided into epochs, each marked off from the one before it by an event which in the technical language of this kind of historiography is called epoch-making.[2]

Now it seems to me that these paragraphs accurately describe Shakespeare's view of history, not only in this play, but all his plays; yet in no play is it so evident as in *Antony and Cleopatra*, because he never touched on a subject so epoch-making as this. The victory of Octavius over Antony and Cleopatra is the necessary prelude to the birth of Christ – in its turn, the most epoch-making of all events in time.

Octavius's victory was epoch-making from the Roman point of view, too, as anyone with even superficial knowledge of Roman history (like myself) will know. It put an end to the disastrous civil wars, and established an imperial system. Moreover, it brought practically the entire world under one government: not since Alexander the Great had one man's sway or renown reached so far. But most important, it was central to a view of history propounded by a poet who was to wield enormous influence on the mind of medieval Europe: Virgil. He made the Cumaean Sibyl foretell the peaceful reign of Augustus; he also wrote an eclogue which foretold the birth of a marvellous child, who for centuries was taken to be Christ. Virgil, for those and other reasons, was 'Christianised', listed as one of the three pagan prophets.

The victory of Octavius over Antony and Cleopatra was important to a very different group as well – the early Church Fathers. They looked at the emergence of Rome as necessary and preordained by God, but there was a serious difference in their viewpoint, and to explain this we have to look a little more closely into the *periodic* presuppositions of their historical thinking. This lands us in the lap of a national poet and prophet very different from Roman Virgil – the Hebrew Daniel. How do Virgil and Daniel become brother prophets of the same great event: the emergence of Rome as a world power? Charles Homer Haskins notes,

Christian Europe, far down into modern times, took its philosophy of history from Augustine and its chronological system from Eusebius ... as heirs to both the classical and Jewish tradition, the early Christian historians faced the task of combining and co-ordinating two histories which had grown up in entire independence of each other. The effort to reduce to a common denominator the materials found in the Roman historians and the Old Testament was in the first instance a question of chronology, which the cannons of Eusebius of Caesarea solved for subsequent Christian Ages ... St. Augustine added to this the theory

---

[2]   R.G. Collingwood, *The Idea of History* (Oxford: Oxford University Press, 1956), p. 49.

of the Six Ages of the World. In the pages of Orosius, who wrote his *Seven Books Against the Pagans* in AD 417, the sixth age coincided with the Roman Empire, the last of the four monarchies in the vision of the prophet Daniel, so that the persistence of Rome was assured until the end of all things earthly. The complement of all was Augustine's distinction between the earthly city of Rome which would pass away and the eternal city of all the faithful, the city not made of hands, invisible in the Heavens, whose builder and maker is God. Thenceforth Christendom had its philosophy of history, turned away from the world that now is fixed on the world to come, and this dualism of thought dominates the Middle Ages.[3]

A glance at Daniel and his four kingdoms is helpful, particularly if one looks at that version of the Bible which we believe Shakespeare used (the Bishop's Bible) and note the rubrics and marginal glosses which provide the then-accepted historical interpretation of his prophesies. In a synopsis of the book ('The Argument') we read,

> Daniel above all others had most special revelations of such things as should come to the church, even from the time they were in captivitie, to the last end of the world, and to the generall resurrection, as of the four Monarchies and empires of the world, to wit, of the Babylonians, Persians, Grecians, and Romans. Also *the certain number of the times* even unto Christ.[4]

Then, in Daniel 2:31–5:

> O King, thou sawest, and behold there was a great image: this great image whose glory was so excellent, stoode before thee, and the forme thereof was terrible. This image's head was of finest gold, his breast and armes of silver, his bellie and thighs of brasse, His legges of yron, and his feet were part of yron, and part of clay. Thou beheldest it till a stone was cut without handes, which smote the image upon his feete, that were of yron and clay, and brake them to pieces. Then was the yron, the clay, the brasse, the silver and the golde broken all together, and became like the chaffe of the sommer floures, and the winde caried them away, that no place was founde for them: and the stone that smote the image, became a great mountaine, and filled the whole earth.

These lines are glossed:

---

[3]   Haskins, *The Renaissance of the Twelfth Century* (Cambridge, MA: Harvard University Press, 1955), p. 227. This is, arguably, the view of Cleopatra herself at the end of the play.

[4]   Bishop's Bible (Bib. Eng. 1591 & 1. Bodleian Library), *The Bible*, Christopher Bankes, 1589. See also the introduction to the book of Daniel in the Bishop's Bible (Bib. Eng. 1588 dl, Bodley): 'Daniel, above all other, had most speciall revelations of such things as shoulde come upon the Church, even from the time that they were in captivitie, to the last ende of all the world, and to the general] resurrection, as of the foure Monarchies and empires of al [*sic*] the world, to wit, of the Babylonians, Persians, Grecians and Romans.'

By golde, silver, brasse and yron are meant the Chaldean, Persian, Macedonian and Roman Kingdomes, which should successively rule all the world till Christ (which is here called the stone) come himself, and destroy the last, and this was to assure the Jewes that their affliction should not end with the empire of the Chaldeans, but that they should patiently abide the coming of the Messiah, which should be at the end of this fourth Monarchie.

This doctrine of the four monarchies dominated historical writing far into the seventeenth century. Newton accepted it, and there are traces of it in Gibbon himself.

In medieval history, the most epoch-making events are those which mark the end of one kingdom and the beginning of another. Such an event was the defeat of Darius by Alexander the Great, which marked the end of the Persian Kingdom, and the arrival of the Greek or Macedonian Kingdom. And *Antony and Cleopatra* is concerned with the Roman conquest of the heirs of the Macedonian Empire – the entire 'near East'. Let us remember that Cleopatra is a Ptolemy, a descendant of one of Alexander's heirs, and that in identifying himself with her, Antony becomes the last champion of the falling kingdom, and Augustus the first king of the new kingdom. (Some would give the honour to Julius Caesar.) Medieval writers differed as to the exact moment when the fall of the old kingdom took place – some placed it at the death of Antony, some at the death of Cleopatra.[5] Shakespeare favoured the former. As Antony lies dying, the soldiers form themselves into a little chorus and cry: 'The star is fall'n / And time is at his period' (4.14.6–7). I can find no other explanation for these words than this.

We saw that Daniel's great image had feet of clay; we saw, too, what Augustine thought of the city of Rome. But it is something of a surprise to hear Antony, in the first scene of the play, state that 'Kingdoms are clay' (when he is teased by Cleopatra into snubbing the ambassadors from Rome):

Let Rome in Tiber melt, and the wide arch
Of the ranged empire fall! Here is my space.
Kingdoms are clay. Our dungy earth alike
Feeds beast as man. The nobleness of life
Is to do thus –

(1.1.33–7)

He then embraces her. In hyperbolic language he has condemned the world's greatest city, the extent of whose power is evoked by a grand architectural image, to dissolution and collapse into water, clay and dungy earth. All the space he needs and claims is that on which he and Cleopatra can embrace. Yet he is not embracing Cleopatra only but also the whole of Egypt. This public erotic gesture is reckless and prophetic. In the course of the play, the lovers' 'space' is taken from them,

---

5   See John Leeds Barroll, *Shakespeare and Roman History* (Princeton: Princeton University Press, 1956), p. 331.

raising the question: does the 'nobleness of life' continue when the space belongs to Caesar, the 'universal landlord' (3.13.72)?

A little earlier in the opening scene Antony has claimed, again in hyperbolic language, that love is not subject to mundane measurement. The heroine challenges him with reductive questions and gets transcendent answers.

CLEO: If it be love indeed, tell me how much.

ANT: There's beggary in the love that can be reckoned.

CLEO: I'll set a bourn how far to be beloved.

ANT: Then must thou needs find out new heaven, new earth.

(1.1.14–17)

This prophetic juxtaposition of a new heaven and a new earth has a long and prominent biblical ancestry (e.g., Isaiah 65:17, 2 Peter 3:13 and particularly Revelation 21:1). There is a substantial Elizabethan and Jacobean literature interpreting contemporary astral and other events as portents of doomsday – the Day of Judgement, and of the inauguration of the new heaven and new earth. A good example is Samuel Gardiner's 1606 *Doomes-Day Book or An Alarum for Atheists, A Watchword for Worldings, A Caveat for Christians*. In the third chapter, while he concedes 'the uncertain and unknowne time of the world's end', he asserts that 'it is not far off we are sure.'[6] Antony's 'new heaven, new earth' would have woken religious echoes in many of the Bible-saturated Jacobean audience. Ethel Seaton has argued convincingly that 'the undertones of Revelation, like sunken bells under the tide, surge and swell through the poetry' of the play.[7] Paul Cantor refers at some length to discussions of the 'puzzling Biblical allusions in Antony and Cleopatra' – most forays into this field seem to justify his concluding remarks:

> One could go on uncovering Biblical allusions in *Antony and Cleopatra*, but these are enough to make the point that Shakespeare may be trying to remind us of what was happening contemporaneously with the Roman drama he unfolded, a drama on another plane that was soon to eclipse in importance the history of Rome, or at least turn it in a new direction.[8]

There would be little point in revealing further biblical allusions merely to reinforce Cantor's general observation. But the recollection of a yet-to-be-performed, well-known event in the Christian gospels, by throwing a contrasting light on

---

[6]   Gardiner, *Doomes-Day Book or An Alarum for Atheists, A Watchword for Worldings, A Caveat for Christians* (London: E White, 1606), p. 15.

[7]   Seaton, '*Antony and Cleopatra* and the Book of Revelation', *Review of English Studies* 22 (1946): p. 222.

[8]   Cantor, *Shakespeare's Rome: Republic and Empire* (Ithaca: Cornell University Press, 1976), p. 221.

an analogous pre-Christian scene, can be both moving and illuminating. Andrew Fichter's comment on the doomed Antony's invitation to his companions to serve him at a final gaudy night (4.2.9–45) leads to a valuable critical suggestion:

> Antony here begins the imaginative revision of Plutarch's narrative that Christianity will eventually complete. Antony's language, that is, contains logical and visual discrepancies that cannot be resolved in terms accessible to the world of the play, but which become meaningful in the context of a future discourse [the Last Supper]. The hermeneutic method which Antony and Cleopatra asks us to adopt is one that implies the inadequacy of the knowledge available in the dramatic present to unlock the enigmas of the text.[9]

In the section that follows, I will attempt to unlock one particular enigma in the text through close reference to the prophet Daniel, before returning in the third section to the enigmatic Octavius/Augustus.

2.

The book of Daniel is not indicated as a source for the play by Seaton, Fichter or Cantor, nor indeed by Kenneth Muir.[10] Yet Daniel was available and well known to Elizabethans and Jacobeans, so the enigma is complicated by the lack of awareness in modern readers of what would, we believe, have been commonplace in Shakespeare's time.

Before his final battle with Octavius, Antony ascends a hill from which he 'shall discover all' (4.12.2). From that height, he observes the sea battle, fatal to his fortunes. He returns to cry,

> All is lost:
> This foul Egyptian hath betrayed me.
> My fleet hath yielded to the foe, and yonder
> They cast their caps up and carouse together
> Like friends long lost.
>
> (10–14)

This scene is the climax of the sequence of desertions and betrayals set in motion by Cleopatra's flight at Actium. He has witnessed the dissolution of his power, the end of an empire in the eastern Mediterranean which he had built for himself and for Cleopatra. He is overcome by a sense of unreality. He cannot believe that he is still himself, that he still exists, asking Eros, 'thou yet behold'st me?' (4.14.1). He then descants upon the inconstant images presented by clouds:

---

[9]   Fichter, 'Antony and Cleopatra and the Time of Universal Peace', *Shakespeare Survey* 33 (1980): p. 106.

[10]   See Muir, *The Sources of Shakespeare's Plays* (London: Methuen, 1977).

Sometime we see a cloud that's dragonish,
A vapour sometime, like a bear, or lion,
A towered citadel, a pendent rock,
A forked mountain, or blue promontory
With trees upon't, that nod unto the world
And mock our eyes with air. Thou hast seen these signs;
They are black vesper's pageants.
...
That which is now a horse, even with a thought
The rack dislimns, and makes it indistinct
As water is in water.
...
My good knave Eros, now thy captain is
Even such a body: here I am Antony,
Yet cannot hold this visible shape, my knave.

(3–14)

This passage inspired William Hazlitt to rhapsodic admiration: 'Without doubt one of the finest pieces of poetry in Shakespeare. The splendour of the imagery, the semblance of reality, the lofty range of picturesque objects hanging over the world, their evanescent nature, the total uncertainty of what is left behind, are just like the moundering schemes of human greatness.'[11] M.R. Ridley, in his Arden edition, devotes a long footnote to this passage but confines himself to its first two lines only, informing us that 'Several passages have been suggested as the sources of this fancy, but its beautiful and striking use to illustrate man's unstable hold on his very entity seems to occur here only.'[12] He then gives examples from Aristophanes, Pliny, Chapman, Du Bartas, Tasso and Ford. In none of them are these three animals mentioned together. Nor, as he himself admits, are any of them are used, as here, 'to illustrate man's unstable hold on his very entity'. Footnotes in other editions are also not helpful. I propose the prophet Daniel as source, not only for these animals in conjunction but also for their use as symbols of the transience of worldly power and glory.

A brief reminder: what modern readers may take as an obscure allusion, or a reference to something more or less remote, may have been familiar knowledge to most Elizabethans. We are dealing here with an all-but-forgotten commonplace. Spenser treats the division of history into four great monarchies familiarly in his "The Ruins of Time" (1591) and Sir Walter Raleigh, in the final pages of his massive but incomplete *History of the World* (1614), tells us: 'By this which we have set down, is seen the beginning and the end of the three first monarchies of the world, whereof the founders and erectors thought that they could never have ended. That of Rome, which made the fourth, was also at this time at the highest ...

---

[11] Hazlitt, *Characters in Shakespeare's Plays* (London: Dent, 1906), p. 98.

[12] Ridley (ed.), *Antony and Cleopatra*, Arden edition (London: Methuen, 1965), p. 172.

but after some continuance it shall lose the beauty it had.'[13] The rise and fall of these four monarchies form the background of Jewish and Christian history in the Old and New Testaments. During the Reformation, conflicting interpretations of the prophets, and particularly of Daniel, attracted the attention of Catholic and Protestant scholars alike. In England the prophetic debate centred on a powerful, learned, dogmatic personality, Hugh Broughton (1549–1612). A redoubtable linguist, he published his views on these great issues in *A Concent of Scripture* in 1588. He and his views were attacked, but after an appeal to Queen Elizabeth, he was allowed to conduct a series of weekly lectures in his own defence in St Paul's Cathedral, using his *Concent* as a textbook.

Let us recall the vision described in the second chapter of Daniel. The four monarchies or kingdoms appear in Nebuchadnezzar's first great dream, which he keeps to himself; Daniel, however, reveals the dream, confounding the official wizards. The feet of that 'great image' of the kingdoms of this world are struck by the stone, the rock of truth, and, as the feet are partly of clay, it crumbles into chaff. We are surely entitled to see in this vision of kingship the origin of Antony's succinct judgement that 'kingdoms are clay.' This is not a Roman sentiment, but a biblical one. In his *Concent of Scripture*, Broughton transforms the vague symbolic sequences of the vision to statistics. Broughton's dating and accompanying genealogies may have been disputed, but no one questioned a sequence of world powers, or their splendour, authority and beauty, unstable as they might be. Broughton's illustration of the vision is handsome; the posture and expression of the 'great image' emit power, emphasised by the spacious world of grand natural and architectural features in the imperial background – which it dwarfs. It is possible that Shakespeare had Broughton's or similar illustrations in mind when writing Cleopatra's great panegyric of Antony.

Nebuchadnezzar's great image composed of metals is, however, only one man's dream. In Chapter 7:1–7, Daniel has a dream of his own in which he abandons the single metallic image of worldly power and endows the four constituents with individual animal forms (for convenience I have included the marginal glosses below each line):

1. In the first yeere of Belshazzar king of Babel, Daniel sawe a dreame, and there were visions in his head, upon his bedde: then hee wrote the dreame, and declared the summe of the matter.

2. Daniel spake and sayde, I sawe in my vision by night, and beholde, the foure windes of the heaven strove upon ᵇthe great sea:

b. Which signifieth that there should be horrible troubles in all corners of the world at sundry times.

3. And foure great beasts came up from the sea one divers from another.

---

[13] See Spenser, 'The Ruins of Time', in *Spenser's Minor Poems*, ed. Ernest de Selincourt (Oxford: Clarendon Press, 1910), lines 64–77, and Raleigh, *The History of the World*, book 5 (London: Walter Burre, 1614), p. 668.

Fig. 8.1   Nebuchadnezzar's vision of worldly powers (Hugh Broughton, *Concent of Scripture*, 1588).

4. The first was as a ᶜlyon, and had eagles wings: I behelde, till the wings thereof were pluckt off, and it was lifted up from the earth, and set upon his feete as a man, and a mans heart was given him.

c. Meaning, the Assyrian and Chaldean Empire which was most strong and fierce in power.

5. And beholde, another beast which was the seconde, was like a ᵈbeare and stoode upon the one side: and he had three ribs in his mouth betweene his teeth, and they sayde this unto him, rise and devoure much flesh.

d. Meaning, the Persians, which were barbarous and cruell.

6. After this, I beheld, and loe, there was an other like a ʰleoparde, which had upon his backe ⁱfoure wings of a foule: the beast had also foure heads, and ᵏdominion was given to him.

h. Meaning, Alexander of Macedonie.

i. That is his four chief captains which had the empire among them after his death: Seleucus had Asia the great, Antigonus the less, Cassander and after him Antipater was king of Macedonie, and Ptolemeus of Egypt.

k. It was not of himself nor of his owne powers that he obtained all these countries: for his armie continued but thirtie thousand men, and he overcame in one battell Darius which had ten hundredth thousand.

7. After this I saw in my visions by night, and beholde, the ˡfourth beast was fearefull, and terrible, and very strong. It had ᵐgreat yron teeth: it devoured, and brake in pieces and stamped ⁿthe residue under his feete: and it was unlike to the beastes that were before it: for it had °tenne hornes.

l. That of the Romane empire, which was a monster and could not be compared to any beast, because the nature of none was able to express it.

m. Signifying the tyrranie and greedinesse o f the Romanes.

n. That which the Romanes could not quietly enjoy in other countries, they would give it to other Kings and rulers, that at all limes when they would they might take it agin, which liberalitic is here called the stamping of the rest under the foot.

o. That is sundrie and divers provinces which were governed by the deputies and proconsuls whereof every one might be compared to a king.

Daniel returns to the fourth beast's iniquitous indeterminate reign of terror against the Saints (the Christians) again and again. We need only concern ourselves with verses which contain details that justify the term 'dragonish' (e.g., in verse 19, added to its 'unlikeness to any other beast' and 'tenne horns' are 'teeth of yron' and 'nails of brasse'). These prophetic images invited speculation particularly concerned with the coming of the Messiah, the day of doom, and the new heaven and earth. Some might have disputed the idea of an end to the Fourth Kingdom of Anti-Christ (whom some Protestants equated with the Pope) but they did so in defiance of Daniel:

26. But the ʹjudgement shall sit, and they shall take away his dominion, to consume and destroy it to the end.

r. God by his power shall restore things that were out of order.

...

27. And the Kingdome, and dominion, and the greatnesse of the Kingdome under the whole heaven shall be given to the holy people of the most High, whose Kingdome is an everlasting Kingdome and all ʹpowers shall serve and obey him.

t. that is some of every sort that beare rule.

This dream became a popular subject with illustrators. For example, see Hans Holbein's (1549) illustration for Daniel 7 (Figure 8.2, on page opposite).

If Broughton was primarily concerned with locating the kingdoms in time, others were concerned with space. A map of the Eastern Mediterranean, which heads the same chapter in a Bible of 1568, depicts irregular land masses allocated to the four symbolical beasts.[14] A curious point is that these animals are all facing inwards across bodies of land and water. The heavy forked vertical line in the middle of the lower foreground must be the Nile (which correctly splits into two). That territory must be Egypt, occupied by the indeterminate beast. This is plausible because it places the other three symbolical beasts in their correct areas geographically: the Greek or Macedonian beast is appropriately placed in Macedonia, in the north-west, facing the Lion of Babylon and the Bear of Persia across the Aegean in the east.

Furthermore, in the space between the four beasts, too obvious to be ignored, is what appears to be a large body of cavalry and spearsmen. This detached military presence is a puzzle. It is not in Daniel. With no authority to quote, I would offer the suggestion that it symbolises the military power to which all world empires must look and upon which they all depend. Before each great battle in *Antony and Cleopatra*, much is made of the soldiers, their disposition and their loyalty or otherwise. We watch Antony's forces disintegrate step by step. It is therefore not impertinent to suggest that references to horses and to armed forces in civilian scenes, which seem to be quite straightforward, may have symbolical weight – for instance, the scene (1.5.39–50) in which Cleopatra's attendant Alexas describes how Antony, about to leave for Rome, hands over a priceless pearl to him to give to Cleopatra. The pearl is an earnest of more to follow: Antony will make Cleopatra mistress of all the East. Alexas's diplomatic acknowledgement of this gift of half the world to Cleopatra is 'dumbed' (50) in beastly fashion by the neigh of his horse. And the last deliquescent cloud shape which Antony sees is of a horse.

If in this scene Shakespeare makes Antony use three of Daniel's four beasts (bear, lion and dragon) as symbols of inconstancy and change, why does he omit the fourth, the Grecian or Macedonian leopard? One can only guess at reasons.

---

[14]   1568 Bib. Eng 61(2) clxxiiij. Bodleian Library, Oxford.

Fig. 8.2   *Daniel's Vision of the Four Beasts* (Hans Holbein, 1549).

Perhaps the symbolical leopard with four heads was too unusual and bizarre to gain credence with any cloud gazer. There is, however, another pictorial source which might account for the cloud shapes that follow upon 'a bear or lion':

> A towered citadel, a pendent rock,
> A forked mountain, or blue promontory
> With trees upon't, that nod unto the world
> And mock our eyes with air.
>
> (4.14.4–7)

Broughton devotes another dream illustration (see Figure 8.3, on page following) to verses 7–9 of Daniel 8, in which the Grecian or Macedonian monarchy appears as a goat with many horns. In the gloss the four large horns are allocated to Alexander of Macedon's four great generals and heirs, one of whom is Ptolemeus of Egypt.

Of interest here, however, is the presence in the background of an impressive 'towered citadel', a striking 'pendent rock' and possibly a 'forked mountain'. There are trees but no blue promontory. Symbolical significances for these individual items are elusive, but together they compose a grand landscape with evidence of imperial architecture and civilisation.

Fig. 8.3   Illustration of the dream in the book of Daniel 8 (Hugh Broughton, *Concent of Scripture*, 1588).

I noted above that Antony uses an architectural image – 'the wide arch of the rang'd empire' – to evoke an imperial grandeur which he dismisses as fated to return to water, to clay and dungy earth. The conjunction appears again towards the end of the play when Cleopatra reduces Caesar, the emperor of Rome, to the same nugatory status: ''Tis paltry to be Caesar' (5.2.2). He too will have become a corpse, 'Which sleeps, and never palates more the dung, / The beggar's nurse, and Caesar's' (7–8). The dissolution of empires in earthy clay and water is complemented by the insubstantiality of clouds, passages which may be seen as precursors of Prospero's:

> The cloud-capp'd towers, the gorgeous palaces,
> The solemn temples, the great globe itself,
> Ye all which it inherit, shall dissolve
> And, like this insubstantial pageant faded,
> Leave not a rack behind.
>
> *(The Tempest, 4.1.152–6)*

We have not yet accounted for the absence of a fourth beast among the clouds. Why does Shakespeare not make his Antony refer, in however a symbolic manner, to the Macedonian or Greek Empire, of which he had become the champion by his alliance with Cleopatra? Because that monarchy has disappeared with his defeat. He cannot, as it were, be allowed to see himself, even in cloud form. His empire gone, who is he? Man's 'unstable hold on his very entity' is conflated with the insubstantiality of the world into which he was born, and out of which he has, as it were, made himself. Shakespeare has given Antony three of Daniel's four images of empires; the fourth cloud shape is, of course, Antony himself:

> That which is now a horse, even with a thought
> The rack dislimns, and makes it indistinct
> As water is in water.
>
> (4.14.11–13)

Most editors explain the coinage 'dislimns' as deriving from 'limn', to paint. To my knowledge only Michael Neill (1994) points to the pun on 'limb'. Antony has just referred to a cloud shaped like a horse; a dis-limbed horse is useless, quite unable to 'bear the weight of Antony' (1.5.20).

If the tentative suggestion that we are shown a single armed troop of spear-horsemen as the centre of attention of all four transitory kingdoms is accepted, we must conclude that all kingdoms depend ultimately on military power. We must also accept that such power is unreliable, which the whole play amply demonstrates. Antony, the champion of one of these powers, 'cannot hold [his] visible shape'. He has become as 'indistinct / as water is in water', and has been supplanted by the champion of the new empire, the Roman monarchy, Caesar:

My good knave Eros, now thy captain is
Even such a body: here I am Antony,
Yet cannot hold this visible shape, my knave.
1 made these wars for Egypt, and the queen, ...
Pack'd cards with Caesar, and false-play'd my glory
Unto an enemy's triumph.

(4.14.12–20)

In the map shown in Figure 8.3, the fourth symbolical animal in the bottom left segment is clearly the Roman beast: 'It was unlike to the beastes that were before: for it had ten horns' (Daniel 7:7). In *Antony and Cleopatra*, Shakespeare dramatises not only the greatest of love affairs but also the passing of primacy from one world power to another.

The ancient belief that major historical events, involving as they usually did the defeat of a great man, were foretold by astral events, was still commonly held by Shakespeare's contemporaries ('When beggars die there are no comets seen: / The heavens themselves blaze forth the death of princes,' as Calpurnia tells us in *Julius Caesar* 2.2.30–31). Antony's lack of cosmic favour is noticeable in *Antony and Cleopatra*. True, there is the mysterious midnight music which the soldiers take to be the god Hercules deserting Antony, but this is a mild portent compared with those that precede the death of Julius Caesar – so mild that it calls for a comment from Octavius:

The breaking of so great a thing should make
A greater crack. The round world
Should have shook lions into civil streets,
And citizens to their dens.

(5.1.13–16)

Yet Ethel Seaton, in her commentary on echoes of Revelation in *Antony and Cleopatra*, focuses attention on the stars: the 'apocalyptic suggestion' of many phrases in the play 'draws one's mind to the great sentences scattered throughout Chapters 8 to 10 of the book of Revelation: "And there fell a great star from heaven, burning as if it were a torch" (*Rev.*, viii.110 Genevan).'[15] Seaton rightly observes that the falling of stars is a consistent apocalyptic event and symbol. The most remarkable astral reference in the play is the curious, short, cosmic lament uttered by the soldiers who find Antony dying:

GUARD 1: The star is fall'n.

GUARD 2: And time is at his period.

ALL: Alas, and woe!

(4.14.106–7)

_____

[15]   Seaton, '*Antony and Cleopatra* and the Book of Revelation', 219–20.

The 'time' that has come to an end with Antony is the Macedonian kingdom; they lament the end of the Grecian monarchy. Shakespeare's authority for this astral placing of the action is not in his source (North). At the time these lines were first spoken (1606–1607), a star, Kepler's nova, which had appeared in October 1604, had recently disappeared from the sky (in February 1606). Even if Shakespeare had no historical authority for suggesting that the heavens might have blazed forth the death of Antony, or for attributing cosmic reaction to his death, it seems that the heavens themselves obliged.[16] Kepler's nova of 1604–1606 had been preceded by one in 1572, discovered by Tycho Brahe, who published his findings and speculations in Latin from Hufniae (Copenhagen) in 1573. An English translation appeared in London in 1632, but there is no reason to doubt that by 1603 all astronomers and astrologers of note had read the Latin version or heard of the new star. Although Brahe spells out the new star's destructive implication for traditional Ptolemaic astronomy, he does not abandon entirely the traditional belief that the appearance and disappearance of stars can be prophetic of great changes on earth. In support of this view, he quotes the prognostication of a Greek astronomer, which was fulfilled in the world-shaping historical event that is the material of *Antony and Cleopatra*:

> Yet it is probable that as the star which Hypparchus beheld did foresignifie the declining of the Grecian monarchy, and the enlarging of the Roman Empire, so far that the whole world should be in subjection to this one city; so likewise, some strange alteration in the public government of Estates and Common-weales shall ensue in the following years.[17]

Such views would have been encouraged by the appearance and then disappearance of Kepler's nova.

By making Antony the unwitting reminder of Daniel's four kingdoms, Shakespeare emphasises not only the interrelation between Roman and Christian history but also the transience and imperfection of all earthly splendour and grandeur. This helps to endow the action with resonances from different cultural cosmologies, resonances which embraced ancient and contemporary astronomy. Discovering the source of the cloud-animals enlarges rather than diminishes the complexity of the play.

---

[16] The appearance of the new star was also employed in plays by Chapman, Jonson and Marston; the most memorable reference is in *King Lear*, where the bastard Edmund dismisses astral influences on character ('Fut! I should have been that I am had the maidenliest star in the universe twinkled on my bastardising'; 1.2.138).

[17] Cited in Murdin and Murdin, *Supernovae* (Cambridge: Cambridge University Press, 1978), p. 14.

3.

Let us return, then, to Augustus/Octavius – and, in particular, to the way in which he was portrayed on the medieval stage in a piece of popular drama that was part of the Chester cycle of mystery plays.[18] This play has come down to us in four manuscripts, all written in Shakespeare's lifetime; one of them is preceded by a 'banes', which tells us something about the origin of the plays in the mid-fourteenth century and devotes a stanza to each individual play, and the company or guild who was responsible for its performance (in this case, the slaters – the carpenters and workers in slate). Significantly, it is assumed by the Tudor writer (1604–1606) of the banes that the audience will know who Octavius and Sybil the Sage are.

It is noteworthy how fluid the stage is: there are lightning switches of locality from Nazareth, to Bethlehem, to Rome, back to Bethlehem and then back to Rome. Although there is a gothic looseness of plot and gargoyle proliferation of barely relevant detail, the artistry is considerable: the contrast between the domestic, village simplicity of Mary and Joseph's affairs and those of the great emperor of Rome; the subsequent dwarfing, and elevation, of both by the incursion of the timeless into time. The play starts with Gabriel announcing to Mary the stupendous news that she will bear the Messiah and the story proceeds in a fashion familiar to those who know the gospels: Mary expresses her amazement and fear, and Gabriel reassures her, pointing to the miraculous pregnancy of her cousin, Elizabeth. Gabriel leaves, and the next scene is devoted to Mary's visit to Elizabeth, where we hear the Magnificat sung, as it were, for the very first time – in some 72 lines. After a three-month stay with Elizabeth, Mary returns home, her condition now apparent to all. Joseph, depicted as an old man, who is not yet married to her, is naturally disturbed. Depressed he lies down to sleep; an Angel appears to reassure him.

A Nuntius then takes possession of the stage, and with much noise, shifts us from Jerusalem to Rome.

> All this world, withoutten weare,
> King, prince, Baron, Bachler,
> I may destroy in great danger
> through virtue of my decree.
> – My name Octavian called is –
> all me about, full in my bliss;
> for wholly all the world, I wis,
> is ready at my owne will.
> ...
> for I have multiplied more
> the Citie of Rome, sith I was bore,
> then ever did any me before,

---

[18]   *Chester Plays VI, The Nativity* (Harl. 2124).

sith I had this Kingdom
for what with strength and strokes sore,
leading lordship, lovelie lore,
all this world now has been yore
tributary unto Rome.
...
Sith I was soverayne, war can cease
and through this world now is peace,
for so dreade a duke sat never on dais
in Rome, that may you trust.

(189–248)

In order to know the extent of his power, he decides to conduct a census of the whole world and he orders his bedill (beadle) to travel to Judea once, emphasising the power of Rome:

When this is done thus in Judye
that in the middest of the world shlbe,
to each land, shire, and citye,
to Rome make them so thrall.
Warne them, boye – I command thee –
Then do the same, saie this from me;
so all this world shall wit that we
bene soveraigne of them all.

(273–80)

There is then a bit of a broad low comedy backchat between Caesar and his beadle or boy (Preco), whose reward for this undertaking is Caesar's provision to choose and take 'an Ladie' he fancies for himself. Now the Senators enter with a petition from all Rome:

Thy men here have each one iment
as a god to honour thee;
and to that pointe we be sent,
poor and rich in parliament,
for so loved a lord, verament,
was never in this citye.

(307–12)

A second Senator adds,

Peace hath been so long and yet is,
no man in thy time lost ought of his,
therefore their will is now, I wis,
to quite you this your meede.

(317–20)

Octavius, however, is modest, hesitant:

> but in folly it were, by many a waye,
> such soveraigntie for to assail
> sith I must dye I wot not what daye,
> to desire such dignitye.
>
> For of fleshe, blood and bone
> made am I, borne of woman;
> and sicker other wathr none
> sheweth not ryht in me;
> nether of yron, tree, nor stone
> am I wrought, you wot each one;
> and of my most part is gone,
> age shewes him so, I see.
>
> And godhede askes in all thinge
> tyme that hath no beginning,
> ne never shall have ending;
> and none of these have I.
>
> Wherefore, by very proofe shewinge,
> though I be highest worldlie King,
> of godhead have I no knowing,
> it were unkindlie.
>
> (325–44)

He consults the Sybil who has the ghost (or spirit) of prophesy:

> Sybble, the sage, tell me this thinge
> for thou wyt hast no man lyving:
> shall ever be any earthly King
> to passe me of degree?
>
> (353–6)

Without hesitation she replies:

> A barne shall be borne blisse to bringe
> The which that never hasse beginning;
> And never shall neded be.
>
> (357–60)

Octavius asks when this child will be born. The Sybil does not know, but consents to discover the answer by prayer. With that we are switched from the dilemma of Augustus in Rome to the difficulties of the Holy Family in Judea. The preco/beadle shouts out that his lord Octavius demands tribute from each man. Joseph, bust with his carpenter's tools, which are mentioned in detail, complains of the injustice of imposing taxes on the humble, honest and poor. But there is no tax exemption, and Joseph has to go to Bethlehem with Mary. There the nativity scene is played out, after which an expositor enters (a Brechtian interruption of the dramatic action) to tell us of another incident 'That befell that ilke daye / that Ihesu Christ was borne' (583–4). He tells us of a precious temple in Rome that was worth a third part of the world's gold and jewels. Images of the gods of all the provinces of the Roman Empire were present there, but in the midst of all, the God of Rome was set as King. About this building moved a brazen man on a brazen horse with a spear in his hand, guarding the image. If any corner of the empire threatened to rebel, the brazen horseman would point his spear in the direction of the rebellious land, and an army was dispatched there at once; it was through the art of necromancy that the world was made to bow down before Rome. This temple was called the Temple of Peace, but it collapses on the day of Christ's birth because it is the work of the Devil. Its ruins, we are told, are still visible in Rome, but no one likes to visit them. There is thus a certain ambivalence in the author towards Rome – necromancy and the Devil are responsible for its power, but Octavius is likeable, humble and a bringer of peace.

We are returned to Rome; and the next character to speak is the Sybil, who has prayed to good effect. The stage direction reads: '*Then they display the star, and the Sybbil approaches the Emperor.*' She invites him to look aloft, and behold the star, which is the sure sign of the birth of the King who surpasses him in power. Octavius sees the Virgin and Child in the star, and offers to honour Him with incense:

> Incense bring, I command in hie
> to honour this child, king of mercy.
> Should I be god? Nay, nay! witterly
> great wrong, I wis, it were.
> For this child is more worthye
> than such a thousand as am I,
> therefore to god, most mightie,
> Incense I offer here.
>
> (665–72)

The Sybil tells Octavius he is wise to acknowledge the lordship of Christ; Octavius then turns to his senators and dismisses them with instructions to follow his suit and worship the Holy Child. The senators are also impressed by the wondrous star, and the child and the maiden in it. The expositor ends with the assurance that all that we have seen is truth; for in Rome when this event took place, a noble church was built in honour of Mary, which is there today for all to see:

> The church is called St. Mary
> the surname is Ara Gaeli
> that men know well thereby
> that this was full true.
>
> (721–4)

This Octavius of the miracles has the entire world at his feet, but he refuses to be deified, insisting on his mortality – his finite, temporal nature. He adheres to prophesy and accepts the Sybil as being in touch with the ultimate Ruler of the world, to whom he is subject. Not only is he viewed sub specie aeternitatis, he views himself that way. Ultimately, he falls into line with the medieval view of history outlined above.

Obviously, Shakespeare's Octavius and the medieval Octavius are very different characters. Shakespeare has read his Roman histories and, above all, his Plutarch, and he himself is the product of the reformed school syllabus introduced into Britain by Erasmus and the humanists. His Latin and Greek classics may have been small, but they were, by comparison with most medieval writers, considerable. There was in him an acute perception and appreciation of the Roman portraits he found in his reading; yet – and this is the main point – there was no alternative historiography to the medieval yet available. Tudor history was still, largely, on the old universal pattern. One might fill in the details, change many facts, see characters in a different light, but one could not, really, change the role of someone like Augustus. He was part of the scheme of things. Yet there were at least two rivals to the medieval view, both of which, in their different ways, appealed to classical world views. First were the English classicists, such as Jonson and Chapman, both of whom wrote Roman plays that were in general anti-Caesar and pro-Pompey (they were republicans and not monarchists). The portraits they paint of Julius and Octavius are not flattering and owe something to the other, greater enemy of the medieval view of history and statecraft – Machiavelli.

In his tragedies and history plays, Shakespeare's extensive historical studies had helped him produce portraits of power seekers, governors and intriguers: Bolingbroke and Prince Hal, Claudius, Iago, Edmund and Cornwall. He had also, before his eyes, plenty of living examples at the court, such as Bacon, whose essays are full of sentiments of which the Florentine would have approved. Shakespeare was intelligent and tough-minded, and it seems that he accepted the view that the princes of this world are likely to be *of this world*, worldly. His other-worldly kings – like saintly Edward VI, or aesthetic Richard II – make a right mess of things. Kings could not afford the luxuries of personal honours, or other vanities; power, real power, was their first concern. Nor were they to love or to inspire love, except in a controlled and calculating way. Fear and awe, yes. They might not be likeable, but they were necessary. And that is what his Octavius is, necessary. He is a curious mixture: the Renaissance Machiavel, with scraps of pure Plutarch, but thoroughly medieval in his concern for the monarchy, the rule of one, and the liquidation of 'rival houses' to the Caesars (this is why Cleopatra calls him 'the Universal landlord').

It is left to Antony to express the medieval contempt for kingdoms; to talk of corruption, of the gnawing effects of time. Shakespeare's Octavius consults no oracles, fears no Gods; he believes in his own destiny: 'let determined things to destiny / Hold unbewailed their way,' he tells Octavia (3.6.84–5). He is 'full-fortuned Caesar' (4.15.24). But Shakespeare, like all good Elizabethans – including

Sir Walter Raleigh – knew that fortune was the instrument of Divine Purpose. Thus Cleopatra, in her newfound transcendence after the death of Antony, can say,

> I hear him mock
> The luck of Caesar, which the Gods give men
> To excuse their after wrath.
>
> (5.2.284–6)

Or, apostrophising the second asp: 'O couldst thou speak, / That I might hear thee call great Caesar ass / Unpolicied!' (305–7).

4.

If Shakespeare's Octavius never speculates upon the old *sic transit gloria mundi* theme or talks of eternity, as both Anthony and Cleopatra do, what does he share with them? First, a preoccupation with this world and its government. Second, a belief in being a chosen instrument – but, whereas the others talk in terms of divinity and believe in prophesies, his categories are luck and destiny: 'Our fortune lies / Upon this jump' (3.8.4–5, before Actium). The medieval Octavius is made to be overtly conscious of his place within the great scheme of universal (as against Roman or Greek) history, and to be the willing tool of the Christian God. Not so Shakespeare's Octavius. Both Antony and Cleopatra frequently resort to ideas and images which have distinctly Christian associations. But Octavius does not: there is no transcendence in him. And yet he is given words – crucial words – which would have meant much more to an Elizabethan audience than they do to us.

Before dealing with them, however, we must glance at Shakespeare's preparation for them. Act I, scene 2, the fortune-teller scene (in Egypt), is *not* from Plutarch – it is Shakespeare's invention. The soothsayer insists that he cannot 'make' a person's fortune good or bad: 'I make not, but forsee' (1.2.18). The delightful, flippant, easy-going Charmian imagines the following fortune for herself: 'Good now, some excellent fortune! Let me be married to three Kings in a forenoon and widow them all; let me have a child at fifty, to whom Herod of Jewry may do homage. Find me to marry me with Octavius Caesar, and companion me with my mistress' (27–31). Apart from its immediate dramatic purpose, this little speech places the action historically for the audience, by an effective shorthand appeal to their general knowledge. Herod of Jewry is alive, then. And this Egyptian *bona roba* hopes to have a son who will king it over Judea. But Herod, as remarked above, was a notorious figure; notorious precisely because he hypocritically promised the Wise Men to do homage to the Child, and then tried to murder him. And Octavius's mention here, next to Herod, would remind the audience of their common appearance in the New Testament and, I believe – for many – on the medieval stage. The play has thus been deliberately placed in some sort of relation to the all-important, impending event in Judea. To determine *what* sort of relation would take a longer study of the whole play, but here are one or two further hints.

In Act III, scene 3, Cleopatra is recovering from the news of Antony's marriage:

CLEO: Whence is the fellow?

ALEXAS: Half afeard to come.

CLEO: Go to, go to: come hither sir.

Enter the Messenger as before

ALEXAS: Good Majesty,
Herod of Jewry dare not look upon you
But when you are well pleased.

CLEO: That Herod's head
I'll have; but how, when Antony is gone,
Through whom I might command it?
(3.3.1–7)

Once more, there is a reminder of what 'period' we are in, by an inverted reference to a well-known biblical incident (Herod had John the Baptist beheaded at the instigation of Herodias).

Then, as it becomes obvious that there will be war between Octavius and Antony, Caesar comforts Octavia with the words:

Cheer your heart
Be you not troubled with the time, which drives
O'er your content these strong necessities;
But let determined things to destiny
Hold unbewail'd their way.
(1.6.81–5)

We are reminded forcibly that 'the time' is moving towards the fulfilment of a predetermined destiny. Octavius does not specify what this destiny is to be. Why not? Because the audience knew: his victory, and the birth of Christ. But the most remarkable utterance of Caesar is this, just before the final series of battles:

The time of universal peace is near:
Prove this a prosperous day, the three nook'd world
Shall bear the olive freely.
(4.6.4–6)

It seems to me that if Octavius had been speaking in character, and not prophetically, he would have used the indefinite and not the definite article: '*A* time of universal peace is near.' '*The* time' makes it quite inescapably the time of peace which, all his audience knew, coincided with the birth of Christ. The words were a commonplace of medieval and Elizabethan usage; in Milton's nativity ode, the birth 'strikes a universal peace through sea and land' (Hymn, III.8).[19] These are small but significant pieces of evidence, which, taken with many others throughout the play, indicate that Shakespeare – unlike Jonson or Chapman – wanted his audience to relate this drama to the universal Christian drama: it was part of his artistic intention that his Tudor audience should be consciously Christian, watching a drama of the epoch-making events that preceded the birth of Christ.

The Christian view of Rome has, of course, undergone several modifications. For the early Christian fathers, the 'tyrannie and greediness of the Romanes' were self-evident: the Roman Empire was 'a monster' that 'could not be compared unto any beast, because the nature of none was able to expresse it'. This view was to be modified as persecution dictated and only to be pushed into the background when the Church became the official Church of the Empire, and the Roman Empire became 'Holy'. But in Protestant countries during the Reformation, it became popular to identify the pope and Papal Rome with the fourth monarchy of Daniel and Revelations. Shakespeare's view of Rome was highly critical and unromantic (there is ample evidence of this in the Roman plays); the texts that were a common feature of Tudor education in the classics and in history corroborate this point.[20]

T.S.B. Spenser affirms that, 'In writing his Roman Plays, Shakespeare was touching upon the greatest and most exciting as well as the most pedantic of Renaissance studies, of European Scholarship.'[21] He also criticises those who, confused by the ambitions of Caesar and Brutus in *Julius Caesar*, try to settle the matter by appealing to a 'traditional' view of them:

> this, it seems to me, obscures the fact that the reassessment and reconsideration of such famous historical figures was a common literary activity in the Renaissance, not merely in poetry and drama (where licence is acceptable) but in plain prose, the writing of History. It seems hardly legitimate to talk about 'tradition', to refer to 'traditional' opinions about Caesar and Brutus, when in fact the characters of each of them had been the subject of constant discussion.[22]

Now, the medieval view of history allowed for much flexibility. A man's character or motives mattered little, for in spite of them, he would fulfil his divinely predetermined role. According to this attitude, writes Collingwood,

> the historical process is the working out not of man's purposes, but of God's; God's purpose being a purpose for man, a purpose to be embodied in human

---

[19] John Milton, 'Ode on the Morning of Christ's Nativity', in F.T. Prince (ed.), *Milton: Comus and Other Poems* (Oxford: Oxford University Press, 1968), p. 4.

[20] See Watson, *The English Grammar Schools to 1660* (Cambridge: Cambridge University Press, 1908), p. 534, and Clarke, *Classical Education in Britain 1500–1900* (Cambridge: Cambridge University Press, 1959), p. 12.

[21] T.S.B. Spenser, 'Shakespeare and the Elizabethan Romans', *Shakespeare Survey* 10 (1958): p. 29.

[22] Ibid., p. 33.

life and through the activity of human wills, God's part in this working-out being limited to predetermining the end and to determining from time to time the objects which human beings desire. Thus each human agent knows what he wants and pursues it, but he does not know why he wants it: the reason why he wants it is that God has caused him to want it in order to advance the process of realising his purpose. In one sense man is the agent throughout history, for everything that happens in history happens by his will; in another sense God is the sole agent, for it is only by the working of God's providence that the operation of man's will at any given moment leads to *this* result, and not to a different one.[23]

So it did not alter the medieval system if you were pro-Caesar or anti-Caesar; indeed, there had been a double attitude towards Caesar among educated men in the Middle Ages, who knew their Lucan and Sallust. It did not matter much – ultimately – what the characters were, provided their deeds still supported the scheme of salvation. But Octavius presents a slightly different problem to Caesar and Brutus. For one thing, important as he was, he was not comparable story material when set beside, say, Julius or Alexander. Plutarch has no life of Octavius – an appalling pagan omission which the Middle Ages promptly made good by a forgery. This spurious 'Life' is a mixture of Sallust and medieval legend, and Shakespeare did not draw upon it for details. Nor did he, obviously, draw upon the miracle plays. No one can imagine his Octavius kneeling at the crib and being transported by celestial music. What then persuaded him to create so curious and so unexpected a figure?

The answer is, of course, the demands of the total artwork. But essential to that work was the conflict between Egypt and Rome, Caesar and Cleopatra, with Antony torn between them. One is tempted to make a daring suggestion, not to be taken too literally. Caesar is the Machiavel, and Rome is not Rome the Great, but the cruel Rome of Daniel – the iron and clay monarchy whose emblematic beast is the dragon – Rome, the kingdom of *this* world. Certainly Rome is presented in an unfavourable light in *Antony and Cleopatra*, and no one has ever called Octavius dynamic or attractive. Cleopatra and Egypt are of *this* world too, but with a difference: the life of enjoyment, lust, desire, as against the life of the intellect and order; fickle, unpredictable, but moist and warm, fecund, 'alive' in terms of Shakespeare's own time – the gorgeous Renaissance excitement with this life, voluptuous, luxurious.

And Antony? It is Antony who has inherited the medieval values of personal honour (Octavius has none), who has a real sense of the limits of man, of Octavius, of kingdoms that are 'clay'. Both the Renaissance (Cleopatra) and the Middle Ages (Antony) go down before the lucky, pragmatic Caesar (Machiavelli, Thomas Hobbes).

This suggestion may not be developed any further. But let me close with one or two quotations to support it, as far as Octavius is concerned. First, from Federico

---

[23]   Collingwood, *The Idea of History*, p. 48.

Chabod in *Machiavelli and the Renaissance*. The Renaissance, he maintains, 'destroyed an organically Unitarian vision of the world' and sought 'a system that can replace, wholly and completely, the disrupted theological system of the schoolmen':

> Each of the aspects of life is self-contained; and the consequence is an unresolved dramatic conflict. It is enough to mention the problem raised by Machiavelli – the problem that is, of the relationship between politics and ethics. This problem remained outside the purview of the Florentine secretary ... But it soon presented itself to his contemporaries and followers ... Thus we find them grappling long and painfully with the question implicit in the phrase *raison d'etat*, for the precise reason that Renaissance thought, having unlocked the door to various branches of human activity, was subsequently unable to re-integrate them, in spite of the fact that human nature is constantly tormented by its need for a comprehensive vision.[24]

In Richard III, Bolingbroke and Henry V, in Claudius, Iago and Edmund, Shakespeare had grappled long and painfully with the question Machiavelli had raised. Thus, his study of Caesar is a study in merely political man – whose triumph he uncannily divined. And like his contemporary, Samuel Daniel, he saw the hollow heartlessness of such men. Listen to this Renaissance Daniel's Caesar (from his 1599 *Tragedie of Cleopatra*):

> CAESAR: Kingdoms I see we winne, we conquer climates,
> Yet cannot vanquish hearts, nor force obedience;
> Affections kept in close concealed limits
> Stand farre without the tears of sorrow and violence,
> Who forced to pay us duty, pay not love;
> Free is the heart, the temple of the mind,
> The sanctuary sacred from above
> Where nature keeps the keys that loose and bind.
> No mortal hand force open can that doore,
> So close shut up, and lockt to all mankind.
> I see men's bodies only ours, no more,
> The rest, another's might, that rules the mind.
>   (2.2.1–12)

---

[24]   Chabod, *Machiavelli and the Renaissance* (Cambridge, MA: Harvard University Press, 1958), p. 191.

Chapter 9
Butler's *Lear*

Laurence Wright

Investigating neglected scholarship must be one of the least strategic moves in the arsenal of academic gamesmanship. Michael Jensen adverts to 'the current allergy too many scholars have to reading anything more than seven years old'.[1] Even so, treasures of thought, research and writing deserve exhumation when they add to our knowledge and understanding of important works of art. This is the case with Butler's *Lear*.

At the time of his passing I wrote that

> Guy Butler's greatest Shakespearean legacy probably lives in the aural memory of generations of his students – sadly, therefore, a fleeting asset to humanity, but one which has infected many of those who sat in his lectures with a love for the protean zest of Shakespearean language ... He had a marvellous talent for reading verse. Syntactic obscurities melted. Stuff which to the student mind lay dead on the page, suddenly lifted into meaning like the blaze of aloes on an Eastern Cape hillside. Who could forget him leaning over the rostrum, with spectacles intermittently lost, sucked, twirled and perched on his nose, growling out in rich, gravelly tones lines such as:
>
> > Golden lads and girls all must,
> > As chimney-sweepers, come to dust.
> > (*Cymbeline*, 4.2)[2]

But, as well as being a compelling teacher, and among a huge array of other interests and undertakings,[3] Butler was also a Shakespearean scholar of stature, though much of his work went unpublished or appeared as scattered articles in disparate journals so that it never achieved critical mass. Nevertheless, his scholarly acuity was profound.

His deepest interest was reserved for the great tragedies, *Othello*, *Lear*, *Macbeth* and *Coriolanus*, though he also had a special place for *Julius Caesar*, *Troilus and*

---

[1]   Michael P. Jensen, 'John W. Velz, Shakespeare Scholar: Reflections on a Friend', *Shakespeare Newsletter* 58.2 (2008): pp. 41, 52.

[2]   Laurence Wright, 'Guy Butler: 21 January 1918 – 26 April 2001', *Shakespeare in Southern Africa*, 1999/2000, pp. vi–ix.

[3]   See Chris Thurman, *Guy Butler: Reassessing a South African Literary Life* (Scottsville: University of KwaZulu-Natal Press, 2010), for an overview of his manifold engagements.

Cressida and *Antony and Cleopatra*. His long-time friend, the poet Don Maclennan, recalled that at one time he had the whole of *Richard II* by heart.[4] His productions at Rhodes University were legendary: *Julius Caesar* (1952), *A Midsummer Night's Dream* (1956), *Othello* (1957), *Hamlet* (1959), *Henry IV Part 1* (1962), *Everyman* (1963), his own *Cape Charade* (1967), *Dr Faustus* (1968), and a last magnificent production of *Noye's Fludde* to the music of Benjamin Britten in the Cathedral of St Michael and St George in 1970. Butler's work as a theatrical director helped catalyse the university's decision to create a drama department, and it led to his undertaking an extensive research tour of the United States in 1958 as a Carnegie Fellow to examine drama and English curricula and ascertain best practice in university theatre architecture, the results of which were influential in the design of the Rhodes University Theatre, inaugurated in 1966.

Acknowledging this grounding in direction and theatre architecture, as well as his authorship of more than 11 plays, most of which have been staged or broadcast,[5] becomes important when we turn to Butler's Shakespearean scholarship. While not a theatre professional by any means (such beings barely existed in South Africa's Eastern Cape in the 1950s and 1960s), he was no mere armchair critic, no academic diagnostician of the kind familiar today, using Shakespeare selectively to buttress historical arguments about Jacobean culture. His focus was unwaveringly on Shakespeare's play texts as drama to be realised in performance. This chapter sets out to assess the particular quality of his scholarly work on Shakespeare, focusing on *King Lear*.

***

Guy Butler's *Lear*, two bulky companion typescript volumes, lies unread in the National English Literary Museum in Grahamstown. There are multiple copies and different versions in draft, partly corrected and amended in holograph, with references missing or incomplete.[6] The project upon which it was based, funded by the South African Human Sciences Research Council, occupied him in his retirement (or what passed as retirement for this tireless cultural dynamo), for roughly 10 years, between 1978 and 1988, though he continued reshaping and

---

    [4]   Personal communication.

    [5]   These include *The Dam* (1953), *The Dove Returns* (1956), *Remembrance Day*, radio play (broadcast 1956, published [1965]), *Judith*, radio play, written in blank verse (1957), *Cape Charade or Kaatjie Kekkelbek* (1968), *A Scattering of Seed*, radio play (1968), *Take Root or Die* (1970), 'One Night at Clay Pits' (1980), *Richard Gush of Salem* (1982), *Demea* (1990), and a number of unpublished works never performed, such as *Silver Spoon: A Farcical Romance*, *Two-Timers*, a modernised version of *Everyman*, and several others. The dates are those of first publication, or first performance in the case of unpublished works.

    [6]   See South African National English Literary Museum, Butler Collection, 2004. 19.5.1.1–2004 19.5.10. The present chapter is based on a copy left to the Institute for the Study of English in Africa in Butler's will.

publishing extracts from the research more or less to the end of his life. Indeed, he had been deeply preoccupied with this play as a teacher and lecturer for most of his career. While the core research was underway, few attending tea in the convivial Rhodes University English Department Common Room could escape knowing just where he was in his thinking on the play, his concerns passing through several obsessive phases; among them, the cosmic bond, the family, clothing, iconology, and the play's mythic foundations. He never attempted a production, believing with A.C. Bradley that '*King Lear* is too huge for the stage,'[7] but even in the case of *Lear* Butler looked to theatrical practicalities as the final arbiter in adjudicating interpretations. This was a perennial emphasis of his Shakespearean criticism.

To illustrate the point, Butler's study coincided with the editing and production of the Wells and Taylor Oxford edition, whose editorial rationale was buttressed by *The Division of the Kingdoms*, a collection of essays edited by Gary Taylor and Michael Warren (1983), urging with some vigour that Folio and Quarto were best regarded as separate plays.[8] Butler corresponded with Stanley Wells concerning the text on which he should base his study[9] and concurred with Wells's advice that he should use 'any ... modern edition that is strongly based on the Folio'.[10] In the end, Butler decided to go with Muir's Arden text, despite its problems. In 11 succinct pages of discussion, he courteously demolishes the cogency for his purposes of regarding Quarto and Folio as separate plays (a decision in which, for literary-critical purposes, many have concurred).[11] Butler uses either dramatic or theatrical criteria, or both, to assess cuts and additions in the two texts, the exception being the change from 'coining' to 'crying' at 4.6.83, which he argues was politically motivated. He lauds improved dramatic writing in Folio's version of Cordelia's responses during the love contest, especially in their rhythm and timing. In the 'stripping' scene in Act III, he admires Folio's embellishment of clothing figures already established in Quarto. He endorses Muir's view that the complete omission of 4.3 was an effort to curb length, suggesting that 'the cutting of the gentleman's account of Cordelia follows a well-known theatrical rule of thumb: eloquent reports of what has happened elsewhere, and off stage, and long messengers' speeches are the first to go.'[12] In line with the excision of bit parts (in Quarto three gentlemen arrive to arrest Lear, in Folio only one; after Gloucester's blinding two servants are cut), he attributes the reduced prominence of music and

---

[7]   A.C. Bradley, *Shakespearean Tragedy* (London: Macmillan, 1952), 247. Quoted in Guy Butler, *King Lear in Shakespeare's Time*, unpublished manuscript, vol. 1, p. 24.

[8]   Gary Taylor and Michael Warren (eds), *The Division of the Kingdoms: Shakespeare's Two Versions of* King Lear (Oxford: Clarendon Press, 1983).

[9]   Letters: Butler to Wells, 22 November 1983; and reply, Wells to Butler, 30 November 1983; draft letter from Butler to Wells 22 December 1983 (NELM, Butler Collection, 2004. 19.8.3.331).

[10]   Letter, Wells to Butler, 30 November 1983, ibid.

[11]   Guy Butler, *King Lear in Shakespeare's Time*, pp. 18–29.

[12]   Ibid., 26.

musicians in Folio to the need for thrift in both money and stage time, supporting the theory 'that the Folio text was revised for the reduced team of a touring company.'[13] Butler's 'take' on the full complex issue emphasises the possibility that Shakespeare revised the text for artistic and theatrical reasons, a view long ago articulated by Harley Granville-Barker in his preface to the play (1927), and Madeleine Doran in her monograph *The Text of King Lear* (1931).[14] His overall conclusion is as follows:

> No single cut or addition, nor the sum of them all, warrants the view that Shakespeare's Folio is a re-created *King Lear*. Much of Folio is nevertheless a heightening and refinement of Quarto. As for the major cuts: as I believe them to have been motivated either by the practical need to increase the pace, or by censorship, and not by any change in thematic intent, I have included readings of them.[15]

The focus of Butler's *Lear* is an effort to explicate the play's full meaning and significance. Oddly enough, one of the reasons publishers gave for refusing to publish Butler's study (others were sheer bulk, focus on a single play, and the work's arrangement as an introductory sequence of scholarly orientations and interventions, followed by a sequential reading in the form of extended critical notes) was his avoidance of close-quarter contention with contemporary Shakespearean scholarship. Throughout his life, Butler was chary of combative intellectual sparring, viewing it as an egoistic distraction from the real point of scholarship, which was to illuminate its intended object. This might seem rather odd coming from someone who contributed vigorously to newspaper polemic throughout his career and stirred up a number of politically controversial hornets' nests.[16] But ad hominem controversy, especially in scholarship, he regarded as both nugatory and demeaning. While the study illustrates healthy command of then-recent works of Lear scholarship as well as older scholarly material, and wide acquaintance with the dramatic and philosophical literature current in the period, these ancillary voices are enlisted to support arguments about the play, rather than to fuel scholarly debate. Butler's study of Lear is throughout an explicit effort 'to see the object as in itself it really is' (to borrow Arnold's take

---

[13]   Ibid., 10.

[14]   Harley Granville-Barker, *Prefaces to Shakespeare: King Lear* (London: Nick Hern Books; Royal National Theatre, 1993), p. 111; Madeleine Doran, *The Text of King Lear* (Stanford, CA: Stanford University Press, 1931).

[15]   Butler, *King Lear in Shakespeare's Time*, 11. Butler contests Gary Taylor's dating of the revision to 1610–11, proposing that the cutting of the trial scene, the addition of the Fool's prophecy, and the change from 'coining' to 'crying' suggest a later date of October–November 1612, 'with an unusual degree of accuracy' (p. 29).

[16]   See Jeanette Eve's compilation of journalism and polemic, *Guy Butler: Fifty Years of Press-Clippings* (Grahamstown: National English Literary Museum, 1994).

on Plato, adapted from Joseph Butler),[17] a procedure which certainly involved disabusing readers of misapprehensions foisted on the play by fellow critics, but not at their personal expense. Despite this scholarly tact, Butler can be startlingly forthright. In response to opinions attributing difficulties in the play's opening scene to their submerged origins in folklore and fairy tale he responds, 'Rubbish; they are nearly all of Shakespeare's own devising,' and proceeds to demonstrate.[18] Butler's revisionary focus addresses, not the ballooning undergrowth of critical scholarship, but misapprehensions distorting our sense of the play itself, as the arbiter of what is intrinsically significant.

The study's title, *King Lear in Shakespeare's Time* (a belated rejoinder to Maynard Mack's *King Lear in Our Time*, 1965) strikes the keynote. In laying the groundwork for his reading, Butler is concerned to show that far from avoiding contemporary political controversy by indulging a form of anachronistic pastoral, *King Lear* speaks directly to the realities of Jacobean Britain: 'If we need an historical model for Lear's kingdom, we simply step outside the Globe, and it is all about us; Jacobean England, collapsing into decadence after the death of Gloriana.'[19] By pooh-poohing any exaggerated emphasis on the *King Lear* source and the influence of fairy tale in the play's opening scene, Butler makes the point that Lear's political folly in dividing his kingdom intentionally flatters the wisdom of King James who was engaged in putting it back together.[20] The royal proclamation concerning 'the Kings Majesties Stile' (1604), proposes the inauguration of 'a blessed Union, or rather Reuniting of these two mightie, famous and ancient Kingdomes of England and Scotland under one Imperiall Crowne'.[21] Scotland, of course, had been a problem throughout Elizabeth's reign, and the play's opening implicitly compliments James for reconstituting what his ancient predecessor, Brut, had torn apart.

But this ingratiating surface gesture smuggles in a much more telling and damaging critique of the King. Look deeper, Butler argues, and it is obvious that the ills infecting Lear's kingdom echo those that prevailed in James's court, to the distress of many of his subjects. The transition from Elizabeth to James in this regard had been shocking in the extreme, and the new King's unprepossessing physical appearance was a very superficial part of the problem. More seriously,

---

[17] Matthew Arnold, 'The Function of Criticism at the Present Time', *The Complete Prose Works of Matthew Arnold*, ed. R.H. Super, vol. 3 (Ann Arbor: University of Michigan Press, 1960–77), p. 258. Cf. Joseph Butler, *The Analogy of Religion* (London: Thomas Tegg and Sons, 1838), p. 152: ' a mind which sees things as they really are'.

[18] Butler, *King Lear in Shakespeare's Time*, p. 86.

[19] Ibid., p. 580.

[20] Ibid., pp. 85–6.

[21] 'Proclamation concerning the Kings Majesties Stile, of King of Great Britaine, &c.', ed. Paul H. Hughes and James L. Larkin, *Stuart Royal Proclamations*, vol. 1, *Royal Proclamations of King James 1, 1603–1625* (Oxford: Clarendon Press, 1973–1983), p. 95. Quoted in Butler, *King Lear in Shakespeare's Time*, p. 36. (Reference incomplete in Butler.)

his notion of kingship showcased many of the flaws which scar Lear's deluded notion of his office. Chief of these was James's narcissistic self-regard. As Butler remarks, 'Lear can be seen as enjoying himself as he divides and gives his kingdom away; [James] as preening himself as he joins his two kingdoms. Both remain firmly in love with their titles, and what they do to their kingdom is done to please their royal selves.'[22] Both show themselves susceptible to flattery. Lear insists on retaining his retinue even when he has relinquished the divinely bestowed duties – and the responsibilities – it symbolises. There is a similar self-regarding quality in James's attachment to royal pomp. Both kings, the real and the fictional, indulge an exaggerated sense of regal dignity focused on themselves, and lack the humility Shakespeare demanded of his worthy kings (Butler compares, for instance, Henry V's ordering the singing of *Non nobis* and *Te deum* after Agincourt).[23]

Of even greater concern was what Butler calls the king's 'painfully pathetic sexual behaviour'.[24] His homosexuality as such was not the issue, but rather the consequent sidelining of his queen:

> What is the status of a Queen when the King claims he is omnipotent and God's lieutenant? James effectively rejected the regality of his Queen; she had a separate establishment, a small court of her own ... There was no proper symbiosis of King and Queen, of Male and Female in the Jacobean court.[25]

All well and good, the reader might respond, but had the lack of any such symbiosis been missed under Elizabeth? Not really; for a 'Virgin Queen' the issue didn't arise. But James's reckless infatuation with a succession of male favourites, the sheer lack of decorum in his roistering personal conduct, and his callous rejection and undermining of his queen, placed exactly the kind of negative pressure on the ideology of kingship that might register in a play where the queen is not only sidelined but absent. Furthermore, *Lear's* lavish subplot excoriates base debauchery in a manner which precisely complements the critique of kingly deficiencies adumbrated in the main plot. Both strands speak eloquently to a severe view of James in his person, and as king.

Secondly, Butler urges that the legendary ancient Britain foregrounded in various modern accounts of the play (and seen in many a contemporary production) is a scholarly phantasm. Elizabethans and Jacobeans lacked the historical imagination to conceive of ancient Britons as being other than they were themselves. Neither the society portrayed in the text, nor that discernible in the legendary sources, conforms to the fanciful image of a society emerging from barbarism: 'The historical knowledge of Elizabethans and Jacobeans was extremely limited and faulty. They were simply not aware of Neolithic or ancient Celtic culture.'[26]

---

22   Ibid., p. 37.
23   Ibid., p. 38.
24   Ibid., p. 40.
25   Ibid., p. 43.
26   Ibid., p. 56.

King Lear could not evade Jacobean England by fabricating mystical cultural and political roots or romanticising an ancient society on the cusp of the primitive. 'The play presents the corruption and collapse of an advanced culture, saturated in western, Hellenic and Judaic thought.'[27] The *translatio imperii* which informs the play's contemporary relevance was innocent of modern notions about historical development or progress: 'The ancient Britons, for them, were little different from the ancient Trojans, Greeks or Romans, or indeed themselves.'[28] By rejecting the notion of Jacobeans believing in a primitive, barbaric ancient Britain, Butler impugned the earnest humanist and existentialist readings and productions of the play which became de rigueur in the 1960s and 1970s (many of them influenced by Jan Kott's *Shakespeare Our Contemporary* [1964]; though, typically, Butler refrains from mentioning this theatrically influential text):

> One must reject the popular absurdist view that this is a play about a martyrdom inflicted by an alien universe upon innocent humanity ... Even those inclined to interpret events in terms of Fortune or Fate (like Gloucester) behave with responsibility, and, indeed, noble courage. If terrible sacrifices are made, the victims are wide-eyed volunteers. Cordelia chooses to invade Britain. Nor are the villains instinct-driven beasts of the wild wood. Their actions proceed rationally from naked egotism; they are cool and explicit about their motives. There is nothing primitive whatever about their thought processes.[29]

Butler's reading is particularly rich in its treatment of the contemporary conviction that the natural world was reaching its limit. According to most contemporary schemes, such as Samuel Gardiner's in his *Doomes-Day Book* (1606) or Godfrey Goodman's in *The Fall of Man* (1616) – Butler's account invokes a rich chorus of similar diagnoses – the natural world was about to return to its native nothingness, consumed by fire. More immediately telling to the popular mind were accompanying signs and portents. The physical ageing of the world, adumbrated by writers such as Samuel Purchas, or Sir Thomas Browne, or Samuel Gardiner again (in *General Signes of Christ Coming to Judgement*), and several others, was accompanied by un-ignorable astronomical portents. Butler's study pays particular attention to the significance of eclipses in the plays written between 1598 and 1606, and especially to the 'nova' discovered by Kepler on 17 October 1604 and immediately put to dramatic use by Chapman, Jonson and Marston.[30] It would have shone throughout 1605, so that when the first actor to play Edmund referred to the 'maidenliest star in the universe' (1.2.129), his audience may even have seen it. Historical precedents such as the noonday eclipse at the crucifixion, or the signs accompanying Julius Caesar's death, or the great comet of 1528 (also marking a period of significant political upheaval) fuelled this climate of seasoned credulity. Butler writes,

---

27 Ibid, pp. 59–60.
28 Ibid.
29 Ibid., p. 58.
30 Ibid., pp. 199–205.

'a coincidence of political disaster and astral portents produced in many sensitive minds – and not least in Shakespeare's – a state bordering on conviction that the end of the world was at hand'.[31]

The increased viciousness and industry of the Devil were everywhere evident, detailed, for instance, by the industrious puritan Phillip Stubbes in his *Anatomie of Abuses* (1583). Turmoil markedly similar to that described by Stubbes, and many others, appears in *Lear*, 'the elements raging in storm, the planets and eclipses perpetually ominous, the earth trembling, and nature in revolt, producing monsters'.[32] The turn of the new century passed pacifically enough, but equanimity was soon ruptured by the Essex Rebellion and the death of the queen in 1603. Festivities to welcome James to the throne had to be delayed because of the worst outbreak of plague in living memory; and this was followed by the prodigiously disturbing Gunpowder Plot of 1605. Antony Nixon's *The Black Year* (1606) excoriates the very hypocrisy and economic excess pilloried in *King Lear*, several passages chiming remarkably with the Fool's prophecy (3.2.80–94), for instance, 'Such as be rich shall be sure of friends ... Those that have no Mittens in Winter, may blow their nails by authoritie, for no man will pittie them that are needy,' and so on.[33] Chapter 4 of Gardiner's *Doomes-Day Book*, mentioned above, with its provocative and inclusive subtitle, *An Alarum for Atheists, A Watchword for Worldlings, A Caveat for Christians*, 'reads like a précis of events and omens in *King Lear*'.[34]

All this, and much more, is richly documented in the opening movement of the study, which establishes foundations for the detailed reading which follows. But the informing principle in Butler's *Lear* is not one of straightforward historical contextualisation, adventitiously agitating the echo-chamber of the textual archive. He sees the play as resonating within a sequence of informing myths. The theoretical inspiration comes from Northrop Frye, whose *Anatomy of Criticism* (1957) was an important precursor to that vogue for explicit theory which dominated large swathes of socio-literary study from the 1970s to the early 1990s. Frye's major work offered an inclusive reading of Western literature in a complex system of myth ultimately rooted in the cycle of the seasons.

Butler never bought into this scheme in its entirety. He liked Frye's idea that putting works of literature in such a context 'gives them an immense reverberating dimension of significance ... in which every literary work catches the echoes of all other works of its type in literature, and so ripples out into the rest of literature and thence into life'.[35] But he was cautious: mythical reverberations 'can confuse

---

[31]   Ibid., pp. 77–8.

[32]   Ibid., p. 71.

[33]   Quoted ibid., p. 72.

[34]   Ibid.

[35]   Northrop Frye, *Fables of Identity: Studies in Poetic Mythology* (New York: Harcourt, Brace & World), p. 37. Quoted in Butler, *King Lear in Shakespeare's Time*, p. 100.

the impact of a great work into a spiral of serpents in a Marabar cave'.[36] The worry was possible dissipation of the play's specificity, losing the sequential process of meaning-making on the stage by subordinating it to myth. This was a not uncommon response to Frye's vision of literature.[37] Butler nevertheless accepted Frye's assertion that myths 'show an odd tendency to stick together and build up bigger structures'.[38]

He saw the deep substructure of the play as following a sequence of four informing myths. The myth of Ixion and Juno speaks to the initial critique of the twin corruptors, power and sex, examined in the early parts of the main and subplots. King Ixion, elevated by Jove to the status of steward in his celestial palace, ungratefully attempts seduction of Jove's wife, Juno, patroness of women and marriage but also of wealth and regality. Ixion succeeds, not with Juno herself, but with a cloud of illusion in her shape. From this union of a false servant and a false image, the centaurs, harbingers of political and familial disaster, are born. Jove's punitive thunderbolt blasts Ixion from heaven 'to a kingdom of ruins and monsters, and thence into hell, to spin forever on a fiery wheel of remorse'.[39] Lear is an Ixion attracted to the status and sheer glamour of Juno's power; Gloucester to her body alone.

Lear's subsequent political and psychic dissolution, his retreat into the wilderness, literal and mental, followed by his restoration, is grounded in the myth of the Abasement of the Proud King, typified in the legendary stories of Robert of Sicily, of the Emperor Jovinian in the *Gesta Romanum* and, especially, the humbling and restoration of Nebuchadnezzar in the Old Testament, probably the archetype of the story-complex. Butler summarises Ralegh's analysis of Nebuchadnezzar's downfall in his *History of the World* (1614) to indicate its relevance to the Lear story: 'Ralegh sees [Nebuchadnezzar] as a perfect example of 1) pride preceding a fall; 2) stubborn refusal to heed repeated admonitions; 3) an astounding reversal of fortune; not into death or torture at the hands of enemies, but into self-induced madness and bestial exile from society; 4) of restoration to sanity through suffering, humiliation, and acknowledgement of his mere humanity.'[40]

The profound spiritual changes subsequently wrought in both Lear and Gloucester, as well as the contrasting behaviours of Cordelia and various servant figures in the main and subplots, are related to the diffuse but powerful myth of the Suffering Servant, in its Judaic, Christian and ancient Greek dimensions; and for the play's resolute confronting of death, Butler resorts, with some equivocation, to

---

[36]   Butler, *King Lear in Shakespeare's Time*, p. 100.

[37]   I recall Bernard Bergonzi expressing similar reservations in theory classes at Warwick University in the early 1970s: cyclical mythic structures might be there, but were they interesting? Did they operate at the level for which people came to literature?

[38]   Northrop Frye, *Fables of Identity*, p. 31. Quoted in Butler, *King Lear in Shakespeare's Time*, p. 14.

[39]   Butler, *King Lear in Shakespeare's Time*, p. 102.

[40]   Ibid., p. 113.

the morality tradition of *Everyman* and the medieval literature on death and dying. These four sequential myth matrices speak in detail to the progress of the action in *King Lear*, though there is no space here to explicate their cogency in full.

Butler's *Lear* is first and foremost a work of synthesis. Many of the perspectives it elaborates had been expressed in earlier scholarship, and Butler duly acknowledges his debts: O.B. Hardison for the myth of Ixion, Maynard Mack and Lilian H. Hornstein for Robert of Sicily, Madeleine Doran on Lear's culpability, John W. Hales for popular British history, Muir, Stone and Urkowitz on textual matters, and so on. Even more are derived directly from that capacious echo chamber mentioned earlier, the literature of the age, in Chapman, Dekker, Jonson, Marlowe, Marston, Montaigne, Munday, Burton, Erasmus, Ralegh's *History of the World*, Cooper's *Thesaurus*, Purchas, and a host of other major and minor figures. Butler's particular emphasis on *Everyman* as the fable underlying the play's final unrelenting portrayal of suffering, dying and death may be original (I return to the question of originality below); but while pervasive, the influence is not textually as tangible. Butler's earliest publication focusing wholly on *Lear* contains this seminal sentence: '*King Lear*, I suggest, is Shakespeare's *Everyman*, but infinitely more complex and profound.'[41] To be sure, the play 'provides a paradigm of the late mediaeval view of man as destined to judgment which was still paramount in the 16th and 17th centuries',[42] and *Lear* indeed follows the stages of Everyman's surrender to death: broadly, dissolution of social ties and status; the struggle with conscience; the preparation for death; and the process of dying. But the influence may be more a matter of common social apprehension than literary influence. More recently, John W. Velz has pondered why Shakespearean judgement scenes based on doomsday pageants and moralities abound in the comedies, but are seemingly avoided in the major tragedies.[43] Butler's answer in the case of *Lear* would be as follows: 'The action of *Lear* takes place shortly before the great assizes begins. It is part of the great cunning of the work to make the audience sit on the bench.'[44]

Though I have conveyed neither the richness and originality of insight, elaboration of thought, nor the extensiveness and cogency of the source material marshalled in support of the study's groundwork, such are the bald premises of Butler's study. It is at this point that his detailed reading of the play begins, in the second part of the text. Instead of following its course, we must turn now to the awkward business of assessment, a task made more challenging and ambivalent when the full evidence is not before the reader.

***

---

[41]   Guy Butler, '*King Lear*', *Rhodes University Department of Education Bulletin* 2.2 (November 1973): p. 1.

[42]   Guy Butler, *King Lear in Shakespeare's Time*, p. 122.

[43]   John W. Velz, 'Eschatology in the Bradleian Tragedies: Some Aesthetic Implications', *The Shakespeare Newsletter* 58.2 (Fall 2008): pp. 41, 62.

[44]   Guy Butler, *King Lear in Shakespeare's Time*, p. 131.

Towards the end of his project, Butler showed himself fully aware that this major work of scholarship was unlikely to see the light of day. Writing to Stanley Wells in May 1987 for advice about 'this monstrous big book which I have written, a mere 220 000 words', he observes with polemical forthrightness:

> I suspect it is quite unpublishable, not only because of its size but because it is so oldfashioned [*sic*]: an attempt to read the play and let it speak for itself in its entirety, rather than use it as a source of ammunition in the latest polemic among the philosophers of literature – many of whom, alas, can't read a text with any perception.[45]

(Butler was evidently no fan of the New Historicist and Cultural Materialist readings then in vogue, with their 'presentist' penchant for claiming authoritative centrality for historically marginal and tangential perspectives.) Wells responded perceptively, urging that the two parts of the study belonged to different genres. He was correct. The first part, with its rather uninspiring title 'General Comments', is directed to a scholarly audience and, indeed, many of its key arguments and original discoveries subsequently appeared as scholarly articles. The second part, with an equally reticent title, 'Notes on Key Phrases in the Text', also yielded a number of innovative scholarly articles, but commits itself to a more or less continuous reading, necessarily covering ground which academics familiar with the play might take for granted.[46] Wells urged that this was probably more suited to a general audience or perhaps a broader educational market.

I suspect that the writing of Butler's unwieldy magnum opus was motivated less by the desire to publish a book than to put on paper his passion for the play and, while he was about it, to be comprehensive and exhaustive in its explication. The Casaubon factor was in play. On the surface at least, as Wells had indicated, the problem was one of genre. There was a blatant – and somehow rather winning – disregard for strategic academic publishing imperatives in Butler's project. His eye was on the universe of *Lear*, not on what Thomas Pepper calls 'the current eutropic-entropic bloom of the critical supermarket'. Urging the imperative of Truth over method, Pepper writes, 'It used to be that classification systems were constructed in order to classify books; now books are written, subjects – in all senses – are produced, in order to conform to the standards of those systems' – a situation he regards, with Hamlet-like scorn, as demonstrating 'the decadence and profound lack of imagination of this time'.[47]

He notes that in current publications, seductive scholarly titles encapsulating 'more or less wittily the thematic concern of the book' are followed routinely by a colon 'which indicates to the cursor of the potential scanning mechanism that the words that follow are names or subjects to be catalogued for access in storage-and-

---

[45] Letter, Butler to Wells, 4 May 1987 (NELM, Butler Collection, 2004. 19.8.3.331).

[46] For the scholarly articles mentioned, see note 59.

[47] Thomas Pepper, *Singularities: Extremes of Theory in the Twentieth Century* (Cambridge: Cambridge University Press, 1997), pp. xi–xii.

retrieval systems'. In this fashion, academics find themselves trapped in the toils of a mechanical Nietzschean perspectivism. The whole stays forever beyond the horizon, because the academic publishing system requires only the unique angle, and this necessitates marginalising what is already known, however adequate or compelling it might be. As a result, not only are the subjects (the objects of study) distorted but so are the authors (who become 'subjects' of the system, as the Ph.D. factories grind relentlessly on), in pale mimicry of John Ruskin's impassioned outcry in the nineteenth century against specialisation and the division of labour: 'It is not, truly, the labour that is divided, but the men.'[48]

I am not arguing that Butler constructed his study in the manner he did out of postmodern disdain for generic convention; rather, that he saw the world in terms of the play and wanted to share this understanding with his audience. *Lear* was to be returned to Shakespeare's time, as theatre, so that it could speak to ours. The simple metaphor he used was that of spectacles. By accepting the profound historical adjustment required to respond properly to the text (putting on the corrective lenses that brought English Renaissance drama into focus), not only was the play illuminated but one could then see *through* the play to aspects of humanity's permanent predicament in the cosmos. Butler wrote his study of *Lear* not only out of a sense of awe and amazement that such a work exists but because to a remarkable extent he identified with the play.

This is absolutely not the way today's university-trained academics approach works of art, except perhaps in unguarded moments before an undergraduate audience. Butler's acceptance of 'old-fashioned' historicity as a means of interpreting not only its meanings but the contemporary significance of art has been widely supplanted by supine thraldom to various *historicisms*. These modes of perception keep readers or audiences shuttling helplessly between hybrid 'historicist' and 'presentist' perceptions, fulfilling their managed role as distanced spectators caught up in the intellectual simulacra created by our culture's predicament of late literacy. No longer are they independently questing participants sharing life-changing artistic and intellectual experiences in one amazing circumambient universe.

It may be that an upbringing remote from what Jacques Barzun has dubbed 'The House of Intellect'[49] – metropolitan art and culture – sometimes nurtures an independence of mind, an originality, denied those reared within its portals. This happens because a rich relationship with the natural world survives as a powerful counterbalance to later cultural complexities. Butler's childhood in the small Eastern Cape town of Cradock in the opening decades of the twentieth century (recounted in *Karoo Morning*, 1977, the first volume of his autobiography), with its joyful openness to the rugged world of nature, to the rigours of small-town life, and to the austere intellectual and religious stimulus of a cultivated family

---

[48]   John Ruskin, *The Stones of Venice*, vol. 2, *Sea Stories*, 1886 (New York: Cosimo, 2007), p. 165.

[49]   Jacques Barzun, *The House of Intellect* (New York: Harper Collins, [1957]).

background combining Anglican and Quaker influences (the town newspaper, the *Midland News*, was a family business), meant that Butler developed an extraordinarily free and robust sense of intellectual adequacy:

> We watched ... marvelling each year when the first tree blossomed – usually an almond; and we waited for the first leaves to turn red on the pear trees. Between these miracles and the marvels in books – particularly those in the Bible – there was no cleavage. Life was all of a piece. The facts we were slowly learning in school and from our environment were still particles floating in the sunlight of our happy subjectivity. Things might be removed by time or distance ... but they were not gone, never taken away. Nothing was alien and there were no exiles. The world was whole.
> So it seemed, for most of the time.[50]

This outlook left Butler with an enduring feeling of fundamental kinship with the natural environment, a healthy trust in the competence of human intelligence, and a rich sense of the importance of human sociality. Religious and philosophical doubt encroached from an early age (the *Collected Poems* supply abundant evidence of these wrestlings), but his upbringing formed in him a strong bastion of intellectual self-confidence, of faith in possible human agency. Experience in World War II challenged all this (the story is told in the second volume of his autobiography, *Bursting World*, 1983) and he struggled with the contrast between industrial modernity and this solid familial matrix for the rest of his life.

In his response to art, the open universe of his early years was still present to Butler. An awkward passage in the third volume of autobiography, *A Local Habitation* (1991), which focuses on Butler's mature struggles to renovate South African culture, indicates his disquiet with the tortured politicisation of art which characterised South Africa's apartheid years:

> I have always felt uneasy about attempts to turn literature into politics or ethics or a substitute for religion. Literature is literature, a major human activity which should be studied in its own right, rather as we study music or painting. Of course it has moral and political dimensions, as have all human activities, but these are not its main concern.[51]

This sounds like the manifesto of a convinced and self-indulgent aesthete. Far from it. True, he affirmed that 'literature's purpose, like that of all other arts, is to create pleasures and joys for mankind which the social and other sciences can't provide,' but he also demanded artistic responsibility. Artists must be 'conscientious citizens and, like everyone else, they have a responsibility towards their hungry neighbours'.[52] Butler maintained this position because he already had before him a world view in which he believed. The *Lear* study shows

---

[50]   Guy Butler, *Karoo Morning* (Cape Town: David Philip, 1977), pp. 51–2.

[51]   Guy Butler, *A Local Habitation* (Cape Town: David Philip, 1991), p. 239.

[52]   Ibid., pp. 239–40.

him arguing for a profoundly Christian reading of the play, not out of abstract doctrinal conviction (or not simply so), and not because the play's intellectual foundations are rooted in the Hellenic-Judeo-Christian matrix, as they obviously are, but because the play uses its religious framework to wrestle with what Butler apprehended to be fundamental realities of human experience. It was not merely that Christian theology found ample means of accommodating pagan philosophy and ethical insight (the issue is thoroughly aired in the *Lear* study),[53] but that Butler recognised and believed in the *Lear* world as a profound representation of his world, and our world.

Two poems in the *Collected Poems* explore his personal identification with the play. 'The Divine Underground' evokes the Lear universe to describe Butler's often bootless search for clear-sighted political and cultural allies – 'those who wear / a habit of discipline on every gesture, armed / in still affection, steel-bright after years' – in the wastelands of South Africa's apartheid turmoil:

> I find them poorly disguised as morons,
> under distorting stars,
> lost in the lands of their birth, quite ousted by
> smooth bastards or daughters in gorgeous gowns
> ...
> they know what they have lost,
> they guess at what they have gained;
> divining an innocent justice, they endure
> our grand and murderous razzmatazz
> as if they were God's spies.[54]

A second poem develops an incident when the *Lear* study itself, specifically work on the story of Nebuchadnezzar, the abasement of the proud king, illuminates a poignant transaction between Butler and an old black man, 'The Acorn Man', under the oak trees outside his home in Grahamstown's High Street. The sheer luxury of being in a position to devote time and energy to literary study, including a year-long overseas fellowship, contrasts strikingly with the courteous old man's abject struggle for bare survival, and its probable defeat. The poem concludes in Lear-like penitence, 'O! I have ta'en / too little care of this'.[55]

These are published poems, their sentiments masked in the reserve of formal utterance for public dissemination. Among the relics of the *Lear* project in the National English Literary Museum are drafts of two, more intimate, poems which never made it into the *Collected Poems*, either on grounds of quality or because they were never finished. They offer less guarded insight into the intensity of Butler's relation with *King Lear*, revealing the sense in which the *Lear* universe

---

53   Guy Butler, *King Lear in Shakespeare's Time*, pp. 132–5.
54   Guy Butler, *Collected Poems* (Cape Town: David Philip, 1999), p. 178.
55   Ibid., pp. 259–61.

was for him the South African world in which he lived. The first juxtaposes 'ripeness' from *Lear* with 'readiness' from *Hamlet*:

> Hearing of his King's defeat
> The derelict duke of Gloster
> Old, blind, superfluous, lust-dieted
> Refused further flight:
> 'A man may rot even here.'
> But his divinely deceitful son replies
> 'Men must endure their going hence
> Even as their coming hither
> Ripeness is all'
> But I, old, etcetera
> Wide eyed but nonetheless blind
> Think rather of a young prince in a rotten kingdom
> Conquering disgust, who finds
> Divinity shaping our ends, and
> Knowing his own end imminent, says
> 'The readiness is all.'[56]

The 'ripening' metaphor invokes natural processes, ineluctable, unasked for; 'readiness', by contrast, is a human state involving personal preparedness in the face of fundamental uncertainties.[57] But is 'readiness' a genuine human possibility, faced with one's own end? The second unpublished poem, scribbled on the back of a page from a critical article on *Lear*, and very probably written during the preparation of the *Lear* study, seems closer to the truth:

> I am now about as old as Gloucester
> Blind in no man's land
> Agreeing with his son in disguise after the battle was lost
> That men must endure their going hence
> That ripeness is all.
> But I must confess that I do not feel
> What ripeness implies – fullness, sweetness
> Fruitfulness, completion of the purposes for which I was made –
> Instead, feeling the evil auguries in my time, my place
> my aging flesh, I envy a younger man
> On the brink of a fatal duel saying
> The readiness is all.
> What am I ready for? Fit for what?[58]

---

56   NELM, Butler Collection, 2004. 19.2.1.124.

57   Some implications of these two words for the plays concerned are usefully explored in Yves Bonnefoy and John T. Naughton, 'Readiness, Ripeness: *Hamlet, Lear*', *New Literary History* 17.3 (Spring 1986): pp. 477–91.

58   NELM, Butler Collection, 2004. 19.2.1.124.

That last raw line – is it part of the poem? I think not. But in his shrinking from the *Lear* universe towards the young Prince Hamlet's, there could be few clearer indications of Butler's visceral identification with Shakespeare's unruly masterpiece.

Scholars deprived of access to the original typescript lodged in the National English Literary Museum can gain a fragmentary sense of the work by perusing the sequence of research articles which flowed from it.[59] I can only recommend that readers who want to understand *King Lear* more fully take the time to sit and read Butler's *Lear*. Much of the work is beautifully written, its diction choice and apposite, and there is insight on almost every page. In all, an enriching exercise, provided we take seriously these words from the preface:

> There can be no one meaning for such a work as *King Lear*, no possible consensus as to its philosophical or religious significance. It is not a piece of profound discourse. It is not a sublime debate or Neo-platonic dialogue, nor proto-Marxist tract. It is a dynamic experience with which we have to engage, generation after generation, and try to come to terms, terms which will never be final.[60]

---

[59]   'Notes and Documents: Shakespeare's Cliff at Dover and an Emblem Illustration' (1984); 'The Barbarous Scythian in *King Lear*' (1985); 'King Lear and Ancient Britain' (1985); 'Blessing and Cursing in King Lear' (1986); 'The Orthodoxy of King Lear's Prayer' (1986); 'Who Are King Lear's Philosophers? An Answer, with Some Help from Erasmus' (1986); 'William Fulbecke: A New Shakespeare Source?' (1986); 'Jacobean Psychiatry: Edgar's Curative Stratagems' (1988); 'Lear's Crown of Weeds' (1989); 'Some Aspects of Elizabethan Psychiatry in Two of Shakespeare's Plays' (1991); 'The Topicality in 1606 of Lear's One Hundred Knights' (1992); 'The Death's of Cordelia and Lear' (1993).

[60]   Guy Butler, *King Lear in Shakespeare's Time*, p. 6.

Bibliography

Abbot, George. *A briefe description of the whole worlde wherein are particularly described all the monarchies, empires, and kingdomes of the same, with their seuerall titles and situations thereunto adioyning*. London: Iohn Browne, 1599.

Anderson, M.D. *Drama and Imagery in English Medieval Churches*. Cambridge: Cambridge University Press, 1963.

Archer, William. T*he Theatrical World of 1896*. London: Walter Scott, 1897.

Arnold, Matthew. *Culture and Anarchy* [1869]. New Haven and London: Yale University Press, 1994.

———. 'The Function of Criticism at the Present Time'. In R.H. Super (ed.), *The Complete Prose Works of Matthew Arnold*, Vol. 3. Ann Arbor: University of Michigan Press, 1960–1977.

Ashcroft, Bill. *Caliban's Voice: The Transformation of English in Postcolonial Literatures*. London: Routledge, 2009.

Badiou, Alain. *Ethics: An Essay on the Understanding of Evil*. Trans. Peter Hallward. London: Verso, 2001.

———. *Saint Paul: The Foundation of Universalism*. Trans. Ray Brassier. Palo Alto, CA: Stanford University Press, 2003.

Barroll, *John Leeds. Shakespeare and Roman History*. Princeton: Princeton University Press, 1956.

Bartolovich, Crystal. 'Shakespeare's Globe?' In Jean Howard and Scott Cutler Shershow (eds), *Marxist Shakespeares*. London and New York: Routledge, 2001, pp. 178–205.

Barzun, Jacques. *The House of Intellect*. New York: Harper Collins, 1957.

Bate, Jonathan. *The Genius of Shakespeare*. London and Basingstoke: Picador, 1997.

Bate, Jonathan and Rasmussen, Eric, eds. *The RSC Shakespeare: Complete Works*. Basingstoke: Macmillan/Random House Modern Library, 2007.

Beerbohm, Max. *Around Theatres*. London: Rupert Hart-Davis, 1953.

Belsey, Catherine. *The Subject of Tragedy: Identity and Difference in Renaissance Drama*. London and New York: Methuen, 1985.

———. *Why Shakespeare?* Hampshire and New York: Palgrave Macmillan, 2007.

Benjamin, Walter. 'The Task of the Translator' [1923]. In Lawrence Venuti (ed.), *The Translation Studies Reader*. London and New York: Routledge, 2000, pp. 16–25.

Boas, F.S. *An Introduction to the Reading of Shakespeare*. London: Oxford University Press, 1927.

———. *Shakespeare and His Predecessors*. London: Oxford University Press, 1896.

Bond, R.W. 'The Puzzle of Cymbeline'. In *Studia Otiosa: Some Attempts in Criticism*. London: Constable, 1938.

Bonnefo, Yves and John T. Naughton. 'Readiness, Ripeness: *Hamlet, Lear*'. *New Literary History* 17.3 (Spring 1986): pp. 477–91.

Borges, Jorge Luis. *Labyrinths*. Harmondsworth: Penguin, 1970.

Bowen, Barbara. 'Beyond Shakespearean Exceptionalism'. In Lloyd Davis (ed.), *Shakespeare Matters: History, Teaching, Performance*. Newark: University of Delaware Press, 2003, pp. 209–32.

Bradbrook, M.C. *Shakespeare the Craftsman: The Clark Lectures 1968*. Cambridge: Cambridge University Press, 1969.

Bradley, A.C. *Shakespearean Tragedy*. London: Macmillan, 1952.

Brahe, Tycho. *De nova, et nullius aevi memoria prius visa stella, jam pridem anno a nato Christo 1572 mense Novembrj primum conspecta contemplatio mathematica*. Copenhagen: Hufniae, 1573.

———. *Tycho Brahe, his astronomical conjecture of the new and much admired star which appeared in the year 1572*. London: BA and TF, 1632.

Brandes, G. *William Shakespeare*. London: Heinemann, 1902.

Bride, Douglas. *Shakespeare in the Movies: From the Silent Era to* Shakespeare in Love. New York: Oxford University Press, 2000.

Bridges, R. *Collected Essays: The Influence of the Audience on Shakespeare's Drama*. London: Oxford University Press, 1927.

Brink, André. *Destabilising Shakespeare*. Grahamstown: Shakespeare Society of Southern Africa, 1996.

Bristol, Michael. *Shakespeare's America, America's Shakespeare*. London and New York: Routledge, 1990.

Brooks, Cleanth. *The Well Wrought Urn*. New York: Harcourt Brace, 1947.

Broughton, Hugh. *A Concent of Scripture*. London: Simson and White, 1588.

Brown, John Russell. 'Introduction'. In William Shakespeare, *The Merchant of Venice*. Cambridge, MA: Harvard University Press, 1955, pp. xi–lviii.

Buchanan, Judith. *Shakespeare on Silent Film: An Excellent Dumb Discourse*. Cambridge: Cambridge University Press, 2009.

Butler, Guy. 'The Barbarous Scythian in King Lear'. *English Studies in Africa* 28.2 (1985): pp. 73–9.

———. 'Blessing and Cursing in King Lear'. *UNISA English Studies* 24.1 (1986): pp. 7–11.

———. *Bursting World: An Autobiography 1936–1945*. Cape Town: David Philip, 1983.

———. *Cape Charade or Kaatjie Kekkelbek*. Cape Town: Balkema, 1968.

———. *Collected Poems*. Ed. Laurence Wright. Cape Town: David Philip, 1999.

———. *The Dam: A Play in Three Acts*. Cape Town: Balkema, 1953.

———. 'The Death's of Cordelia and Lear'. *Shakespeare in Southern Africa* 6 (1993): pp. 1–12.

———. *Demea*. Cape Town: David Philip, 1990.

———. *The Dove Returns: A Play in Three Acts*. Cape Town: Balkema, 1956.

————. *Essays and Lectures 1949–1991*. Ed. Stephen Watson. Cape Town: David Philip, 1994.

————. *Everyman*. Unpublished Manuscript. South African National English Literary Museum (NELM), Butler Collection, 1950. 73.400.1.

————. 'The Fair Queen who liked Blacks'. In *Shakespeare Across Cultures: Conference Papers*. Grahamstown: Shakespeare Society of Southern Africa, 1994, pp. 12–54. And in *Shakespeare in Southern Africa* 9 (1996): pp. 1–21.

————. 'Jacobean Psychiatry: Edgar's Curative Stratagems'. *Shakespeare in Southern Africa* 2 (1988): pp. 15–30.

————. *Judith*. Radio Play, in Blank Verse. NELM, Butler Collection, 1957. 73.395.3.

————. *Karoo Morning: An Autobiography 1918–1935*. Cape Town: David Philip, 1977.

————. *'King Lear'*. *Rhodes University Department of Education Bulletin* 2.2 (November 1973): pp. 1–15.

————. *'King Lear* and Ancient Britain'. *Theoria* 65 (1985): pp. 27–33.

————. King Lear *in Shakespeare's Time*. Unpublished Manuscript. NELM. Butler Collection, 2004. 19.5.1.1–2004. 19.5.10.

————. 'Lear's Crown of Weeds'. *English Studies* 70.5 (1989): pp. 395–406.

————. Letter to Stanley Wells, 27 November 1983: NELM. Butler Collection, 2004. 19.8.3.331.

————. Letter to Stanley Wells. Draft. 22 December 1983: NELM. Butler Collection, 2004. 19.8.3.331.

————. *A Local Habitation: An Autobiography 1945–1990*. Cape Town: David Philip, 1991.

————. 'Notes and Documents: Shakespeare's Cliff at Dover and an Emblem Illustration'. *Huntington Library Quarterly* 47 (1984): pp. 226–31.

————. 'Notes on Seeing and Hearing Shakespeare's Plays in South Africa'. In *Guy Butler: Essays and Lectures 1949–1991*. Ed. Stephen Watson. Cape Town: David Philip, 1994.

————. 'One Night at Clay Pits'. In *Plays from Near and Far: Twelve One Act Plays*. Cape Town: Maskew Miller, 1980.

————. 'The Orthodoxy of King Lear's Prayer'. *New Fire* 9.4 (1986).

————. 'Remembrance Day'. *Eleven One-Act Plays: South African and Others*. Ed. A.D. Dodd and F.O. Quinn. Cape Town: Juta & Co., Ltd, 1965, pp. 181–211.

————. *Richard Gush of Salem*. Cape Town: Maskew Miller, 1982.

————. *A Scattering of Seed* [1968]. Radio Play. Unpublished Manuscript. NELM. Butler Collection, 2004. 37.204.

————. *Silver Spoon: A Farcical Romance*. Manuscript Play. NELM. Butler Collection, 1965.

————. 'Soldier Heroes in Corrupt Societies: A Comparison of N.P. van Wyk Louw's Germanicus and Shakespeare's Coriolanus'. Booklet: N.P. van Wyk Louw Lecture, Rand Afrikaans University, 13 September 1976.

————. 'Some Aspects of Elizabethan Psychiatry in Two of Shakespeare's Plays'. *Adler Museum Bulletin* 17.2 (July 1991): pp. 2–12.

————. *Take Root or Die*. Cape Town: Balkema, 1970.

————. 'The Topicality in 1606 of Lear's One Hundred Knights'. *English Studies in Africa* 35.1 (1992): pp. 1–7.

————. *Two-Timers*. Undated Manuscript Play. NELM. Butler Collection 94.2.4.25.

————. 'Who Are King Lear's Philosophers? An Answer, with Some Help from Erasmus'. *English Studies* 67.6 (1986): pp. 511–24.

————. 'William Fulbecke: A New Shakespeare Source?' *Notes and Queries* 33.3 (1986): pp. 363–5.

Butler, Joseph. *The Analogy of Religion*. London: Thomas Tegg and Sons, 1838.

Butler, Judith. *Antigone's Claim: Kinship Between Life and Death*. New York: Columbia University Press, 2000.

————. *Gender Trouble: Feminism and the Subversion of Identity*. London and New York: Routledge, 1999.

Cantor, Paul A. *Shakespeare's Rome: Republic and Empire*. Ithaca: Cornell University Press, 1976.

Cartmell, Deborah. *Interpreting Shakespeare on Screen*. Basingstoke: Macmillan, 2000.

Chabod, Federico. *Machiavelli and the Renaissance*. Cambridge, MA: Harvard University Press, 1958.

Chadwick, Hubert. *St Omers to Stonyhurst: A History of Two Centuries*. London: Burns & Oates, 1962.

Chambers, E.K. *The Medieval Stage*, Vol. 2. Oxford: Oxford University Press, 1903.

————. *Shakespeare: A Survey*. London: Sidgwick & Jackson, 1925.

Clarke, M.L. *Classical Education in Britain 1500–1900*. Cambridge: Cambridge University Press, 1959.

Clifford, James. *Routes: Travel and Translation in the Twentieth Century*. Cambridge, MA: Harvard University Press, 1997.

Cohen, Walter. *Drama of a Nation: Public Theater in Renaissance England and Spain*. Ithaca, NY, and London: Cornell University Press, 1985.

————. 'The Merchant of Venice and the Possibilities of Historical Criticism'. *English Literary History* 49.4 (1982): pp. 765–89.

Collingwood, R.G. *The Idea of History*. Oxford: Oxford University Press, 1956.

Collins, C. 'Poetry and Symbolism: A Study of The Tempest'. *Contemporary Review* 93 (January 1908): pp. 65–83.

Comaroff, Jean and Comaroff, John. *Theory from the South: Or, How Euro-America Is Evolving Toward Africa*. London: Paradigm, 2012.

Cooper, Thomas. *Thesaurus Linguae Romanae et Britannicae*. London: 1565.

Coulton, G.G. *Art and the Reformation*. Oxford: Oxford University Press, 1928.

Damrosch, David. *What Is World Literature?* Princeton and Oxford: Princeton University Press, 2003.

Danby, J.F. *Poets on Fortune's Hill: Studies in Sidney, Shakespeare, Beaumont & Fletcher*. London: Faber & Faber, 1952.

De Kock, Leon. 'South Africa in the Global Imaginary: An Introduction'. *Poetics Today* 22.2 (2001): pp. 263–98.

Delabastita, Dirk. '"If I Know the letters and the Language": Translation as a Dramatic Device in Shakespeare's Plays'. In Ton Hoenselaars (ed.), *Shakespeare and the Languages of Translation*. London: Thomson, 2004, pp. 31–52.

Derrida, Jacques. 'Des Tours de Babel'. Trans. Joseph P. Graham. In *Difference in Translation*. Ithaca, NY, and London: Cornell University Press, 1985, pp. 165–207.

———. *The Ear of the Other: Otobiography, Transference, Translation*. New York: Shocken, 1985.

———. *Of Grammatology*. Baltimore: Johns Hopkins University Press, 1976.

———. *Limited Inc*. Evanston: Northwestern University Press, 1988.

Desai, Ashwin. *Reading Revolution: Shakespeare on Robben Island*. Pretoria: Unisa Press, 2012.

Desmet, Christy and Sawyer, Robert, eds. *Shakespeare and Appropriation*. London and New York: Routledge, 1999.

Dionne, Craig and Kapadia, Parmita, eds. *Native Shakespeares: Indigenous Appropriations on a Global Scale*. Aldershot: Ashgate, 2008.

Distiller, Natasha. *Fixing Gender: Lesbian Mothers and the Oedipus Complex*. Madison: Fairleigh Dickinson University Press, 2011.

———. '"The Mobile Inheritors of Any Renaissance": Some Comments on the State of the Field'. *English Studies in Africa* 51.1 (2008): pp. 138–44.

———. 'Shakespeare and the Coconuts'. *Shakespeare Survey* 62 (2009): pp. 211–21.

———. *Shakespeare and the Coconuts: On Post-apartheid South African Culture*. Johannesburg: Wits University Press, 2012.

———. *Shakespeare, South Africa, and Post-Colonial Culture*. Lampeter: Edwin Mellen, 2005.

———. 'South African Shakespeare: A Model for Understanding Cultural Transformation?' *Shakespeare in Southern Africa* 15 (2003): pp. 21–7.

Dobson, Michael. *The Making of the National Poet: Shakespeare, Adaptation, and Authorship, 1660–1769*. Oxford: Clarendon Press, 1992.

Dollimore, Jonathan. *Radical Tragedy*. Hertfordshire: Harvester Wheatsheaf, 1989.

Dollimore, Jonathan and Sinfield, Alan, eds. *Political Shakespeare: New Essays in Cultural Materialism*. Manchester and New York: Manchester University Press, 1985.

Doran, Madeleine. 'Elements in the Composition of King Lear'. *Studies in Philology* 30.1 (1933): pp. 34–58.

———. *The Text of King Lear*. Stanford University Publications, Language and Literature, Vol. 4, No. 2. Stanford, CA: Stanford University Press, 1931.

Dover Wilson, J. *The Essential Shakespeare*. Cambridge: Cambridge University Press, 1932.

Dowden, Edward. *Shakespeare: A Critical Study of His Mind and Art*. London: Kegan Paul, French, Trubner & Co., 1892.

Drakakis, John. 'Shakespeare and Venice'. In Michele Marrapodi (ed.), *Italian Culture in the Drama of Shakespeare and His Contemporaries*. Aldershot: Ashgate, 2007, pp. 169–86.

Dubrow, Heather. *Echoes of Desire: English Petrarchism and Its Counter-discourses*. Ithaca, NY, and London: Cornell University Press, 1995.

Eagleton, Terry. *After Theory*. London: Allen Lane, 2003.

———. *Literary Theory: An Introduction* [1983]. Oxford: Blackwell, 1996.

Edwards, Francis. *Robert Persons: The Biography of an Elizabethan Jesuit*. St Louis: Institute of Jesuit Sources, 1995.

Edwards, Philip. 'Shakespeare's Romances: 1900–1957'. In Nicoll, A. (ed.), *Shakespeare Survey* 11 (1958).

Elam, Keir. '"At the Cubiculo": Shakespeare's Problems with Italian Language and Culture'. In Michele Marrapodi (ed.), *Italian Culture in the Drama of Shakespeare and His Contemporaries*. Aldershot: Ashgate, 2007, pp. 99–110.

Eliot, T.S. *Selected Essays*. London: Faber & Faber, 1951.

Ellis-Fermor, Una. *The Jacobean Drama: An Interpretation*. London: Methuen, 1936.

Evans, Joan. *Art in Medieval France 987–1498*. Oxford: Oxford University Press, 1948.

Evans, Michael. *Signifying Nothing: Truth's True Contexts in Shakespeare's Texts*. Hertfordshire: Harvester Wheatsheaf, 1989.

Eve, Jeanette, ed. *Guy Butler: Fifty Years of Press-Clippings*. Grahamstown: National English Literary Museum, 1994.

Evenden, Elizabeth and Freeman, Thomas S. 'Print, Profit and Propaganda: The Elizabethan Privy Council and the 1570 Edition of Foxe's "Book of Martyrs"'. *English Historical Review* 119 (2004): pp. 1288–307.

———. *Religion and the Book in Early Modern England: The Making of John Foxe's 'Book of Martyrs'*. Cambridge: Cambridge University Press, 2011.

Everyman. Ed. Geoffrey Cooper and Christopher Wortham. Nedlands, Western Australia: University of Western Australia, 1980.

Fedderson, Kim and Richardson, J.M. 'Looking for Richard in *Looking for Richard*: Al Pacino Appropriates the Bard and Flogs Him Back to the Brits'. *Postmodern Culture* 8.2 (1998).

Felperin, H. *Shakespearean Romance*. Princeton: Princeton University Press, 1972.

Fichter, Andrew. 'Antony and Cleopatra and the Time of Universal Peace'. In *Shakespeare Survey* 33 (1980): pp. 99–122.

Fineman, Joel. *Shakespeare's Perjured Eye: The Invention of Poetic Subjectivity in the Sonnets*. Berkeley: University of California Press, 1986.

Foxe, John. *Actes and Monuments of matters most speciall and memorable, happening in the Church, with an universall history of the same.* London: Peter Short, 1596.

Friedman, Susan Stanford. *Mappings: Feminism and the Cultural Geographies of Encounter.* Princeton: Princeton University Press, 1999.

Frye, Northrop. *Anatomy of Criticism: Four Essays.* Princeton: Princeton University Press, 1957.

———. *Fables of Identity: Studies in Poetic Mythology.* New York: Harcourt, Brace & World, 1963.

———. *A Natural Perspective: The Development of Shakespearean Comedy and Romance.* New York: Columbia University Press, 1965.

Fuss, Diana. *Essentially Speaking: Feminism, Nature and Difference.* New York and London: Routledge, 1989.

Gajowski, Evelyn, ed. *Presentism, Gender, and Sexuality in Shakespeare.* Basingstoke: Palgrave Macmillan, 2009.

Garber, Marjorie. *Shakespeare After All.* New York: Anchor Books/Random House, 2004.

Gardiner, Samuel. *Doomes Day Booke.* London, 1606.

———. *Doomes-Day Book or An Alarum for Atheists, A Watchword for Worldings, A Caveat for Christians.* London: E. White, 1606.

———. *General Signes of Christ Coming to Judgement.* London, 1625.

Garuba, Harry. 'Review of Post-Colonial Shakespeares'. *Research in African Literatures* 33.1 (2002): pp. 218–20.

Gentili, Vanna. 'A National Idiom and Other Languages: Notes on Elizabethan Mabivalence with Examples from Shakespeare'. In Michele Marrapodi and Giorgio Melchiori (eds), *Italian Studies in Shakespeare and His Contemporaries.* Newark: University of Delaware Press, 1999, pp. 187–205.

Gerhardt, Sue. *Why Love Matters: How Affection Shapes a Baby's Brain.* London and New York: Routledge, 2008.

Gevisser, Mark. *Thabo Mbeki: A Dream Deferred.* Johannesburg: Jonathan Ball, 2007.

Gilbert, A.H. 'The Tempest: Parallelism in Characters and Situations'. *Journal of English and Germanic Philosophy* 14 (1915): pp. 63–74.

Gollancz, Israel, ed. *A Book of Homage to Shakespeare.* Oxford: Oxford University Press, 1916.

Goodman, Godfrey. *The Fall of Man.* London, 1616.

Gordon, Colette. 'What's Hecuba to Him, or "Kupenga" to Them? Syncretic Theatre, Global Shakespeare'. Seminar paper, 'Global Shakespeares' Seminar, World Shakespeare Conference, Prague, July 2011.

Granville-Barker, H. 'Preface'. In *Shakespeare's Tragedie of Cymbeline Printed from the Folio of 1623.* London: Ernest Benn, 1923.

———. *Prefaces to Shakespeare. King Lear* [1927]. London: Nick Hern Books/ Royal National Theatre, 1993.

————. *Prefaces to Shakespeare:* The Winter's Tale – Cymbeline. London: B.T. Batsford, 1984.

Greenblatt, Stephen. *Shakespearean Negotiations: The Circulation of Social Energy in Renaissance England.* Berkeley: University of California Press, 1988.

————. *Will in the World: How Shakespeare Became Shakespeare.* London: Jonathan Cape, 2004.

Grisell, H.D. and Pollen, J.H., eds. 'Four Papers Relative to the Visit of Thomas Sackville, afterwards Earl of Dorset, to Rome in 1563–64'. *Catholic Record Society Miscellanea II*, CRS 2. London: Catholic Record Society, 1906.

Gross, John. *The Rise and Fall of the Man of Letters: Aspects of English Literary Life since 1880.* London: Penguin, 1991.

Hacksley, Malcolm. 'Shakespeare in CRUX, 1967–1991: An Overlooked Resource for Teachers of Shakespeare?' *Occasional Papers and Reviews Shakespeare Society of Southern Africa* 7.1 (1992): pp. 14–20.

Hales, John W. *Notes and Essays on Shakespeare.* London: G. Bell and Sons, 1884.

Haraway, Donna. *Primate Visions: Gender, Race and Nature in the World of Modern Science.* London and New York: Routledge, 1989.

Hardison, O.B. 'Myth and History in King Lear'. *Shakespeare Quarterly* 26 (1975): pp. 221–42.

Harpsfield, Nicholas. *Dialogi Sex contra Summi Pontificatus, monasticae vitae, sanctorum, sacrarum imaginum oppugnatores, et pseudomartyres.* Antwerp: Christopher Plantin, 1566.

Haskins, Charles Homer. *The Renaissance of the Twelfth Century.* Cambridge: Harvard University Press, 1955.

Hastings, Francis. *An Apologie or Defence of the Watch-word.* London: Felix Kingston, for Ralph Jackson, 1600.

————. *A Watchword to all religious, and true hearted English-men.* London: Felix Kingston, for Ralph Jackson, 1598.

Hawkes, Terence. *Meaning by Shakespeare.* London and New York: Routledge, 1992.

Hayward, John, ed. *Donne: Complete Verse and Selected Prose.* London: Nonesuch, 1929.

Hazlitt, William. *Characters in Shakespeare's Plays* [1817]. London: Dent, 1906.

Helgesson, Stefan. 'Provincialising English: Rethinking Literature'. *English Studies in Africa* 51.1 (2008): pp. 123–9.

Heywood, Thomas. *An Apology for Actors.* London, 1612.

Hind, Arthur Mayger. *Hans Holbein, The Younger: His Old Testament Illustrations, Dance of Death, and Other Woodcuts.* New York: Frederick A. Stokes, 1912.

Hoenselaars, Ton, ed. *Shakespeare and the Languages of Translation.* London: Thomson, 2004.

————. 'Translation Futures: Shakespearians and the Foreign Text'. *Shakespeare Survey* 62 (2009): pp. 273–82.

Hofmeyr, Isabel. 'The Black Atlantic Meets the Indian Ocean: Forging New Paradigms of Transnationalism for the Global South – Literary and Cultural Perspectives'. *Social Dynamics* 33.2 (2007): pp. 3–32.

———. 'Universalizing the Indian Ocean'. *PMLA* 125.3 (May 2010): pp. 721–9.

Holbein, Hans. *Images of the Old Testament with English and French Text* [1549]. Bern and Frankfurt: Herbw Lang, 1973.

Holderness, Graham. *Cultural Shakespeare: Essays in the Shakespeare Myth.* Hatfield: University of Hertfordshire Press, 2001.

———, ed. *The Shakespeare Myth.* Manchester: Manchester University Press, 1988.

Holinshed, Raphael. *Chronicle of Scotland.* 1587.

Hornstein, Lilian H. 'King Robert of Sicily: Analogues and Origins'. *PMLA* 79 (1964): pp. 13–21.

Houliston, Victor. 'Breuis Dialogismus [text, with translation, commentary, and textual notes]', *ELR* 23 (1993): pp. 382–427.

———. *Catholic Resistance in Elizabethan England: Robert Persons's Jesuit Polemic, 1580–1610.* Aldershot: Ashgate, 2007.

———. 'St Thomas Becket in the Propaganda of the English Counter-Reformation'. *Renaissance Studies* 7 (1993): pp. 43–70.

Huang, Alexander C.Y. *Chinese Shakespeares: Two Centuries of Cultural Exchange.* New York: Columbia University Press, 2009.

Hughes, Paul H. and James L. Larkin, eds. *Stuart Royal Proclamations*, 2 Vols. Oxford: Clarendon Press, 1973–1983.

Jackobson, Roman. 'The Linguistic Aspects of Translation' [1959]. In Lawrence Venuti (ed.), *The Translation Studies Reader.* London and New York: Routledge, 2000, pp. 113–18.

James, D.G. *Scepticism and Poetry: An Essay of the Poetic Imagination.* London: George Alien & Unwin, 1937.

James, H. *Selected Literary Criticism.* London: Heinemann, 1963.

Jensen, Michael P. 'John W. Velz, Shakespeare Scholar: Reflections on a Friend'. *Shakespeare Newsletter* 58.2 (2008): pp. 41–52.

Johnson, David. *Shakespeare and South Africa.* Oxford: Clarendon Press, 1996.

Johnson, Samuel. *Johnson on Shakespeare: The Yale Edition of the Works of Samuel Johnson*, Vol. 8. Ed. A. Sherbo. London: Yale University Press, 1968.

Jonson, Ben. 'To the Memorie of my beloued, the Avthor, Mr William Shakespeare: And what he hath left vs'. In *Mr. William Shakespeares Comedies, Histories, and Tragedies.* London: Isaac Iaggard and Edward Blount, 1623.

Joughin, John, ed. *Shakespeare and National Culture.* Manchester: Manchester University Press, 1997.

Kendon, Frank. *Mural Paintings in English Churches during the Middle Ages.* London: J. Lane, 1923.

Kermode, Frank. Introduction. *The Arden Edition of The Works of William Shakespeare*: The Tempest. London: Methuen, 1979, pp. 81–8.

Kiernan, Victor. *Shakespeare: Poet and Citizen.* London: Verso, 1993.

Kinney, Arthur F. *Shakespeare and Cognition: Aristotle's Legacy and Shakespearean Drama*. New York and London: Routledge, 2006.

Kipling, Rudyard. 'The Vision of the Enchanted Island'. In Israel Gollancz (ed.), *A Book of Homage to Shakespeare*. Oxford: Oxford University Press, 1916, pp. 200–203.

Kolve, V.A. *The Play Called Corpus Christi*. London: Arnold, 1965.

Kott, Jan. 'Prospero's Staff'. In D.J. Palmer (ed.), *Shakespeare:* The Tempest*: A Casebook*. London: Macmillan, 1989, pp. 244–58.

———. *Shakespeare Our Contemporary*. London: Methuen, 1964.

Lablanc, Michael, ed. 'Excerpts from the Criticism of William Shakespeare's Plays and Poetry from the First Published Appraisals to Current Evaluations'. *Shakespearean Criticism* 77. Detroit: Gale Research, 2002.

Lawrence, W.W. 'The Wager in Cymbeline'. *PMLA* 35.4 (1920): pp. 391–431.

Leavis, F.R., ed. *A Selection from Scrutiny: Volume 2*. Cambridge: Cambridge University Press, 1968.

Lee, John. 'Shakespeare, Human Nature, and English Literature'. *Shakespeare* 5.1–4 (2009): pp. 176–89.

Lefevere, André. *Translation, Rewriting, and the Manipulation of Literary Fame*. London and New York: Routledge, 1992.

LeVay, Simon. *The Sexual Brain*. Cambridge, MA, and London: MIT, 1994.

Levin, Carole and Watkins, John, eds. *Shakespeare's Foreign Worlds: National and Transnational Identities in the Elizabethan Age*. Ithaca: Cornell University Press, 2009.

Looking for Richard. Film. Directed by Al Pacino. Fox Searchlight, 1996.

Loomba, Ania. 'Speaking of the Moor: From "Alcazar" to "Othello"'. Review of *Remapping the Mediterranean World in Early Modern English Writings*. *Shakespeare Studies* 38 (2010): pp. 266–79.

Loomba, Ania and Orkin, Martin, eds. *Post-colonial Shakespeares*. New York: Routledge, 1998.

Loomie, Albert J. 'The Armadas and the Catholics of England'. *Catholic Historical Review* 59 (1973): pp. 385–403.

Luce, M., ed. 'Introduction'. *The Arden Shakespeare:* The Tempest. London: Methuen, 1926, pp. ix–lxx.

Mack, Maynard. *King Lear in Our Time*. Berkeley: University of California Press, 1965.

Male, Emile. *Religious Art from the 12th to 18th Century*. London: Routledge and Kegan Paul, 1949.

Marrapodi, Michele, ed. *Italian Culture in the Drama of Shakespeare and His Contemporaries*. Aldershot: Ashgate, 2007.

Marrapodi, Michele et al., eds. *Shakespeare's Italy: Functions of Italian Locations in Renaissance Drama*. Manchester: Manchester University Press, 1997.

Massai, Sonia, ed. *World-Wide Shakespeares: Local Appropriations in Film and Performance*. New York: Routledge, 2005.

Melchiori, Giorgio, ed. *William Shakespeare's* The Merry Wives of Windsor. Surrey: Nelson, 2000, pp. 1–117.

Milward, Peter. *Religious Controversies of the Elizabethan Age: A Survey of Printed Sources*. London: Scolar Press, 1978.

Moorman, F.W., ed. 'Introduction'. *The Arden Shakespeare:* The Winter's Tale. London: Methuen, 1912.

Moretti, Franco. *Atlas of the European Novel, 1800–1900*. New York: Verso, 1998.

Moulton, R.G. *Shakespeare as a Dramatic Thinker: A Popular Illustration of Fiction as the Experimental Side of Philosophy*. New York: Macmillan, 1912.

Mousley, Andy. 'Introduction: Shakespeare and the Meaning of Life,' *Shakespeare* 5.1–4 (2009): pp. 134–43.

Muir, Kenneth, ed. *The Arden* King Lear. London: Methuen, 1975.

———, ed. *The Arden* Macbeth London: Methuen, 1970.

———. *The Sources of Shakespeare's Plays*. London: Methuen, 1977.

———. 'The Text of *King Lear*'. In *Shakespeare, Contrasts and Controversies*. Brighton: Harvester Press, 1985, pp. 51–66.

Mullaney, Steven. 'Strange Things, Gross Terms, Curious Customs: The Rehearsal of Cultures in the Late Renaissance'. *Representations* 3 (1983): pp. 40–67.

Murdin, Paul and Murdin, Lesley. *Supernovae*. Cambridge: Cambridge University Press, 1978.

Murry, J.M. *Shakespeare*. London: Jonathan Cape, 1936.

Neill, Michael. 'Post-colonial Shakespeare? Writing Away from the Centre'. In Ania Loomba and Martin Orkin (eds), *Post-colonial Shakespeares*. New York: Routledge, 1998, pp. 165–85.

———. *Putting History to the Question: Power, Politics, and Society in Renaissance Drama*. New York: Columbia University Press, 2000.

Nicoll, A. *Stuart Masques and the Renaissance Stage*. London: George G. Harrap & Co., 1937.

Nixon, Anthony. *The Black Year*. London, 1606.

Nosworthy, J.M., ed. *The Arden Edition of The Works of William Shakespeare:* Cymbeline. London: Methuen, 1955.

Nussbaum, Damian. 'Reviling the Saints or Reforming the Calendar? John Foxe and his "Kalender" of Martyrs'. In Susan Wabuda and Caroline Litzenberger (eds), *Belief and Practice in Reformation England: A Tribute to Patrick Collinson from his Students*. Aldershot: Ashgate, 1998, pp. 113–36.

Oakley-Brown, Liz, ed. *Shakespeare and the Translation of Identity in Early Modern England*. London and New York: Continuum, 2011.

Orkin, Martin. *Drama and the South African State*. Manchester: Manchester University Press, 1991.

———. *Local Shakespeares: Proximations and Power*. London and New York: Routledge, 2005.

———. *Shakespeare Against Apartheid*. Craighall: Ad. Donker, 1987.

O'Toole, Emer. 'Shakespeare, Universal? No, It's Cultural Imperialism'. *Guardian*, 21 May 2012.

Pafford, J.H.P., ed. 'Introduction'. *The Arden Edition of The Works of William Shakespeare:* The Winter's Tale. London: Methuen, 1981, pp. xxxvii–xliv.

Pally, Regina. *The Mind-Brain Relationship*. London and New York: Karnac, 2000.

Parker, Patricia. *Shakespeare from the Margins: Language, Culture, Context*. Chicago and London: University of Chicago Press, 1996.

Pearce, Brian. 'Beerbohm Tree's Production of The Tempest, 1904'. *New Theatre Quarterly* 11.44 (1995): pp. 299–308.

——. 'Granville Barker's Production of The Winter's Tale, 1912'. *Comparative Drama* 30.3 (1996): pp. 395–411.

——. 'The Reception of Shakespeare's Late Plays in the Early Twentieth Century'. *Shakespeare in Southern Africa* 9 (1996): pp. 41–8.

——. 'The Re-evaluation of Shakespeare's Late Plays: 1896–1938'. Ph.D. Thesis. Royal Holloway and Bedford New College, University of London, 1992.

——. 'Sir Henry Irving's Interpretation of Iachimo: The Actor as Literary Critic'. *Speech & Drama* 45.2 (1996): pp. 12–17.

——. 'William Poel and the Elizabethan Drama'. *Shakespeare in Southern Africa* 10 (1997): pp. 44–8.

Pearce, Richard. 'Geography Lessons'. *NOVEL: A Forum on Fiction* 32.3 (Spring 1999): pp. 449–52.

Pepper, Thomas. *Singularities: Extremes of Theory in the Twentieth Century*. Cambridge: Cambridge University Press, 1997.

Persons, Robert. *A Temperate Ward-word, to the turbulent and seditious Wach-word of Sir Francis Hastings knight*. Antwerp: Arnout Conincx, 1599.

——. *A Treatise of Three Conversions of England from Paganisme to Christian Religion*, 3 Vols. Antwerp: Arnout Conincx, 1603–4.

——. *The Warn-word, to Sir Francis Hastinges Wast-word*. Antwerp: Arnout Conincx, 1602.

Pettet, E.C. *Shakespeare and the Romance Tradition*. London: Methuen & Co. Ltd, 1949.

Prince, F.T., ed. *Milton: Comus and Other Poems*. Oxford: Oxford University Press, 1968.

Questier, Michael C. *Catholicism and Community in Early Modern England: Politics, Aristocratic Patronage, and Religion, c. 1550–1640*. Cambridge: Cambridge University Press, 2006.

Quiller-Couch, A. *Shakespeare's Workmanship*. London: T. Fisher Unwin Ltd, 1918.

Quince, Rohan. *Shakespeare in South Africa: Stage Productions During the Apartheid Era*. New York: Peter Lang, 2000.

Raleigh, Sir Walter. *The History of the World*. London: Walter Burre, 1614.

Raleigh, W. *Shakespeare*. London: Macmillan, 1907.

Rhodes, Neil. *Shakespeare and the Origins of English*. Oxford: Oxford University Press, 2004.

Richard III. Film. Directed by Richard Loncraine. MGM, 1995.

Rothwell, Kenneth S. *A History of Shakespeare on Screen: a Century of Film and Television*. Cambridge: Cambridge University Press, 1999.

Roy, Modhumita. 'Writers and Politics / Writers in Politics'. In Charles Cantalupo (ed.), *Ngugi wa Thiong'o: Texts and Contexts*. Trenton, NJ: Africa World Press, 1985.

Ruskin, John. *The Stones of Venice: Volume 11; Sea Stories* [1887]. New York: Cosimo, 2007.

Said, Edward. *Culture and Imperialism*. New York: Knopf, 1993.

———. 'Traveling Theory Reconsidered'. In *Reflections on Exile and Other Essays*. Cambridge, MA: Harvard University Press, 2002.

Sakai, Naoki. 'Translation'. *Theory, Culture & Society* 23.2–3 (2006): pp. 71–86.

———. 'Translation and the Figure of the Border: Toward the Apprehension of Translation as Social Action'. *Profession* (2010): pp. 25–34.

Salingar, Leo. *Shakespeare and the Traditions of Comedy*. Cambridge: Cambridge University Press, 1974.

Samuelson, Meg. 'Oceanic Africa: Thinking from the Cape'. Seminar Paper for 'Thinking Africa and the African Diaspora Differently Workshop'. Centre for African Studies, University of Cape Town, 14 December 2011.

———. 'Oceanic Histories and Protean Poetics: The Surge of the Sea in Zoë Wicomb's Fiction'. *Journal of Southern African Studies* 36.3 (September 2010): pp. 543–57.

Sander, Nicholas. *De origine ac progressu schismatis Anglicani*. Ed. E. Rishton Rheims: J. Foigny, 1585. Ed. R. Persons and W. Allen Rome: Bartholomew Bonfadini, 1586.

Saunders, Mark. *Complicities: The Intellectual and Apartheid*. Pietermaritzburg: University of Natal Press, 2002.

Schalkwyk, David. *Hamlet's Dreams: The Robben Island Shakespeare*. London: Continuum, 2013.

———. *Literature and the Touch of the Real*. Newark: University of Delaware Press, 2004.

———. *Shakespeare, Love and Service*. Cambridge: Cambridge University Press, 2008.

———. 'Shakespeare's Untranslatability'. *Shakespeare in Southern Africa* 18 (2006): pp. 37–48.

Schiebinger, Londa. *The Mind Has No Sex? Women in the Origins of Modern Science*. Cambridge, MA, and London: Harvard University Press, 1989.

———. *Nature's Body: Gender in the Making of Modern Science*. New Brunswick: Rutgers University Press, 2004.

Schulte, Rainer and Biguenet, John, eds. *Theories of Translation: An Anthology of Essays from Dryden to Derrida*. Chicago and London: University of Chicago Press, 1992.

Scofield, M. 'Poetry's Sea-Changes: T.S. Eliot and The Tempest'. In S. Wells (ed.), *Shakespeare Survey* 43 (1991): pp. 121–9.

Seaton, Ethel. 'Antony and Cleopatra and the Book of Revelation'. *Review of English Studies* 22 (1946).

Shaw, George Bernard. *Our Theatres in the Nineties*. London: Constable & Co., 1906.

Simons, Jos, ed. Robert Persons, S.J. *Certamen Ecclesiae Anglicanae: A Study of an Unpublished Manuscript*. Assen: Van Gorcum, 1965.

Simpson, Mary-Helen. 'Shakespeare on the Brink' Review of André Brink, *Destabilising Shakespeare*. *Scrutiny2* 2.2 (1997): pp. 64–6.

Singh, Jyotsna. *A Companion to the Global Renaissance: English Literature and Culture in the Era of Expansionism*. Oxford: Blackwell, 2009.

Smith, Peter. *Social Shakespeare*. Basingstoke: Macmillan, 1995.

Solms, Mark and Turnbull, Oliver. *The Brain and the Inner World: An Introduction to the Neuroscience of Subjective Experience*. London and New York: Karnac, 2006.

Speaight, R. *William Poel and the Elizabethan Revival*. London: Heinemann, 1954.

Spenser, Edmund. 'The Ruins of Time' [1591]. In Ernest de Selincourt (ed.), *Spenser's Minor Poems*. Oxford: Clarendon Press, 1910.

———. *The Shepeards Calender*. London, 1579.

Spenser, T.S.B. 'Shakespeare and the Elizabethan Romans'. *Shakespeare Survey* 10 (1958).

Spurgeon, C.F.E. *Shakespeare's Imagery*. Cambridge: Cambridge University Press, 1935.

Stanivukovic, Govan V., ed. *Remapping the Mediterranean World in Early Modern English Writings*. New York: Palgrave Macmillan, 2007.

Steiner, George. *After Babel: Aspects of Language and Translation*. Oxford: Oxford University Press, 1975.

Stockammer, Robert. 'COsMoPoLITerature'. komparatistik.uni-muenchen.de/personen/professoren/stockhammer/cosmopoliterature1.pdf.

Stoll, E.E. *Art and Artifice in Shakespeare*. Cambridge: Cambridge University Press, 1933.

———. *Shakespeare Studies*. New York: Macmillan, 1927.

———. 'The Tempest'. *PMLA* 47 (1932): pp. 699–726.

Stone, P.W.K. *The Textual History of King Lear*. London: Scolar Press, 1980.

Stow, John. *The Annales of England, faithfully collected out of the most autenticall Authors*. London: R. Newbury, 1600.

Strachey, L. 'Shakespeare's Final Period'. In *Books & Characters*. London: Chatto & Windus, 1922.

Stubbes, Phillip. *Anatomie of Abuses*. London, 1583.

Styan, J.L. *The Shakespeare Revolution: Criticism and Performance in the Twentieth Century*. Cambridge: Cambridge University Press, 1977.

Sutcliffe, Matthew. *A Briefe Replie to a certaine odious and slanderous libel lately published by a seditious Jesuite, calling himself N. D. ... entitled a temperate ward-word*. London: Arnold Hatfield, 1600.

————. *A Full and Round Answer to N. D. alias Robert Parsons the Noddie his foolish and rude Warne-word.* London: G. Bishop, 1604.

Swain, J.W. 'The Theory of the Four Monarchies: Opposition History Under the Roman Empire'. *Classical Philology* 35.1 (January 1940).

Sweetser, Eve. '"The Suburbs of Your Good Pleasure": Cognition, Culture and the Bases of Metaphoric Structure'. In Graham Bradshaw, Tom Bishop and Mark Turner (eds), *Shakespeare International Yearbook* 4. Aldershot and Burlington: Ashgate, 2004, pp. 24–51.

Swinburne, A.C. *A Study of Shakespeare.* London: Chatto & Windus, 1880.

Symons, A. *Studies in Two Literatures.* London: Leonard Smithers, 1897.

Taylor, Gary. 'The Fortunes of Oldcastle'. *Shakespeare Survey* 38 (1985): pp. 85–100.

————. *Reinventing Shakespeare: A Cultural History from the Restoration to the Present.* Oxford: Oxford University Press, 1989.

————. 'William Shakespeare, Richard James, and the House of Cobham'. *RES* 38 (1987): pp. 334–54.

Taylor, Gary and Warren, Michael, eds. *The Division of the Kingdoms: Shakespeare's Two Versions of King Lear.* Oxford: Clarendon Press, 1983.

Tennyson, H. *Alfred Lord Tennyson: A Memoir By His Son – Vol. II.* London: MacMillan, 1897.

Thorndike, A.H. *The Influence of Beaumont and Fletcher on Shakespeare.* Worcester, MA: Oliver B. Wood, 1901.

————. *Shakespeare's Theatre.* New York: Macmillan, 1916.

Thornton Burnett, Mark and Wray, Ramona, eds. *Shakespeare, Film, Fin de Siecle.* Basingstoke: Macmillan, 2000.

Thurman, Chris. *Guy Butler: Reassessing a South African Literary Life.* Scottsville: University of KwaZulu-Natal Press, 2010.

————. 'Lawrence, Leavis and Butler: Some Reflections on Appropriation, Influence, Association and "Redemption"'. In Jim Phelps and Nigel Bell (eds), *D.H. Lawrence around the World: South African Perspectives.* Empangeni: Echoing Green Press, pp. 267–94.

Tiffin, Helen. 'Plato's Cave: Educational and Critical Practices'. In Bruce King (ed.), *New National and Post-colonial Literatures: An Introduction.* Oxford: Clarenden, 1996, pp. 143–63.

Tillyard, E.M.W. *Shakespeare's Last Plays.* London: Chatto & Windus, 1938.

Tinkler, F.C. '*Cymbeline*'. *Scrutiny* 7.l (June 1937).

————. '*The Winter's Tale*'. *Scrutiny* 7.4 (March 1938).

Toulmin Smith, Lucy. *York Plays.* Oxford: Oxford University Press, 1885.

Tuve, Rosemond. *Elizabethan and Metaphysical Imagery: Renaissance Poetic and Twentieth-century Critics.* Chicago: University of Chicago Press, 1968.

Uleman, James S. 'Introduction: Becoming Aware of the New Unconscious'. In Ran R. Hassin, James S. Uleman and John A. Bargh (eds), *The New Unconscious.* Oxford: Oxford University Press, 2005, pp. 3–15.

Urkowitz, Steven. *Shakespeare's Revision of King Lear*. Princeton: Princeton University Press, 1980.

Velz, John W. 'Eschatology in the Bradleian Tragedies: Some Aesthetic Implications'. *Shakespeare Newsletter* 58.2 (Fall 2008): pp. 41–74.

Vendler, Helen. *The Art of Shakespeare's Sonnets*. Cambridge: Harvard University Press, 1997.

Venuti, Lawrence, ed. *The Translation Studies Reader*. London and New York: Routledge, 2000.

Viswanathan, Gauri. *Masks of Conquest: Literary Study and British Rule in India*. New York: Columbia University Press, 1989.

Vladislavic, Ivan. *T'kama-Adamastor: Inventions of Africa in a South African Painting*. Johannesburg: University of the Witwatersrand, 2000.

Walsham, Alexandra. *Church Papists: Catholicism, Conformity and Confessional Polemic in Early Modern England*. Woodbridge, Suffolk: Boydell and Brewer, 1993.

Watson, Foster. *The English Grammar Schools to 1660*. Cambridge: Cambridge University Press, 1908.

Weimann, Robert. *Author's Pen and Actor's Voice: Playing and Writing in Shakespeare's Time*. Cambridge: Cambridge University Press, 2000.

Wells, Stanley. Letter to Guy Butler, 30 November 1983. NELM. Butler Collection, 2004. 19.8.3.331.

———. 'Preface'. In David and Ben Crystal (eds), *Shakespeare's Words: A Glossary and Language Companion*. London: Penguin, 2002.

Welsford, E. *The Court Masque: A Study in the Relationship Between Poetry and the Revels*. Cambridge: Cambridge University Press, 1927.

Weston, J.L. *From Ritual to Romance*. Cambridge: Cambridge University Press, 1920.

Wickham, Glynne. 'Hell-Castle and Its Door-Keeper'. *Shakespeare Survey* 19 (1966).

———. *The Medieval Theatre*. Cambridge: Cambridge University Press, 1974.

Widdowson, Peter, ed. *Re-Reading English*. London and New York: Methuen, 1982.

Willan, Brian. 'Whose Shakespeare? Early Black South African Engagement with Shakespeare'. *Shakespeare in Southern Africa* 24 (2012): pp. 3–18.

Wilson, E., ed. *Shaw on Shakespeare*. Harmondsworth: Penguin, 1961.

Wilson Knight, G. *The Crown of Life*. London: Methuen, 1985.

———. *Shakespeare and Religion*. London: Routledge & Kegan Paul, 1967.

———. *The Shakespearian Tempest*. London: Methuen, 1960.

———. *The Wheel of Fire: Interpretations of Shakespearian Tragedy with Three New Essays*. London: Methuen, 1983.

Wright, Laurence. 'Cultivating Grahamstown: Nathaniel Merriman, Shakespeare and Books'. *Shakespeare in Southern Africa* 20 (2008): pp. 25–38.

————. 'Guy Butler: 21 January 1918 – 26 April 2001'. *Shakespeare in Southern Africa* 12 (1999/2000): pp. vi–ix.

————. 'Introduction: South African Shakespeare in the Twentieth Century'. *Shakespearean International Year Book* 9 (2009): pp. 3–28.

Young, Sandra. 'A Charming, Troubling Circus: Roy Sargeant's Taming of the Shrew'. *Shakespeare in Southern Africa* 23 (2011): pp. 81–3.

————. '"Let your indulgence set me free": Reflections on an "Africanised" *Tempest* and Its Implications for Critical Practice'. *Social Dynamics* 36.2 (June 2010): pp. 315–27.

Index

Page numbers in italics indicate illustrations.

academic publishing system 177–8
Adelman, Janet 13, 14
'Africanisation' of Shakespeare 48–9
Afrikaner nationalism 15
allegorical interpretations of
        Shakespeare 111
Alma-Tadema, Lawrence 125
Almereyda, Michael 85
American literary tradition 83
American Shakespeareans 86
'Anglo-American' Shakespeare films 82–5
anthropomorphic theology 116
apartheid 9, 96, 180
        Bantu Education policies 3
        coming-into-being after 44
        experiences 30
        politicisation of art 179
apolitical Shakespearean tradition 5–6
Archer, William 100, 104, 118, 125
Aristophanes 146
Aristotle 135
Arnold, Matthew 20, 170–71
Ashcroft, Bill 58
astral events
        historical events foretold by 154–5
        as portents of doomsday 144
Augustine of Hippo 129, 141–3
Augustus/Octavius 139, 141, 143, 145,
        156–61
authorship controversy 94–5

Bacon, Francis 160
Bafana Bafana 96
Baldwin, Alec 91, 93
Bale, Christian 84
Bale, John 70
Barrie, J.M. 83
Bartolovich, Crystal 57
Barzun, Jacques 178

Bate, Jonathan 36
Baxter Theatre 49
Beaumont, Francis 100
Becket, Saint Thomas 69
Becket, Samuel 129
Beerbohm, Max 101
Bening, Annette 84
Benjamin, Walter 55–6
Bhabha, Homi 86
biographical criticism 100–103, 111
biology
        and culture 25, 28
        and language 19, 24–5
        and subjectivity 29–32
Bishop's Bible 142
Boas, F.S. 101, 107
Bolingbroke (King Henry IV) 71, 74
Bond, R. Warwick 120–21, 125
'Book of Nature' 130
Borges, Jorge Luis 16
Boutcher, Warren 65
Bradbrook, Muriel 107
Bradley, A.C. 6, 105, 110, 114, 169
Brahe, Tycho 155
Branagh, Kenneth 84, 88, 95
Brandes, George 100
Breight, Curtis 90
Bridges, Robert 105, 117, 118
Brink, André 13–14, 43
Brink, Jan ten 100
British-American tensions over
        Shakespeare 82–95
Brook, Peter 86, 116
Brooke, Sir William 70
Broughton, Hugh 147, *148*, 150–51,
        152, 154
Browne, Sir Thomas 173
Buchanan, Judith 83
Burton, Richard 84
Burton, Robert 176
Butler, Guy 4, 6–15, 69, 167–82

Butler, Joseph 171
Butler, Judith 14, 32, 37
Butler, Samuel 7

Calendar of Saints 78
Cantor, Paul 144, 145
Carey, George 70–71, 78
Carey, Henry 70
Carter, Helena Bonham 84
Castiglione, Baldassare 65
Catholic-Protestant relations 5, 69–79,
    147, 163
Cervantes, Miguel de 16
Chabod, Federico 164–5
Chambers, E.K. 102
Chapman, George 146, 160, 163, 173, 176
Chaucer, Geoffrey 129
Chester cycle of mystery plays 156
Christ, birth of 141, 162–3
Christian theology 10, 129–33, 180
Christianity and Roman history 141, 155,
    160, 163
circular London theatres 134
Close, Glenn 84
Clyde-Curry, Walter 129
cognitive sciences and cognitive literary
    studies 5, 23–33
Coleridge, Samuel Taylor 108
Collingwood, Robin George 140, 163–4
Collins, Churton 111–12
colonialism 15–16, 37, 43, 45–6, 48, 108
Columbus, Christopher 1
Comaroff, Jean and Comaroff, John 1, 2
*Conference about the Next Succession to
    the Crowne of Ingland* (Catholic
    treatise) 71
constructionist/relativist approaches 32
Cooper, Thomas 176
Corpus Christi play, *The Harrowing of
    Hell* 137
corruption 9, 97, 160, 173
court masque 100, 118
Craig, Edward Gordon 99
Cresswell, Joseph 71
criticism of Shakespeare's late plays 99–125
Crystal, Billy 84
cultural materialism 6, 30, 177
cultural norms and cultural change 25, 30,
    43, 51

culture and biology 25, 28
culture/nature binary 30

Damrosch, David 57
Danes, Clare 85, 89
Daniel (biblical prophet) 141–3
    animal forms 147, 150
    book of 145, 147
    Daniel's Vision of the Four Beasts
        (Holbein) *151*
    four kingdoms 142–3, 155
    Illustration of the dream in the book
        of Daniel *152*
Daniel, Samuel 165
Dante (Dante Alighieri) 129
Day of Judgement 144
death
    human anxiety about 23
    medieval literature on 175–6
Dekker, Thomas 176
De Kock, Leon 42
Delabastita, Dirk 61
de Lancey, Guy 48–50
Dench, Judi 84
Derrida, Jacques 16, 54
Desai, Ashwin 3
Dias, Bartholomew 1–2
DiCaprio, Leonardo 85, 89
difference-as-inequality 5
Distiller, Natasha 3, 7, 9, 14, 43
Dobson, Michael 57
doctrine of the four monarchies 143
Dollimore, Jonathan 14, 36
Donne, John 69
Doran, Madeleine 170, 176
Dowden, Edward 76, 100, 111
Downey Jr., Robert 84
Drakakis, John 14
Du Bartas, Guillaume 146

Eagleton, Terry 4, 14, 20
eclipses in Shakespeare's plays 173–4
Edmondson, Paul 94
Edwards, Philip 102, 106, 119
Egypt 135, 143, 149–51, 161, 164
Eliot, T.S. 113
Elizabeth I, Queen 71, 147, 172
Elizabethan/Jacobean historical and
    political events 100, 172

Elizabethan sense of World and Time 130
Elizabethan Stage Society 119, 125
Elizabethan theatre design and practice
    134–7
Ellis-Fermor, Una 120
Emerson, John 83
Emmerich, Roland 94
Englefield, Sir Francis 71
English invasion of France 62
'Englishness'
    construction of 46
    in South African education and culture
        3–4
Erasmus, Desiderius 160, 176
essentialism 25, 32, 40
Essex Rebellion 174
Eurocentrism 27, 40
Everett, Barbara 86, 94
Everett, Rupert 84
Everyman (morality play) 176
evolution 24–5

Fabyan, Robert 73–4, 77
Fanon, Frantz 45
Fedderson, Kim 88, 91, 92
'feminine principle' 13, 14
feminism 13–14, 36
feminist historians of science 30
Fichter, Andrew 145
Fiennes, Joseph 84
FIFA 2010 World Cup 82, 96
Fineman, Joel 29
Finkelstein, Richard 90
First Folio (1623) 39, 82
Firth, Colin 84
Fishburne, Lawrence 84
Fletcher, John 100, 111
Flockhart, Calista 84
Florio, John 65
football (soccer) 5, 82, 85, 96
Ford, John 146
'foreign Shakespeare' 50–51
forgiveness in Shakespeare's plays 50,
    108, 132
form and content, relationship between 19,
    23–6, 32, 34–5
formalism 106–11
Foxe, John 70–72, 73–7, 78
France 62, 63, 135

Freeman, Thomas 72–3, 74
French language 53, 60, 62–5
Freud, Sigmund 118, 129
Friedman, Susan Stanford 40
Friel, Anna 84
Frye, Northrop 174–5
Furnivall, Frederick James 100

Garber, Marjorie 21
Gardiner, Samuel 144, 173–4
Garrick, David 82
Garuba, Harry 51
gender 13, 19–21, 30–33, 37, 43
generation gaps in Shakespeare scholarship
    11–13
'Generation S' 4, 7, 14–16
Gevisser, Mark 15
Gibbon, Edward 143
Gibson, Mel 84
Gielgud, John 86, 87
Gilbert, A.H. 106
Giovanni, Sir 65
global north and global south 1, 2, 52
global Shakespeare 46, 47–8, 50, 56
globalisation 97
Globe Theatre 15, 94, 134, 171
Gollancz, Israel 100, 107
Gollancz, Victor 108
Goodman, Godfrey 173
Gordimer, Nadine 50
Gordon, Colette 50–51
Granville-Barker, Harley 99, 102, 108–10,
    121–2, 123, 125, 170
Grecian or Macedonian monarchy and
    Kingdom 143, 151, 153
Greenaway, Peter 116
Greenblatt, Stephen 14, 62, 83
Gross, John 4
Guazzo, Stefano 65
Gunpowder Plot 174

Hacket, William 77
Hales, John W. 176
Hall, Edward 77
Hardison, O.B. 176
Harpsfield, Nicholas, Archdeacon of
    Canterbury 72–3, 75, 77–8
Hart, F. Elizabeth 24
Haskins, Charles Homer 141–2

Hastings, Sir Francis 76
Hawke, Ethan 85
Hawthorne, Nathaniel 83
Hazlitt, William 104, 146
Helgesson, Stefan 45–6
Hellenic-Judeo-Christian matrix 180
Herod of Jewry 140, 161–2
heterosexuality 31, 33
Heywood, Jasper 69
Heywood, Thomas 59, 60, 61
historicism 118–24, 178
historicist tradition 117, 119, 125
historicity 10, 178
historiography 40, 77, 87, 140–41, 160
HIV/AIDS 9
Hobbes, Thomas 164
Hoenselaars, Ton 55
Hoffman, Michael 84
Hofmeyr, Isabel 40–41, 47
Holbein, Hans 150, *151*
Holinshed, Raphael 77, 122, 136
Holy Writ 130
Hornstein, Lilian H. 176
human
    evolution 25
    idea of the 22
    nature 27
    subjectivity 29
humanism 5, 14, 19–20, 27, 30, 33, 37, 51,
    160, 173
humanities 20, 22, 23
    and sciences 1, 31
humoural theory 29

identity, Shakespeare's narratives
    of 29–30
Ifans, Rhys 94
illusion and reality 125
imagery and image patterns in
    Shakespeare's plays 111, 136
Imogen cult of Victorians 104
imperial architecture 151
Indian Ocean studies 41, 47
internationalisation of Shakespeare 84
intertextual reading 122
Irving, Sir Henry 99, 100, 102, 103–5,107,
    109–10, 112–13, 116, 118, 119,
    120–21, 122, 123, 125
Isle of Dogs (play) 78

Italian language 53, 60, 65
Italy 65

Jacobean court drama 118–19
Jacobean/Elizabethan historical and
    political events 100, 172
Jacobi, Derek 84, 94
James, D.G. 105, 106, 122
James, Henry 102–3, 104–6, 109, 115, 125
Joao II, King of Portugal 1–2
Johnson, David 2, 9
Johnson, Samuel 103–4, 121
Jones, Emrys 86
Jones, James Earl 86
Jonson, Ben 5, 11, 12, 39, 120, 160, 163,
    173, 176
Jovinian (Emperor in *Gesta Romanum*) 175
Julius Caesar 143, 154, 160, 164, 173
justice 35–6, 132–3

Kani, John 9
Kant, Immanuel 58
Keaton, Michael 84
Keats, John 137
Kepler's nova (star) 155, 173
Kiernan, Victor 10
Kimball, Frederic 87, 92, 93–4
Kinney, Arthur 27
Kline, Kevin 84, 86
Knight, G. Wilson 4, 6, 105, 111–19, 121,
    122, 125
Kott, Jan 112, 116, 129, 173
Kozintsev, Grigori 84
Kurosawa, Akira 84

language
    and culture/multiculturalism 56–8,
        86–7
    material, biological aspect 24–5
    multilingualism 59
    and nation 60–61
    unity or body of 55, 58
Lawrence, D.H. 123
Lawrence, W.W. 119, 122
Ledger, Heath 85
Lee, John 21–3, 27–30
Lee, Sir Sidney 100, 107
leisure pursuits, Elizabethan and
    Jacobean 81

Leo Africanus 47
linguistic approach (cognitive, scientific, structural) 19, 25
linguistic and physical violation 62–4
Loncraine, Richard 84, 86–8, 91–4
London Olympics, 2012 15
Looking for Richard (film) 5, 81, 82, 85–6, 88, 91–5, 97
Loomba, Ania 2–3, 47
Lord Chamberlain's Men (Lord Hunsdon's Men) 70
Lucan (Marcus Annaeus Lucanus) 164
Luce, Morton 101–2, 106
Luhrmann, Baz 85, 89
Lukács, Georg 45

Macedonian or Grecian monarchy and Kingdom 143, 151, 153
Machiavelli, Niccolo 160, 164–5
Mack, Maynard 7, 171, 176
Maclennan, Don 168
Madden, John 84
Magnificat 156
mapping
    of Eastern Mediterranean 150
    of literature 39
    of southern Africa 1–2
Marlowe, Christopher 135, 176
Marston, John 173, 176
Martellus, Henricus (Heinrich Hammer) 1–2
Marx, Karl 129
Marxism 14, 25, 36, 45
materialism 20, 37
    of the brain 25
materialist criticisms 31
McKellan, Ian 84
Mda, Zakes 23
Mechanicals, The (theatre company) 49
medieval art and meditation 133, 140
medieval Christian universe 129, 136
medieval theatre 134
medieval view of history 163–4
medieval writers 143, 160
Melville, Herman 83
metatheatrical elements in Shakespeare's late plays 123, 125
'metropolitan' literature and culture 44, 178
Middle Ages 134, 140, 142, 164

Milton, John 129, 162–3
miracle plays 140
misogyny 33–4
'modern' audiences and Elizabethans 26–7
modern nation-state 60–61
modern 'realistic' criticism of Shakespeare's plays 103, 118
modernity 1, 10, 37, 179
Monck, Nugent 125
Monroe, Marilyn 95
Montaigne, Michel 176
Moorman, F.W. 105
moral literary criticism 106
morality plays 140, 176
Moretti, Franco 39
Moulton, R.G. 106
Mousley, Andy 22–3
Muir, Kenneth 9, 145, 169, 176
Mullaney, Steven 60
Munday, Anthony 176
Murray, Bill 85
Murry, John Middleton 112, 121
music 54, 92–3, 116, 134, 154, 164, 168, 169
myth
    of Abasement of the Proud King 175
    of Ixion and Juno 175, 176
    in Shakespeare criticism 100, 106, 111
    of Shakespeare's universality/ 'Shakemyth' 16, 89, 91
    of Suffering Servant 175

National English Literary Museum (South Africa) 168, 180, 182
nativity scene 159
naturalism 104, 118, 138
nature
    law and grace 133
    and nurture 131–2
Nebuchadnezzar 147, 149–50, 175, 180
Neill, Michael 66, 153
neuroscience 5, 23, 27, 31
New Criticism 4, 50, 124
New Historicism 4, 7, 31, 177
'New World' 46–7
Newton, Isaac 143
Nixon, Antony 174
Norman, Marc 84
Nosworthy, J.M. 101, 107, 110

Octavius/Augustus 139–41, 145, 156–62, 164
oikumene (inhabited/'civilised' world) 2
Oldcastle, Sir John (Lord Cobham) 5, 70–79
Olivier, Laurence 84, 95
Orkin, Martin 2–3, 7, 9
Otelo Burning (film) 96
O'Toole, Emer 15–16
Ovid (Publius Ovidius Naso) 35
Oxford English Dictionary 59

Pacino, Al 85, 87–9, 91–4, 97
Pafford, J.H.P. 101, 107
pagan
    historiography 164
    prophets 141
    philosophy 180
Paltrow, Gwyneth 84
Parker, Oliver 84
Pearce, Richard 40
Pepper, Thomas 177
Persian Kingdom 142–3
Persons, Robert 69–70, 71, 72, 76–9
Petrarchism 33–4, 35
Pfeiffer, Michelle 84
Pirandello, Luigi 125
Plaatje, Sol 5
plague 71, 174
Pliny (Gaius Plinius Secundus) 146
Plutarch (Lucius Mestrius Plutarchus) 122, 145, 160, 161, 164
Poel, William 99, 101, 105, 106, 112, 119, 125
Pole, Cardinal Archbishop 72
Pory, John 47
post-apartheid era 4, 9, 44, 48, 50
postcolonialism 3, 12, 40, 41, 47, 48, 51, 54, 58
postmodernism 91–2, 178
postmodernity 1, 3, 37
post-structuralism 25, 31, 32
power
    critiques of 43, 46, 47, 48, 51
    dynamics and asymmetries 5, 13, 30, 41, 48, 63, 64
    'worldly powers' 141, 146, 147, *148*, 149–50, 154
Price, T.R. 107
'primitive' brain 31

Protestant-Catholic relations 5, 69–79, 147, 163
'pseudo-Hellenistic' theology 115
psychoanalysis 13–14, 36–7
Ptolemaic astronomy 155
Purchas, Samuel 173, 176

Quiller-Couch, Sir Arthur 107–8, 112
Quince, Rohan 3
Quinn, Aidan 91

race 3–4, 12–13, 19, 30, 37, 47
racism 9, 15, 48, 51
Raleigh, Sir Walter 102, 107, 146–7, 161, 175, 176
Rasmussen, Eric 36
realistic criticism 100, 103–6, 110, 114, 117–18, 123–4, 125
Redgrave, Vanessa 86, 94
Redmayne, Eddie 95
Reeves, Keanu 84
religious conflict and controversy 70, 76
revenge drama and revenge tragedy 36, 100
Richard II, King 71
Richard III, King 96
Richardson, J.M. 88, 91, 92
Richardson, Joely 94
Ridley, M.R. 146
Robert of Sicily 175
romance
    literature 100, 118, 121–2, 125
    'quest romance' 88
    Shakespearean Romances 101–2, 104, 106–7, 112
romantic criticism 117
romantic legacy 46
Rome
    emergence as world power 141
    Roman conflict with Egypt 164
    Roman and Elizabethan systems 35
    Roman history 140, 155
    Shakespeare's view of 163, 164
Rothwell, Kenneth 91
Royal Shakespeare Company 15, 49–50
Ruskin, John 178
Ryder, Winona 91, 93

Sackville, Thomas 72
Said, Edward 44–5, 46, 59

Saint Augustine (Augustine of Hippo) 129, 141–3
Sakai, Naoki 53, 55, 57, 58, 61
Sallust (Gaius Sallustius Crispus) 164
Samuelson, Meg 40, 41
Saunders, Mark 26
Schalkwyk, David 3, 33, 54–5
school syllabi 2–3, 28, 96–7, 160
Scofield, Paul 84
Scotland 79, 171
Seaton, Ethel 144, 145, 154–5
'Shakemyth' 89, 91
Shakespeare, William, plays of
    All's Well That Ends Well 11
    Antony and Cleopatra 12, 13, 132, 135, 139, 140–47, 149–51, 153–65, 168
    As You Like It 53, 64, 134
    Coriolanus 13, 15, 133, 135, 139, 167
    Hamlet 36, 131, 132, 134, 139
    Henry IV, Part 1 23, 70, 71, 74, 79
    Henry IV, Part 2 72, 74, 139
    Henry V 53, 61–2, 90, 135
    Julius Caesar 26, 139, 154, 163, 167
    King Lear 10, 13, 28, 132, 133, 135, 139, 167
    Macbeth 131, 134, 135, 136–7, 139, 167
    Measure for Measure 11, 132, 133, 134, 139
    The Merchant of Venice 37, 53, 64–5, 132
    The Merry Wives of Windsor 62, 70
    A Midsummer Night's Dream 134
    Othello 12, 37, 47, 133, 136, 139, 167
    Pericles 134
    Richard II 71, 74, 136, 168
    Richard III 81, 96, 134
    The Taming of the Shrew 37, 83
    The Tempest 95, 102, 103, 134
    Titus Andronicus 33, 35, 36
    Troilus and Cressida 130, 132, 167–8
    Twelfth Night 130
    Two Noble Kinsmen 11
    The Winter's Tale 11
Shakespeare Authorship Coalition (SAC) 94–5
Shakespeare Birthplace Trust (SBT) 94–5
Shakespeare and British cultural capital 5, 57, 82–96
Shakespeare in Mzansi (film series) 96

Shakespeare and national identity 44, 55, 60, 96
Shakespeare and resistance 26, 45, 51–2
Shakespeare in Southern Africa (journal) 3, 6, 8–10
Shakespeare on the stage
    and English critical traditions 94–125
    in South Africa 48–50, 168
    see also Globe Theatre
Shakespeare-as-cultural-capital 3, 5
Shakespeare-on-screen, history of 95
Shaw, George Bernard 100, 104–5, 110, 118, 122, 125, 129
sic transit gloria mundi theme 161
Sidney, Sir Philip 122, 125
Simpson, Mary-Helen 13–14
sin, notion of 130
Singh, Jyotsna 46
Sinyard, Neil 91–2
slavery 12, 46–7
Smith, Peter 89
Smith, Zadie 23
soap operas 54
soccer (football) 5, 82, 85, 96
Solms, Mark 31–2
sonnets 33–5
Sophiatown 30, 43
South African literature and literature in South Africa 43, 50
South African Shakespeare and Shakespeare in South Africa 2–16, 21, 40, 42–4, 48–52, 87, 97, 181
space (or world) 150
    of a play 135
    and time 130
Spacey, Kevin 91, 93
Spanish succession 71
Spenser, Edmund 61, 146
Spenser, T.S.B. 163
Spurgeon, Caroline 111–13
stars 144, 154–5, 159, 173
Stiles, Julia 85
Still, Colin 112, 125
Stockammer, Robert 57
Stoll, E.E. 110, 111
Stone, P.W.K. 176
Stonyhurst College (St Omer) 69
Stoppard, Tom 84
Stow, John 77

Strachey, Lytton 99–101, 117, 118, 120, 121, 125
structural/structuralist criticism 106, 115
Stubbes, Phillip 174
Styan, J.L. 110
subjectivity 25, 27, 29, 34, 179
Sutcliffe, Matthew 76
Suzman, Janet 9
Sweetser, Eve 26–7
Swinburne, A.C. 104
Sybil (ancient oracle) 159–60
symbolic criticism 100, 111–18, 123–4, 125
Symons, Arthur 104–5

Tasso, Torquato 146
Taylor, Elizabeth 84
Taylor, Gary 89, 90, 169
Taylor, Jeremy 133
Tennyson, Alfred 104
Terry, Ellen 125
Thompson, Emma 84
Thorndike, Ashley 118–19
Tillyard, E.M.W. 4, 6, 105, 115, 116, 119, 120–23, 125, 129
time 130, 155, 162
    of a play 135
    as primary translator 54
Tinkler, E.C. 111, 113, 121–2
Tolstoy 117, 118
translated Shakespeares 58–66
translation
    as creative process 55–6
    Shakespeare and/in 58–66
transnationalism 5, 40–41
travelling theory 44
Tree, Sir Herbert Beerbohm 83, 99, 105, 125
Tucci, Stanley 84
Tudor audience 156, 163
Tudor history 160
Turnbull, Oliver 31–2
Twidle, Hedley 43

unconscious, theories of the 29, 100, 118, 125
United States of America (USA) 2, 81–96, 168

universality 5, 11, 15–16, 19, 21, 23, 27–8, 31, 33, 39, 41, 45, 89, 97
Urkowitz, Steven 176
Ussher, Archbishop James 130

Velz, John W. 176
Vergil, Polydore 77
Virgil (Publius Vergilius Maro) 141
Viswanathan, Gaudi 20

Walters, Paul 8
Warren, Michael 169
Wars of the Roses 86
Washington, Denzel 84
wealth-poverty gap 9
Weinberg, Joanna 9
Welles, Orson 84
Wells, Stanley 94, 177
Welsford, Enid 120
West, Dominic 84
'Western'
    literature 174–5
    nations 91
    'non-Western subjectivities' 51
    'Westerners' 12, 26–7
Weston, Jessie 113
'white liberals' 3
Whitman, Walt 83
Wickham, Glynne 137
Widdowson, Peter 20
Wilde, Oscar 110, 125
Williams, Michelle 95
Wilson, John Dover 4, 6, 9, 112, 123
Winslet, Kate 84
world literature, definition of 56
World Shakespeare Festival 15
World War II 6, 8, 83–4, 179
Wright, Laurence 3, 43

xenophobia 9

Yeats, W.B. 138
York, Michael 94

Zeffirelli, Franco 84, 94

www.ingramcontent.com/pod-product-compliance
Ingram Content Group UK Ltd.
Pitfield, Milton Keynes, MK11 3LW, UK
UKHW020354010325
455677UK00021B/445

9 781138 272002